The Harbinger
and New England Transcendentalism

THE

HARBINGER,

DEVOTED TO

SOCIAL AND POLITICAL PROGRESS.

" All things, at the present day, stand provided and prepared, and await the light."

VOL. I.

PUBLISHED BY THE BROOK FARM PHALANX.

NEW-YORK:
BURGESS, STRINGER, AND COMPANY.
BOSTON:
REDDING AND COMPANY.
M DCCC XLV.

The title page of Volume I of *The Harbinger* when the magazine was published by the Brook Farm Phalanx (June 1845—June 1847)

The Harbinger
and New England
Transcendentalism

A Portrait of Associationism in America

Sterling F. Delano

Rutherford • Madison • Teaneck
Fairleigh Dickinson University Press
London and Toronto: Associated University Presses

Associated University Presses
440 Forsgate Drive
Cranbury, NJ 08512

Associated University Presses
25 Sicilian Avenue
London WC1A 2QH, England

Associated University Presses
2133 Royal Windsor Drive
Unit 1
Mississauga, Ontario
Canada L5J 1K5

Library of Congress Cataloging in Publication Data

Delano, Sterling F., 1942–
   The Harbinger and New England transcendentalism.

   Bibliography: p.
   Includes index.
   1. Collective settlements—United States—History.
2. American Union of Associations—History.   3. Tran-
scendentalism (New England)—History.   4. Harbinger—
History.   I. Title.
HX653.D44   1983   335'.974   82-48396
ISBN 0-8386-3138-X

Printed in the United States of America

For Maris

Contents

Acknowledgments

This book would never have been written were it not for Sidney P. Moss. It was Professor Moss's seminar in New England Transcendentalism at Southern Illinois University several years ago that first stimulated my interest in the subject. Professor Moss later oversaw an early draft of this study, and he did so with a critical eye that was searching and penetrating at the same time that it was reassuring. Because he combined consistent thoroughness and passion for exactness with a comprehensive sweep of mind, he provided me by his example with my first real insight into what was involved in being, truly, a scholar. I shall never be able to acknowledge fully the extent of my debt to Sidney P. Moss, but I am very grateful for the opportunity of having been able to know and to work with him.

Whenever a book evolves over a period of years—as this one did—a writer incurs many debts of gratitude. I wish there were time and space to cite by name all of the librarians, scholars, and colleagues at such places as the Massachusetts Historical Society, the Boston Public Library, Southern Illinois University, Harvard University, and Yale University who have aided me in this study. I do want to thank particularly, however, the Massachusetts Historical Society and the Boston Public Library for granting me permission to quote from manuscript material in their collections. My sincere thanks as well to the *Colby Library Quarterly* for its permission to reprint material first published there.

Anyone today who seriously explores the orchard of New England Transcendentalism will likely be rewarded with the fruits of Joel Myerson's labors. I certainly have been myself. I know of no individual who has so carefully cultivated such extensive ground, who has—to paraphrase one of Concord's famous residents—cut such a broad swath without failing at the same time to shave close.

It is not only in this regard, however, that I owe a debt of gratitude to Joel Myerson, for it has been my especially good fortune to have had him read a late draft of this book. His insightful and detailed comments contributed a great deal to making the finished draft better, and I wish to extend my sincere thanks to him.

I am fortunate to be on the faculty of an institution that actively encourages and supports research and scholarship. Special thanks go to Rev.

John P. O'Malley, O.S.A., Rev. Lawrence C. Gallen, O.S.A., and Joseph P. McGowan, as well as to the Audio Visual Department and the staff of Falvey Memorial Library for their help and support. The continual support, encouragement, and friendship of Robert E. Wilkinson has also always been greatly appreciated.

I would like to express my gratitude as well to Villanova graduate research assistant Marie Rauscher, typist JoAnn LaVan, Fairleigh Dickinson University Press chairman Harry Keyishian, and Associated University Presses managing editor Katharine Turok.

To my entire family—especially my beloved Maris, Rachel, and Debra—I am deeply grateful for patience, understanding, and support.

Introduction

This is the first full-scale study of *The Harbinger* (1845–49), a magazine that was the official organ of Associationism and Fourierism in America. *The Harbinger* is naturally associated with Brook Farm, perhaps the best-known of American utopian communities of the nineteenth century, for it was there that the magazine was originally conceived by George Ripley, who himself was the founder of that community. For the first two of the four years of its existence, when the Associationist magazine was published at the farm, it received the full-time attention of Ripley and his dedicated associates, Charles A. Dana and John S. Dwight, Dana later achieving considerable celebrity as editor of the New York *Sun,* and Dwight later establishing himself as one of the earliest and foremost critics of music in the United States. Due largely to the efforts of these men, *The Harbinger* was soon established as the most important Associationist journal in America, as evidenced by the fact that, just two years after its inception, the magazine was adopted as the official organ of the American Union of Associationists.

There are many reasons that this study of *The Harbinger* was undertaken. First, it seemed paradoxical that there should be such an abundance of material about Brook Farm and so little information about *The Harbinger.*[1] Since that day in the fall of 1847 when the socialistic community ceased all activities, a wealth of material has emerged illuminating every conceivable aspect of that operation, among them, biographies, autobiographies, diaries, memoirs, personal reminiscences, journals, official records, and letters, not to mention critical essays and books. Significantly, this information, except only in the most summary of ways, reveals little about the operation, publication, and ideology of *The Harbinger.* While it is fortunate that there exists this nearly finished portrait of Brook Farm, that portrait cannot be completed without its main feature, *The Harbinger.*

A far more major reason for this undertaking, however, is the fact that *The Harbinger* attracted some of the very best intellects ever in America. The list of its contributors is one of the most extraordinary among American journals. Besides Ripley, Dwight, and Dana, there were Albert Brisbane, William H. Channing, Christopher Pearse Cranch, George W. Curtis, Parke Godwin, Horace Greeley, James Russell Lowell, John Greenleaf Whittier, William Ellery Channing, James Freeman Clarke, Francis G. Shaw, Henry

11

James, Sr., and Frederic Henry Hedge. A magazine that could engage the energies of men of this caliber must have been remarkable indeed. The obvious question that arises is this: What enabled *The Harbinger* to enlist the efforts of such notable individuals? A large concern of this study is an attempt to answer this crucial question.

Perhaps the most significant reason for this study's being undertaken is that *The Harbinger* was, with *The Western Messenger* and the *Dial,* the chief organ of the Transcendentalists. However, though the *Dial,* for example, has received a great concentration of scholarly scrutiny,[2] little attention has been devoted to *The Harbinger,* despite the fact that it was a magazine to which the majority of Transcendentalists contributed. Emerson, well known for his editorship of and association with the *Dial,* was one of the few Transcendentalists who refused to appear in its pages. His reply to John Dwight's request for a line or two from him was "Though I should heartily rejoice to aid in an uncommitted journal—not limited by the name of any man—I will not promise a line to any which has chosen a patron."[3]

Emerson, of course, was right, for *The Harbinger* did regard Charles Fourier as the foremost authority in the world on industrial reform, and therein lay the fundamental difference between the Transcendentalism of individuals such as Emerson, Thoreau, Bronson Alcott, and Margaret Fuller, with their emphasis on the inherent dignity and sanctity of the individual, and the Transcendentalism of those committed to *The Harbinger,* with its belief in social reform through associative and cooperative labor. The point to be made is that, all too often, we still continue to identify Transcendentalism almost exclusively with Emerson and Thoreau; we forget that the ideas advocated in *The Harbinger* constitute as much, if not more, a part of a definition of Transcendentalism as do the ideas espoused by those two famous residents of Concord, Massachusetts.

By late 1847, when the Brook Farm experiment had ended, Transcendentalism was no longer the passionate cause it had been in the 1830s and early 1840s. *The Harbinger* managed to survive for another year and a half, but with its demise in early 1849 came the end of that brand of Transcendentalism which not only captured the enthusiasm and dedication of some of the ablest minds in the United States, but which caused them to channel their ideas and energies into a publication that offers to us today the key to a fuller understanding of Transcendentalism as it developed on native soil.

The Harbinger
and New England Transcendentalism

THE

HARBINGER,

DEVOTED TO

SOCIAL AND POLITICAL PROGRESS.

" All things, at the present day, stand provided and prepared, and await the light."

VOL. V.

PUBLISHED BY THE AMERICAN UNION OF ASSOCIATIONISTS

NEW YORK:
BURGESS, STRINGER, AND COMPANY.

BOSTON:
REDDING AND COMPANY.
MDCCCXLVII.

The title page of Volume V of *The Harbinger* after publication of the journal was transferred from the Brook Farm Phalanx to the American Union of Associationists (June 1847–February 1849)

1

A History of *The Harbinger*

Brook Farm and *The Harbinger*

It is tempting to argue that George Ripley's inability to allow the Brook Farm community that he had founded in 1841 in West Roxbury, Massachusetts, to enjoy a more central position in the somewhat diffuse socialist movement of the time represented, on his part, a serious failure of understanding, a failure, ironically, that would certainly have to be included among the major contributing factors for the community's eventual demise in the autumn of 1847. Such an argument would claim that the perceptive, ambitious, and intelligent Ripley should have recognized that the one crucial thing lacking in the contemporary social-reform movement in which he and his fellow communitarians were engaged was what the Harvard graduate himself would call a "centre of influence," and that he should have paid closer attention to the appeals of those other reformists in the United States who frequently urged that Brook Farm become just such a center.[1]

Had he done so, the argument would continue, the West Roxbury community would have received, among other things, much greater financial support than it actually did from those individuals scattered throughout New England who were committed, in one way or another, to the socialist reform platform. This, in turn, would have made it considerably easier for the Brook Farmers to cope with the fickleness of some of their New York--based financial supporters (such as Horace Greeley, the powerful editor of the New York *Tribune*), and, more important, it would have considerably lessened the shock of the financial devastion that was represented by the loss by fire in March 1846 of the nearly completed Phalanstery, which was to have become the nerve center of Brook Farm by accommodating all of its approximately 150 regular inhabitants.

All of this, of course, must necessarily remain conjecture. We shall obviously never know what the fate might have been of Brook Farm or of the socialist movement generally had George Ripley adopted a more profound sense of the importance of the community of which he was the driving force. Nor will we ever know whether *The Harbinger*—which was first published at Brook Farm in June 1845—would have developed a radically different character from that which it actually acquired. What we do know, however, is that while it is true that by the mid-1840s the reform fervor that had been earlier brought about, in part, by the financial Panic of 1837 was hardly any longer to be felt, Brook Farm itself was continuing its increasingly successful experiment in living in West Roxbury. It had, of course, been founded in 1841, and now, in 1843, it was showing its first-ever profits. As one of Ripley's biographers has pointed out: "The Brook Farmers boasted that they could produce in one acre what formerly took six acres to grow; and by November, 1843, they could point proudly to a handsome profit. In 1844 the Brook Farmers became more confident and more militant and . . . in March, 1845, Ripley administered the crowning touch by arranging for Brook Farm to be incorporated into the State of Massachusetts."[2]

The year 1845 would prove to be, in fact, the most important in Brook Farm's six-year history, but not because of any petition that George Ripley might carry to the Massachusetts legislature on behalf of the West Roxbury community. Indeed, the summer of 1845 would witness the launching of *The Harbinger,* a new weekly journal that during the four years of its existence would advocate radical and comprehensive social and industrial reform. The autumn would bring smallpox, the outbreak of which would not only break the spirit of many of the Brook Farmers, but would temporarily force the closing of the highly regarded Brook Farm school as well.

The event, however, that would ultimately have the most profound effect on the Brook Farm community was to be none of these. That event had already occurred earlier in the year, and it had to do with the very critical decision to declare openly Brook Farm's allegiance to many of the doctrines propounded by the controversial French social scientist, Charles Fourier. By so doing, George Ripley and his fellow Brook Farmers set a course for their community—as well as for *The Harbinger*—that must, as we shall see, have given them serious cause many times in subsequent months and years to reflect on the wisdom of their decision.

Fourierism, Associationism, and *The Harbinger*

One of the problems relating to Brook Farm that has intrigued scholars and historians alike concerns the exact time at which the socialistic enterprise became a Fourierist Phalanx.[3] We know that on 18 January 1844 a new constitution was drawn up converting "The Brook Farm Institute of Agriculture and Education" to "The Brook Farm Association for Industry and Education," which provided for a system of Groups and Series[4] based on the principles of Charles Fourier. We know too that just a little over a year later, in March 1845, a third constitution was drafted, which changed the name of the community to the "Brook Farm Phalanx."[5]

Despite these facts, there continues to be some confusion regarding the extent to which the West Roxbury community subscribed to Fourier's principles before it openly avowed its allegiance to them in 1845. Amelia Russell, a onetime resident of Brook Farm, long ago suggested that as early as 1841, George Ripley, the founder of the community, had introduced several of Fourier's ideas, namely, cooperative labor, association of families, attractive industry, "integral" education, and "honors according to usefulness."[6] More recently, Charles Crowe has argued that Brook Farm was from its beginning a "thinly veiled Fourierist Phalanx."[7] On the other hand, Arthur E. Bestor, Jr., in a 1941 pamphlet commemorating the centennial anniversary of Brook Farm, said that it was during the winter of 1843–44 that "Fourierist ideas became increasingly influential" at the community.[8] Clarence Gohdes, however, put the time somewhat later. Using a community labor record, Gohdes stated that the association did not decide to become a Phalanx until it had completed a one-year experiment with Fourierism during the period May 1844 to May 1845.[9]

Whatever the time, the fact remains that from the first Ripley's vision of a utopian community was strikingly similar to that which Fourier envisioned. What Ripley lacked, and what Fourier provided for him, was a method and a system to realize his vision. This system Ripley and his fellow Brook Farmers officially adopted in 1845, for with its division of labor according to Groups and Series it enabled them to construct a systematic organization where none had previously existed. Perhaps even more important, the conversion to a Phalanx placed the community squarely in the center of the Fourierist movement in America, not an unimportant consideration to Ripley and his associates.

The decade beginning in 1840 was a period in which more than thirty Fourierist communities appeared in America, for Fourierism had "established itself as one of the leading philosophies of social reform in the United States. It numbered its adherents in the thousands."[10] By the fall of 1844, however, several of these communities had already failed. Their supporters had sent frantic letters to Ripley urging him to stand firm at Brook Farm as an example to other Associationists.[11] In December of the same year, the New York Associationists also turned to Ripley, for they were beginning "to see the need of concentrating their efforts in some one undertaking, and it [was] to Brook Farm" that they looked.[12] Indeed, Ripley himself came to regard Brook Farm as the most concrete symbol in America of the value of Fourierism.[13] Understandably, Ripley decided that if Brook Farm was to be the center of the Fourierist movement in the United States, it should also be the place at which the major organ of Fourierism was published. Thus on 14 June 1845 appeared the first number of *The Harbinger,* a weekly magazine that was to survive for four years, though it was transferred to New York for its last two years of publication.

The story thus far seems to have been straightforward enough. It quickly became complicated, however, by the increasingly important need—not to mention difficulty—of clarifying the distinction between Associationism and Fourierism. For what Ripley and the several thousand ideologically like-minded individuals in the United States at the time were immediately to discover was that it was one thing to be known as an Associationist, but it was quite another to be indiscriminately tarred with the term *Fourierist*. The fact is, Ripley and his fellow Associationists spent considerable time and energy trying to convince a skeptical and even hostile American audience that the terms *Associationism* and *Fourierism* did not mean entirely the same thing. This they did primarily in *The Harbinger,* which in 1846 was declared to be the official organ of Associationism in the United States by the American Union of Associationists. *The Harbinger,* in fact, is today our most valuable source of information on the Associative movement in this country, for it was in its pages that the leading American Associationists recorded their views on and qualifications of Fourier's utopian schemes. It would be wise, therefore, to take a moment to indicate the nature of the problem that would persistently confound Ripley and the Associationists for almost the next four years, a problem that ultimately must be counted among the significant reasons for the eventual collapse of *The Harbinger* in February 1849, as well as for the failure of the Associative movement in America.

According to no less an authority than Albert Brisbane, the foremost expositor of Fourier's principles in America and one of the few men to have studied with the master before his death in 1837, Associationists divided the Frenchmen's works into two categories. The first contained those writings that dealt with industrial association, or the organization of labor, which included elaborate discussions on the systems of commerce, property, and education, and the division of profits in society. Industrial association, it was stated in *The Harbinger* on different occasions, was a practical matter that could be judged by common sense as well as by practical experience. Accordingly, Associationists accepted most of Fourier's ideas in this area, for they believed that the French social scientist had studied human history and human nature more profoundly than any other man with respect to social science. Thus they turned to Fourier for insights on social problems, especially in matters pertaining to industrial reform. As *The Harbinger* observed, Fourier had "in a great measure defined and ascertained the law of this State of Association, or Organic Unity of Interests and Works, to which the world is now so consciously tending" (5:28).[14] And elsewhere it was noted that Fourier "is our guide in the great science of industrial association" (2:93).

The second category of Fourier's works, however, embraced a wide field of scientific speculations and analogical conjectures. Among these apocalyptic visions were the Frenchman's theory on the immortality of the soul, his outline of future orders of society, and his descriptions of the many institutional changes that would occur as the human race progressed. Associationists regarded this second category as sheer romance, as indeed, it was pointed out many times in *The Harbinger,* Fourier did himself. In an article entitled "Fourier's Writings," John Dwight noted that discovery with the Frenchman was based as much on intuition as on anything else. Many of the laws that he announced contained no scientific demonstration; in fact, they involved no demonstration of any kind (1:333). Thus the editors of *The Harbinger*—variously George Ripley, John S. Dwight, Charles A. Dana, and Parke Godwin, who was the son-in-law of William Cullen Bryant—could state:

> As to Fourier's theories of Marriage, of Cosmogony, and the Immortality of the Soul, we do not accept them and this is the position which the Associative School in this country and in Europe, have [*sic*] always taken and never varied from. . . . We consider Fourier as a servant to this cause [social reform], and not its master, and take from him such parts of his system as he has demonstrated to our understandings, and no others [3:153].

But despite the magazine's frequent reiteration of these facts, Fourier's American detractors continued to place Associationists and Fourierists in the same category. This angered the Associationists, for it made them liable to the charge that the ideals that they espoused would, among other things, abolish the institution of marriage and introduce a system of "universal licentiousness" in sexual relationships.[15] The editors of *The Harbinger* were obviously concerned that Associationists not be misunderstood or misrepresented in this area, and they therefore felt required on many occasions to respond to such typical accusations as the following from the New York *Observer* (a Calvinist paper, perhaps the most vocal of all the American papers critical of Associationism): "The Associationists, under the pretence of a desire to promote order and morals, design to overthrow the marriage institution, and in the place of the divine law, to substitute the 'passions' as the proper regulator of the intercourse of the sexes."[16] Moreover, the *Observer* charged that Associationists were "secretly and industriously aiming to destroy the foundations of society, and to introduce a system in which the most unrestrained indulgence of the sensual passions is enjoyed and sanctified by the name of virtue" (3:155). *The Harbinger,* of course, denied such allegations, and it responded to them all in generally the same way. It disclaimed all responsibility for Fourier's theories, except as they related to the organization of industrial association.

Actually, charges of this sort were made even before *The Harbinger* was founded, mainly by what the magazine was later to call the "New York Coalition," which seems to have consisted of the New York *Courier and Enquirer,* the New York *Express,* the New York *Observer,* the New York *Mirror,* and the New York *Herald.* The attacks by these papers on Associationism, inspired mostly by a cursory understanding of Fourier's religious views and sexual attitudes, often were directed at Horace Greeley, himself an ardent Associationist and editor and founder of the New York *Tribune*.[17] Even after *The Harbinger* was launched in June 1845, Greeley continued to refute the various charges against Associationism in the columns of his paper. Perhaps because they had such confidence in Greeley, or perhaps because *The Harbinger* was not yet established in the journalistic world, Ripley and his associates were content to let Greeley in the New York *Tribune* act as the spokesman for American Associationists with respect to the accusations of the "New York Coalition."[18] Obviously they were pleased to have so powerful an ally, and they said as much in their own columns on many occasions (1:189; 2:44; 3:155; 4:245; 5:287, for example). Nevertheless, the editors of *The Harbinger* learned quickly that they could not be indifferent to the assaults on Associative doctrines. For one thing, there were so many; for another, the criticisms were often prejudicial, vindictive, and misinformed, and more harm to the cause would result if they were left unanswered. With the publication in the 8 November 1845 number of a rebuttal titled "The Translator of *The Wandering Jew*," *The Harbinger* joined the New York *Tribune* in its efforts to defend Associationism and explain to detractors the Associative school's position with respect to the doctrines of Fourier.

The "translator" of *The Wandering Jew* (1845), a novel by the French Associationist Eugene Sue, was William Henry Herbert, a little-known American novelist and a frequent contributor to a variety of American magazines. Herbert had devoted fifteen months to translating Sue's novel only to discover—though not very astutely, to be sure—that the work was "utterly subversive of social morality, destitute of religion, and averse to Christianity" (1:349). Accordingly, despite his translation, he denigrated the novel, its author, Fourierism, and Associationism. *The Harbinger* stated that it was responding to Herbert's criticisms because they were aimed directly at Associative doctrines, and not because it felt compelled to defend the Fourierist philosophy embodied in *The Wandering Jew*, or because it had any particular desire to defend Eugene Sue.

Herbert's charge that Associationists were not Christians was, the magazine said, a misleading statement. As Associationists did not form a religious sect, but a school, they subscribed as a group to no particular theology:

> As individuals, we have our own opinions, varying from Rationalism to the deepest and entirest faith in Christ as the Son of God, the Lord of Heaven and Earth. Under our banner are to be found men of almost all denominations, fired by the same enthusiasm for the establishment of Justice and Unity throughout the earth. [1:351].

So far as the doctrines of Fourier were concerned, Associationists did not "adopt either the theories or the statements of Fourier, as to the relation of the sexes, nor [were they] in any way responsible for them" (1:350). Furthermore, the chief aims of Associationism were "the organization of labor, the abolition of war, slavery, and domestic servitude, the guarantee to every person of the best possible education, of constant and congenial employment, and of pecuniary independence" (1:351).

The editors of *The Harbinger* were especially annoyed by what they charged was the vindictiveness of Herbert's remarks, but they promptly discovered that, by comparison, they were relatively tame. For in December 1845, just a month after the magazine published its own remarks on Sue's novel, the *Democratic Review* printed an article on *The Wandering Jew* that was, according to *The Harbinger*, "for barefaced and atrocious misrepresentation of the Associative movement in this country . . . without a parallel among the productions of a partisan and bigoted press" (2:60). The magazine was shocked that a journal with so enviable a reputation as that of the *Democratic Review* would publish an article so obviously designed to "appeal to the most shameful prejudices," an article that "would disgrace the most vulgar writer who could be hired to serve the cause of a vindictive, personal controversy" (2:60). *The Harbinger* could account for its appearance only by the temporary absence of the *Democratic Review*'s editor, John L. O'Sullivan, who, the magazine was sure, would not have lent his name to such a "tissue of error and misrepresentation." This opinion was supported by the *Daily Advertiser,* a leading Democratic paper in Rochester, New York, which criticized the *Democratic Review* for publishing "the meanest, most disgraceful, most contemptible [review] that ever appeared in any journal assuming the name of democratic" (2:79).

The *Democratic Review*'s charges were familiar ones, and Ripley and his colleagues responded to them by repeating in the pages of *The Harbinger,* "perhaps for the thousandth time," that "Fourier is not our Master, but our Teacher." Associative interest in Fourier, it was said, was limited to the Frenchman's theories on industrial reform. These, for the most part, were supported by concrete evidence and observation. So far as Fourier's speculations on other subjects were concerned, Associationists rejected them.

Attacks such as these came with such frequency that the newly formed American Union of Associationists was compelled to issue an official statement of its objects and principles. Apparently, the original Constitution of the American Union of Associationists—which had been drafted and adopted on 27 May 1846 in Boston at the New England Fourier Society meeting—had not been very widely circulated, for that document certainly defined clearly the nature of the Associationist relationship to Fourier. Specifically, Article 7 of the Constitution stated, in part, that

we recognize the invaluable worth of the discoveries of Charles Fourier in the Science of Society, the harmony of that Science with all the vital truths of Christianity, and the promise it holds out of a material condition of life wherein alone the spirit of Christ can dwell in all its fulness;—but *"Fourierists"* we are not, and cannot consent to be called, because Fourier is only *one* among the great teachers of mankind; because many of his assertions are concerning spheres of thought which exceed our present ability to test, and of which it would be presumption for us to affirm with confidence; and because we regard this as a holy and providential movement, independent of every merely *individual* influence or guidance, the sure and gradual evolving of Man's great unitary destiny in the Ages.[19]

In any event, it was noted in the number for 15 August 1846 that the American Union regretfully observed, though without surprise, "that misconceptions, errors, and calumnies are widely circulated in relation to the doctrines of Associationism." Specifically, Associationists had been accused most often of advocating the abolishment of the institutions of marriage, representative government, and the Christian Church. These charges, the Union said, were simply untrue. Associationists would not abolish or significantly alter any of these institutions, though they would try to improve them. Marriage in the present state of society, it noted, was actually a form of "legalized prostitution," but it was also "the most sacred and important of existing social ties, and . . . the pivot on which the order of society depends" (3:153–54). Associationists considered representative government "the greatest step of modern political improvement." Despite its many imperfections, it at least embodied a part of the idea of human liberty. And so far as the Christian Church was concerned, Associationists would like to see the many hostile and scattered religious sects brought together in one Universal Church, though the reform necessary to effect such a change was not within the province of Associationism.

In short, the Union declared that far from aiming at the destruction of these institutions, Associationists regarded their preservation "as an indispensable condition of the reform to which we are devoted." The institutions which Associationists condemned as false, corrupting, oppressive, and brutalizing were slavery; the system of labor for wages, which was a form of slavery maintained by capitalists; the existing system of commerce, which was wasteful and complicated; prostitution in all its forms; monopoly of the soil; pauperism; war; and competition, which caused hatreds, frauds, jealousies, and lies. Regarding Fourier, Associationists thought him to be the discoverer of the laws of universal unity. No other man ever explained so clearly the great principles of harmony or the formulas for "the organization of all the departments of human activity, according to the divine plan" (7:202).

These clarifying statements did nothing, it seems, to lessen the number or intensity of the attacks on Associationism. In fact, assaults on Associationist doctrines continued right up to the concluding numbers of *The Harbinger*. Specifically, the *American Review*,[20] *Brownson's Quarterly Review*,[21] and the New York press generally,[22] especially the New York *Observer*,[23] were most vehement in their denunciations of Associationism. *The Harbinger* even challenged the New York *Observer* to a formal debate on the merits of

Associationist aims, a debate to consist of six or twelve articles of a stipulated length to be published in full in both magazines. The *Observer,* however, did not even acknowledge *The Harbinger*'s invitation.

Some papers and magazines, such as the *National Era* (Washington, D.C.), the New Bedford *Mercury* (Massachusetts), and the *National Anti-Slavery Standard* (New York), were often reasonable in their discussions of Associationism, and the Boston *Chronotype* (which allowed Associationists the use of three of its columns on a weekly basis after the demise of *The Harbinger*) and *The Voice of Industry* (Massachusetts) usually printed articles that commended the utopian socialists and their aims.[24] Even the New York *Herald* and the New York *Mirror,* according to *The Harbinger* (4:179; 5:271), began publishing articles "favorable" to Associationists, though this must have been only a temporary lapse in the usual editorial policy of anti-Associationism in these papers, for Ripley and his fellow editors criticized both of them on ideological grounds more than once in the last three volumes of *The Harbinger.*

Overall, though, it may be said that the general controversy inspired by Associationism did have at least two positive effects: one was that it enabled Associationists such as Ripley, Dwight, and Dana to achieve a degree of publicity for their cause that might not otherwise have been possible. The more that detractors railed against Associative doctrines, the more attention they brought to Associationism. In a sense, the critics inadvertently provided Associationists with a broader-based forum than they might otherwise have had, one that enabled them to discuss contemporary social problems and to suggest Associative methods for eliminating them. It was stated many times in the columns of *The Harbinger* that the best way to make converts to Associationism was by having the issues brought to the attention of the public. People might then recognize the many injustices in society, as well as the ineffectiveness of the existing institutions to alleviate them.

The second positive effect of these battles was the clarity and precision with which *The Harbinger* was compelled to discuss Associationism. The various assaults made it essential for the paper to explain in exact terms the Associative program for the widespread reform that *The Harbinger* advocated. This was especially important since Fourier's own terms were often ambiguous and confusing, even at times to thoroughgoing Associationists.[25] Obviously, Associationist doctrines could not be promoted effectively if adherents were unable to explain them, or be somewhat uniform in their explanations. The magazine, therefore, devoted considerable space in its columns to extended definitions of such Fourierist axioms as "attractions are proportional to destinies" and "the series distribute the harmonies," and such Fourierist concepts as the four affective passions, the three distributive passions, and the distributive or mechanizing attractions.

Finally, it probably ought to be noted that the difference between being an Associationist and a Fourierist was not, perhaps, so dramatic as that between being a Transcendentalist (read individualist) and an Associationist (read communitarian). Still, there was a difference between Associationism and Fourierism, and to Associationists it was obviously a significant one. Apart from the irony that the more trouble they went to to make that difference clear the more muddled it seems to have become, there is a more fundamental point to make: the confusion between Associationism and Fourierism serves to remind us that Transcendentalism as a whole always was an amorphous phenomenon. To be sure, if anything has characterized Transcendentalism, it has been the difficulty of defining it. As Richard Francis pointed out in his article on "The Ideology of Brook Farm": "It is obviously much easier to make certain assumptions about the [Transcendental] movement than to attempt a satisfactory definition of it."[26] The example of the Associationist movement in America—specifically in New England in the 1840s—is certainly a further illustration of the truth of that important point.

Predecessors of *The Harbinger*

The Harbinger was the immediate successor to Albert Brisbane's *The Phalanx* (1843–45), though William Henry Channing's *The Present* (1843–44) may also be said to have been its predecessor.[27] Channing published the first number of his monthly magazine in September 1843. Its purpose was, among other things, "to encourage and note the progress of spiritual and humane enterprises to remove ignorance, vice, and suffering; [and] to record discoveries and inventions which promise to elevate man's condition."[28] Channing apparently thought that the French socialists were the most important contributors in these areas, for he filled the pages of his magazine with their writings.[29]

Channing himself was a man who embraced all the popular reforms of the day, from abolition to temperance.[30] Publishing, however, was not one of his strong points; he failed to issue the February number for 1844, and he managed to publish only seven numbers of *The Present* before its demise with the April 1844 issue. Though he did publish a prospectus for a second volume, it never appeared. Channing announced suspension of his publication due to the "near and sacred" duty of preparing a memoir of his uncle, the venerable Unitarian, Dr. William Ellery Channing.[31] In the same announcement he expressed his obligation to the doctrines of Fourier, and he apologized for the "abstract and 'transcendental'" cast of his previous articles.[32]

With the closing of Channing's magazine, the "friends" of social reform turned their attention to Albert Brisbane's *The Phalanx*. Brisbane was regarded by Associationists as the foremost expositor of Fourier's theories in America, as indeed he was. He traveled in Europe from 1828 to 1832 and

took lessons from the master himself. After his return to America he published a pamphlet, *Two Essays on the Social System of Charles Fourier,
Being an Introduction to the Constitution of the Fourienne Society of New
York* (New York, 1838, 24 pp.), which was the first Fourierist publication in
the United States.[33] Two years later Brisbane published the most thorough
exposition of Fourier in English, *Social Destiny of Man* (1840). Then on 1
March 1842 he began a column in Horace Greeley's New York *Tribune,* for
which he personally paid, and in which he explained and defended Fourier's
theories.[34] That column ran for nineteen months. A year after he began this
column, Brisbane published *Association: or, A Concise Exposition of the
Practical Part of Fourier's Social Science* (New York, 1843), of which
10,000 copies were in print by 1847.[35]

The first notice of Brisbane's *The Phalanx* appeared in the second number
of Channing's *The Present* in a column headed "Signs of the Times."[36] In the
first number, which appeared in October 1843, Brisbane announced that *The
Phalanx* would be the organ of Fourier's theories, and that is precisely what
it was for the next year and a half of its existence. The last number was
published on 23 May 1845, just two weeks before *The Harbinger* issued its
first number.

At this time, Brisbane printed the prospectus of *The Harbinger* and an-
nounced that the subscription lists to *The Phalanx,* as well as to John Allen's
Social Reformer, had been transferred to Brook Farm, for the name of *The
Phalanx* was to be changed to *The Harbinger.* Among the leading con-
tributors to the new magazine, it was announced, would be Parke Godwin,
Albert Brisbane, Osborne Macdaniel, and Horace Greeley, all from New
York; George Ripley, Charles A. Dana, John S. Dwight, L. W. Ryckman,
and John Allen of Brook Farm; and Francis G. Shaw of West Roxbury.[37]

Thus, the press campaign that Brisbane had been waging for some seven
years did not end with the final number of his *Phalanx,* for *The Harbinger*
committed itself to continuing the campaign in its pages, a task that for the
next four years it performed remarkably well, considering the problems with
which it had to contend.

A History of Financial Difficulties

In some respects, it was unfortunate that *The Harbinger* was published at
Brook Farm at all. Had it been initially published in New York, where it was
eventually transferred in November 1847, it might have enjoyed a longer life,
for it did have the makings of a first-rate journal. It counted among its
editorial staff some of the best minds of the era; its contributors were as
talented a group as any that could be found at that time in New England; and
its contents, particularly its musical criticism, were always vigorous, lively,
and high-minded.

The first five of the magazine's eight volumes were published at Brook Farm. As such, *The Harbinger* was directly affected by events occurring in the community. Unfortunately, the timing could not have been worse: by the winter of 1845, just a few months after the publication of the magazine's first number, Marianne Dwight, one of the most prolific letterwriters at Brook Farm, reported that the community had reached its "severest crisis." "We are perplexed," she wrote, "by debts, by want of capital to carry on any business to advantage, [and] by want of our Phalanstery or the means to finish it."[38]

Though there is little indication of the alarming situation involving *The Harbinger* or Brook Farm in the journal's first volume, there was abundant evidence in the correspondence of members of the community.[39] In addition to Miss Dwight's letter of 7 December 1845, there was a letter from Brisbane to Ripley on 9 December 1845, saying that the New York Associationists were seriously considering pledging their support to the recently formed North American Phalanx, located at Red Bank, New Jersey.[40] This letter must have surprised Ripley, for only a year earlier this same group had informed him that their base for propagandizing for Fourierism would be Brook Farm. Indeed, only a few months before, Brisbane himself had personally charged Ripley and *The Harbinger* with continuing the press campaign for the "cause." We can only imagine Ripley's shock, or perhaps despair, when just two weeks after Brisbane's portentous news, a letter arrived from George W. Curtis, a sometime resident at Brook Farm and later the editor of *Harper's Weekly,* in which he told his companions: "My New York friends . . . would christen your sheet 'An Omen Ill' instead of Harbinger."[41]

Of course, it was impossible for the New York Associationists to know how soon their ominous pronouncement would be fulfilled, but less than three months later the Brook Farm Phalanstery burned to the ground. Started in the summer of 1844, the long-awaited structure was near completion when it was destroyed on 3 March 1846. Unfortunately, the Brook Farmers had already invested $7,000 in it. Worse, since "it was not yet in use by the Association, and until the day of its destruction, not exposed to fire, no insurance had been effected" (2:221).

Ripley announced the loss by fire in the 14 March 1846 number. It was the first indication in the magazine itself that the weekly paper was in trouble. Ironically enough, Ripley, just a few months earlier, encouragingly reported that *The Harbinger* had reached a circulation of one thousand (1:79). Now, however, he had to acknowledge that the loss would be "a severe trial of our strength; . . . it may prove more than we are able to bear" (2:22). A week later, in a followup article entitled "To Our Friends," Ripley emphasized Brook Farm's central importance in the Associationist movement in America, but he admitted that the fire was "a total destruction of resources . . . and must inevitably derange our plans for the enlargement of the Association and the extension of our industry" (2:237). A month later, the magazine reported that certain branches of industry at the Farm would have to be suspended, though the press was not to be one of them (2:237). For the following few months, *The Harbinger* repeatedly issued requests for names that could be added to its subscription lists. By June 1846, Ripley finally was required to make a bold and urgent plea:

> We are . . . compelled to make an urgent appeal to the friends of the cause throughout the country to aid our publication. . . .
> We wish it to be clearly understood, that our paper cannot be sustained without the zealous cooperation of our friends. . . . We have never received a sufficient patronage to justify the expense of its [*The Harbinger*'s] publication. . . . We are bound to acknowledge that any material diminution in the number of our subscribers would so far embarrass our proceedings, as to render the continuance of "The Harbinger" difficult, if not impossible. [3:12]

In the months that followed Ripley's appeal, matters seem not to have improved substantially. Life in the community became increasingly more difficult, and by the fall of 1846, a majority of its members had left. About the only thing remaining was *The Harbinger,* and under the present circumstances, it was only a matter of weeks before it too would be discontinued. Realizing this fact, Ripley sent John S. Dwight, his devoted associate and coeditor of the magazine from 1846 to 1847, to a Boston meeting of the newly formed American Union of Associationists. There, on 21 September 1846, Dwight put the matter unequivocally to the organization: either the Union take over the financial burden of publishing *The Harbinger,* or affirm it did not need the organ and let it die.

Dwight's ultimatum confused the directors of the Union, for they knew the Union could not at that time assume such a financial responsibility. There were, however, several individual expressions of faith: Charles Dana pledged to raise $150.00 for the publication of the fourth volume; John Orvis, one of the Union's directors and the future husband of Marianne Dwight, said he would purchase 500 copies of the magazine's next number, and he pledged to raise $50.00 for the next volume; and several members made contributions on the spot (3:268).

These contributions, as well as others, enabled Ripley to raise $464.00 (4:64), and the fourth volume of *The Harbinger* was published, seemingly without any real financial difficulty, for there was practically no mention anywhere in the volume of the need for new subscribers. Eventually, the American Union of Associationists saw its way clear to give the paper the financial backing it had earlier requested. It was announced in the 29 May 1847 number of *The Harbinger* that the next issue would close the fourth volume: "At that time, it [*The Harbinger*] will be transferred from the Brook Farm Phalanx to the American Union of Associationists" (4:400). From 12 June 1847, the first issue of volume 5, until 10 February 1849, the final number, the paper was published by the Union. It should be noted, however, that the entire contents of the fifth volume were printed at Brook Farm.

Thus the actual transfer of the magazine to New York did not occur until November 1847, by which time the Union had established its central office in New York. There *The Harbinger* immediately underwent a few significant changes, including the appointment of Parke Godwin as editor, a leading Fourierist at the time and later editor of the New York *Evening Post*. This position as editor of *The Harbinger* Godwin held until the magazine's demise in 1849. It was also decided that George Ripley and Charles Dana would be Godwin's editorial assistants in New York. John Dwight and William Henry Channing remained in Boston in order to perform what apparently were thought to be less consequential editorial duties in that city.

It was hoped that *The Harbinger*'s removal to New York would result in an expanded reading audience. The New York Associationists quickly discovered, however, that they were no less troubled by financial problems than Ripley had been at Brook Farm. Additionally, there were unanticipated and ultimately unresolvable problems as a result of the transfer: there was a personality clash between Godwin and the Bostonians, Ripley and Dwight[42]; there were publishing delays due to the difficulty of hiring competent foremen; and there were many typographical errors in several issues (a constant source of annoyance) because capable proofreaders were hard to find.

George Ripley, for one, was unaccustomed to these difficulties, for the publishing of the paper had been considerably easier at Brook Farm than it now was in New York. True, there had been financial problems at West Roxbury, but the nature of the community was such that Ripley did not have to go beyond it to insure the appearance of the magazine, for most of those individuals involved in its publication resided at the farm itself. The situation in New York, however, was quite different, and Ripley characterized the initial efforts to publish the magazine there in this way:

> It seems as if all the petty, unexpected little imps and demons that could be produced, were hovering over the first steps of the new *Harbinger,* to give it a most annoying trial, on its entrance to the high, brilliant, and powerful life, to which I am sure it is destined. I should despair giving you an idea of the thousand and one little torments, which we have suffered.[43]

Chief among these so-called torments was the difference between the amount of money expended for *The Harbinger*'s publication (which included such items as printing, folding, and mailing, as well as the salaries of the editors) and the amount of money received for the magazine (not only from weekly sales but from subscriptions and Union dues as well). *The Harbinger* itself published a statement of expenditures for the year May 1847 to May 1848 in which it was stated that the paper operated at a deficit of $1,495.57 for that year (7:30). Expenditures were listed as $2,898.96, of which $826.00

had been paid to the editors and general agent; $2,072.96 of that total had been paid out for the printing of the paper and maintenance of the central office.

By October 1848, Ripley had informed Dwight that "the brethren here [New York City] are getting a good deal discouraged. . . . They all have the feeling that the direct Associative movement is and will be for some time an uphill work in this country, that it will scarce pay the way."[44] Though Ripley was annoyed with his New York associates because he felt they had "little courage, little faith, and little enterprise," he did admit at this time that, proportionately, *The Harbinger* was operating at a greater loss for the previous few months than it had during the year ending May 1848.

With future prospects for the magazine not substantially improved by December 1848, the Union began seriously to consider alternatives for raising funds. Three possibilities were proposed: (1) to reduce the size of the paper; (2) to limit it to a monthly; and (3) to appeal to friends to sustain the present form.[45] On 10 February 1849 *The Harbinger* announced that it would appear in the future either as a monthly magazine or as a weekly newspaper of smaller dimensions (8:116). The purpose for this change, it was stated, was to bring expenditures for the paper more directly in line with its income. The new form, readers were told, would appear in a few days. *The Harbinger,* however, never again appeared in any form. It died with the 10 February 1849 number. So far as is known, subscribers were never provided an explanation, but even the least perceptive of them surely realized the magazine's inability to meet financial exigencies.

A few months after *The Harbinger*'s demise, the executive committee of the American Union of Associationists printed a circular in which it announced that the Union had secured the exclusive use of three columns in the Boston *Daily and Weekly Chronotype.*[46] These columns, under the editorship of John Dwight, were to be devoted to the propagation of Associationist doctrines. Thus, Associationists would once again have an organ that, in addition to W. H. Channing's recently formed *Spirit of the Age* (1849–50), would reach five to six times as many readers as did *The Harbinger.* This plan proved unsuccessful, however, since most of the leading Associationists were shortly to abandon the movement. Nevertheless, these two papers may be said to have been the successors of *The Harbinger.*

General Contents and Contributors

One of the more interesting, if unanswerable, questions pertaining to *The Harbinger* is whether the quality of the magazine diminished or improved with the paper's transfer from Brook Farm to New York in 1847. The answer to that question, of course, depends entirely on one's point of view. Certainly the thoroughgoing Associationist must have considered the New York version of *The Harbinger* to be inferior to the organ published at Brook Farm. During its tenure at Brook Farm, *The Harbinger* had been devoted almost exclusively to propagandizing for Associationism. With its removal to New York, however, the paper acquired a more commercial character, for it was forced to cater to popular tastes in an effort to increase subscription lists. The changes in *The Harbinger*'s format and the increased number of advertisements evidence this fact.

In its years at Brook Farm, the magazine was printed on paper approximately eight inches by eleven inches in size, with sixteen pages to each number, and three columns to a page. Although the design was not fancy or elaborate, it was neat, orderly, and clearly printed. After its transfer, *The Harbinger*'s page size was increased to approximately eleven inches by seventeen and a half, which allowed for four columns to a page. The paper was therefore difficult to read because page size resembled that of a newspaper, the print was small, and the columns were filled with careless typographical errors.

The shift in *The Harbinger*'s advertising policy was no less evident than its change of format. At Brook Farm, the journal published only one advertisement with any consistency, and that pertained to the community's highly regarded school, which was conducted by Ripley and his wife, Sophia. Occasionally it printed advertisements announcing the sale of Associationist works by French authors, but at no time did commercial ads occupy more than one column while the paper was printed at West Roxbury. With its removal to New York, and its added financial difficulties, the paper had to increase the number of advertisements in its pages. Advertisements occupied as many as six to eight columns in most of the New York numbers. This increase was significant, for it directly led to the diminishing quality of *The Harbinger*'s pages.

From the point of view of the more pragmatic Associationist, of course, these changes, as well as others, were both necessary and desirable, for they improved the magazine's chances for survival. The abstract and scientific character of the paper at Brook Farm was not desirable for popular effect. The magazine had to begin selecting its topics for discussion from wider fields of interest. Accordingly, John Dwight's column of musical reviews was expanded to include theater news, foreign-art intelligence, and articles on European and American painters and paintings. Moreover, several columns of "Weekly Gossip" were introduced in an effort to lighten the parochial character for which the paper was known at Brook Farm.[47] No doubt that was the purpose, too, for introducing a weekly column entitled "European Affairs," in which Charles Dana reported significant events taking place in Ireland, France, Italy, and Germany.

In short, the editors of *The Harbinger* made every effort they could to make the New York version of the magazine less parochial and more broadly appealing. Obviously, these efforts were not successful, for the magazine survived in New York only for a year and a half. Quite likely, the terrific competition from other papers had something to do with *The Harbinger*'s failure. In any event, from the magazine's first pages of lofty optimism to its closing plea for reorganization, *The Harbinger* stood (and continues to stand) as a cameo portrait of an experiment that failed, but that failed with a sense of dignity all the same.

The Harbinger began at Brook Farm enthusiastically enough. The first number, which appeared on 14 June 1845, carried two mottoes. The first, "All things, at the present day, stand provided and prepared, and await the light," generally explains the title of the journal. This statement of Emanuel Swedenborg, the Swedish philosopher and theologian, appeared under the masthead of every succeeding number.[48]

The second and more significant quotation came from the great Unitarian minister, Dr. William Ellery Channing, and it became the heading for all of the magazine's editorials:

> Of modern civilization, the natural fruits are, contempt for others' rights, fraud, oppression, a gambling spirit, in trade, reckless adventure, and commercial convulsions all tending to impoverish the laborer and to render every condition insecure. Relief is to come, and can only come from the new applications of Christian principles, of Universal justice and Universal love, to social institutions, to commerce, to business, to active life. [1:8]

It was around these crucial ideas that George Ripley and his associates organized their material for the next five volumes.

In the "Introductory Notice," a lengthy and idealistic manifesto, *The Harbinger* set forth its intentions:

> In meeting our friends, for the first time, in the columns of the Harbinger, we wish to take them by the hand with Cheerful greetings, to express the earnest hope that our intercourse may be as fruitful of good, as it will be frank and sincere, and that we to-day may commence a communion of spirit, which shall mutually aid us in our progress towards the truth and beauty, the possession of which is the ultimate destiny of man.

The notice continued:

> We believe that principles are now in operation, which will produce as great a change on the face of society, as that which caused beauty and order to arise from the chaos of the primitive creation by the movings of the divine Spirit; and to impart these convictions and principles to the hearts of our readers, will be our leading purpose in the columns of this paper. [1:8]

The Harbinger further promised that in its discussions of the social phenomena of the day, it would not be swayed by "prevailing standards of fashion or popular opinion," that it would speak out in all matters with "entire independence of outward authority." The subjects that would most often engage the attention of the magazine would be politics, literature, music, science, and social reform.

In politics, the notice stated, *The Harbinger* would strive to be entirely democratic: "We shall take sides with no party, but proceed from time to time to remark upon all parties, with the frankness and independence which our position fully enables us to exercise." In literature, the magazine's aim would be to improve the taste of the public rather than "gratify the cupidity of booksellers." In music, it noted, there had heretofore not existed in America any such thing as musical criticism. It pledged to contribute something, "if only by our sincerity and impartiality, toward a sound and profitable criticism." Scientific discoveries, it promised, would always be noted, especially those bearing on "the progressive well-being of man."

But however much attention would be given these subjects, *The Harbinger* wanted it to be unmistakably clear that its interest in social reform would be paramount. No love of literature, no enjoyment of abstract discussions, and no delight in intellectual theories would seduce the paper from its "devotion to the cause of the oppressed, the down-trodden, [and] the insulted and injured masses of our fellow men." Because it intended to labor for the equal rights of all people, *The Harbinger* expected to find its audience, not only among "refined" and "educated" citizens, but among "swart and sweaty artisans" and laborers as well.

Obviously the undertakings of *The Harbinger* were numerous, and the aid of several individuals had to be enlisted. Those contributors who helped to fulfill the magazine's lofty promises were, for the most part, of two groups: the Brook Farmers and their friends, and the Fourierists, who had little connection with the American Transcendental movement as it emerged in Boston in the 1830s and 1840s. The following individuals were listed as the authors for the first volume[49]:

Albert Brisbane, New York
William H. Channing, New York
Otis Clapp, Boston
Christopher P. Cranch, New York
George W. Curtis, New York
Charles A. Dana, Brook Farm
A. J. H. Duganne, Philadelphia
John S. Dwight, Brook Farm
George G. Foster, New York
E. P. Grant, Canton, Ohio
Parke Godwin, New York
Horace Greeley, New York
Thomas W. Higginson, Cambridge
James R. Lowell, Cambridge

Osborne Macdaniel, New York
D. S. Oliphant, Batavia, New York
George Ripley, Brook Farm
L. W. Ryckman, Brook Farm
J. A. Saxton, Deerfield, Mass.
Francis G. Shaw, West Roxbury, Mass.
William W. Story, Boston
John G. Whittier, Amesbury, Mass.

The second volume listed these contributors[50]:

Albert Brisbane
William H. Channing, Brook Farm
William F. Channing, Boston
Walter Channing, Boston
James F. Clarke, Boston
Christopher P. Cranch
George W. Curtis
Charles A. Dana
John S. Dwight
George G. Foster
Parke Godwin
E. P. Grant
Thomas W. Higginson
Osborne Macdaniel
John Orvis, Brook Farm
George Ripley
Francis G. Shaw
William W. Story

These individuals made original contributions to the third volume:

S. P. Andrews, Boston
Albert Brisbane
William H. Channing, Boston
William E. Channing, Concord, Mass.
Christopher P. Cranch
George W. Curtis
Charles A. Dana
John S. Dwight
E. P. Grant
Frederic H. Hedge, Bangor, Me.
Thomas W. Higginson
Max E. Lazarus, Wilmington, N.C.
J. H. Pulte, Cincinnati, Ohio

George Ripley
S. D. Robbins, Chelsea, Mass.
Francis G. Shaw
William W. Story

The fourth volume included contributions by:

Albert Brisbane
William H. Channing
George W. Curtis
Charles A. Dana
John S. Dwight
Parke Godwin
Thomas W. Higginson
Max E. Lazarus
James R. Lowell
Osborne Macdaniel
John Orvis
George Ripley
Francis G. Shaw
William W. Story

The fifth volume was written by:

John Allen, Boston
William H. Channing
J. J. Cooke, Providence, R.I.
George W. Curtis
John S. Dwight
Thomas W. Higginson, Newburyport, R.I.
Max E. Lazarus
Osborne Macdaniel
C. Neidhardt, Philadelphia
John Orvis
Jean M. Palisse, Brook Farm
E. W. Parkman, Boston
George Ripley
Miss E. A. Starr, Deerfield, Mass.

The sixth volume, the first to be published in New York, listed these contributors:

George H. Calvert, Newport, R.I.
William H. Channing

J. J. Cooke
Charles A. Dana, New York
John S. Dwight, Boston
Parke Godwin
E. Ives, Jr., New York
Henry James, New York
Max E. Lazarus
Osborne Macdaniel
Jean M. Palisse, New York
Mary S. Pease, Philadelphia
George Ripley, New York
James Sellers, Jr., Philadelphia
Francis G. Shaw, New York
J. J. G. Wilkinson, London

These contributors authored the seventh volume:

Charles A. Dana
John S. Dwight
Edward Giles, New York
Parke Godwin
Henry James
Max E. Lazarus
William H. Meller, Pa.
George Ripley
James Sellers, Jr.
Eliza A. Starr
Edmund Tweedy, New York
J. J. G. Wilkinson

It should be noted that not all contributors were listed in the indexes, perhaps because they wished to remain anonymous. Several of the poems published in the magazine, for example, were signed with pseudonyms such as "Portia" and "One of the Steps," while still other verses were signed only by initials such as "x.," "R. H. B.," and "E. B. B." George H. Calvert, for one, contributed seven poems to *The Harbinger* under the initials "E. Y. T."[51] Additionally, the sixth volume failed to include the name of Poe's friend, Frances Osgood, who contributed a poem entitled "Stanzas for Music" (6:194).

As was noted earlier, *The Harbinger* engaged the talents of several men possessing genuine literary ability. A glance at the list of contributors in the indexes of the magazine is sufficient to indicate this fact. It should be remarked too that eleven of *The Harbinger*'s contributors had earlier written for the *Dial:* William Ellery Channing, William Henry Channing, Clarke, Cranch, Curtis, Dana, Dwight, Hedge, Lowell, Ripley, and Saxton.

Undoubtedly the central problem confronting Ripley and his associates from the outset was that of producing a more or less literary paper, but one that, at the same time, would espouse and advance the cause of Associationism in America. Clarence Gohdes has stated in *The Periodicals of American Transcendentalism* that such items as poems, book reviews, musical criticism, and fiction were merely "a sauce for the weighty editorials dealing with various aspects of socialism, the translations from Fourier, and other French believers in 'Unity,' and the essays by American advocates of the cause."[52] This evaluation of *The Harbinger*'s contents is essentially accurate, for the magazine certainly published many more articles pertaining to Associationism than on any other subject. Gohdes's observation, however, fails to convey the seriousness with which subjects other than those relating to social reform were treated. *The Harbinger*'s *raison d'être* may have been to proselytize for Associationism and Fourierism, but one need only read Dwight's reviews of music, or some of the book reviews and articles on art generally, to realize that such matters were not taken lightly at all.

Indeed, it is somewhat difficult to believe that *The Harbinger*'s serialization of *Consuelo* (French ed., 1845) and *The Countess of Rudolstadt* (French ed., 1846), two works of fiction by George Sand, was intended only to provide "sauce" for weightier matters. Certainly it took some courage to translate and publish these two novels at a time when "American critical journals were almost unanimously hostile to French fiction in general." As one modern critic has noted: "*The Harbinger* stands out in the forties as the staunchest defender of [the] French novel . . . and in particular of George Sand, who was by far the most controversial French literary figure of the time."[53]

Francis G. Shaw, a friend and West Roxbury neighbor of the Brook Farm community, provided his own copyrighted translations of both these works. The serialization of *Consuelo* was spread out over the first three volumes; it appeared in twenty-five numbers of the first volume; in all twenty-six numbers of the second volume; and in three numbers of the third volume. With the conclusion of this novel, *The Harbinger* began serializing the second by Sand, *The Countess of Rudolstadt*. It ran for twenty-three numbers in the third volume and appeared in fifteen numbers of the fourth. These two novels were the only fiction ever published in *The Harbinger*.

Additionally, Shaw translated two other works by Sand for the magazine. One was a short article, "The Scepticism of the Age," printed in the 9 August 1845 number. The other, *Letters of a Traveller*, appeared in five installments in the fifth volume.

To some extent, to be sure, *The Harbinger* relied on translations such as these to help fill its pages, and Sand was only one of several French writers whose translated works appeared in the magazine. In fact, with the exception of Sand, the paper uniformly published translated versions of works by

French Associationists. At the head of the list, of course, was Fourier himself, though the journal did not publish as many of his writings as one would expect. In his book about Brook Farm, Zoltan Haraszti stated that, in December 1845, Albert Brisbane unloaded several unpublished Fourier manuscripts on *The Harbinger*.[54] *The Harbinger,* however, obviously decided not to publish them, for only four of the Frenchman's works in translation ever appeared in the magazine. One of these, "An Unpublished Fragment of Fourier," was reprinted from the leading organ of the French Associationists, *La Démocratie Pacifique,* and it appeared in *The Harbinger* in the 15 August 1846 number. Of the others, "Confirmation of the Doctrine of Association, Drawn from the Holy Evangelists," was published in the numbers for 11 and 18 October 1845. John Dwight translated this work, as he did *Cosmogony,* theretofore an unpublished Fourier manuscript, which appeared in *The Harbinger* in four installments beginning with the first number of the second volume. The most extended writing to appear in the journal was his *Le Nouveau Monde Industriel* (French ed., 1829). Also translated by Dwight, it ran for twenty-three numbers in the second and third volumes.

More popular than Fourier, at least insofar as numbers of translations were concerned, was Victor Considerant, a leading French social scientist and Associationist. Translations of his works appeared in thirty-eight numbers of the paper. Other French Associationists whose works were translated for *The Harbinger* were Victor Hannequin, Matthew Briancourt, H. Gorsse, B. Constant, V. Meunier, and Mme. D'Alibert.

Yet another feature that occupied *The Harbinger*'s columns was poetry, a rather convenient filler for the half-columns that the paper's weighty prose articles had an uneconomical habit of leaving blank. Early in its career the magazine announced that it was "proud to number among our contributors some of our best American poets" (1:112). While this may in some sense have been true (James Russell Lowell and John Greenleaf Whittier were listed as contributors), that fact certainly did not substantially alleviate *The Harbinger*'s difficulty of publishing original verse. Of the more than 440 poems published during the magazine's existence, slightly less than one-fourth were original; the remainder was reprinted from various sources.

While the editors of *The Harbinger* obviously had difficulty filling the columns of the magazine with original verse, they certainly had no such trouble with book reviews. In all, the magazine published approximately 356 such reviews and literary notices, all of which were original, and most of which were written by Dana, Dwight, and Ripley. Many of these reviews were characterized by their critical acumen, though they often were, as one might expect, occasions to proselytize for Associationism. Typically, it mattered little to *The Harbinger*'s reviewers whether the book being considered concerned euthanasia, the water cure, or life in the South Sea islands, for they had little difficulty injecting extraliterary considerations into their discussions. Thus, the fact that the magazine regularly reviewed books on such diverse subjects as Charles Kraitsir's *Significance of the Alphabet* (1846), Captain Henry Keppel's *Expedition to Borneo* (1846), and A. J. Downing's *The Fruits and Fruit Trees of America* (1845) is more an indication of the magazine's desire to discuss Associationism whenever possible than an evidence of the paper's catholicity of taste.

Frequently, a less propagandistic attitude was adopted when books by noted American and European authors were reviewed. Among the American authors discussed in *The Harbinger*'s columns were Poe, Melville, Hawthorne, Emerson, Longfellow, Lowell, and Whittier, to mention a few. European authors reviewed in the magazine included, among others, Dickens, Charlotte Brontë, Shelley, Hood, and Tennyson from England; Goethe, Fichte, and Schlegel from Germany; and George Sand and Eugène Sue from France. A great deal of critical attention was paid Emanuel Swedenborg, the Swedish theologian, scientist, and philosopher. In fact, he was the subject of no fewer than seventeen reviews.

If anything, however, *The Harbinger* distinguished itself at the time of its publication, as well as in the years since its demise, by its music criticism. Unquestionably, that was one of the chief merits of the paper. In fact, it may be claimed with some justice that *The Harbinger* was the first magazine in the history of American journalism to present anything resembling a consistent body of criticism on this particular art form.

In charge of this feature was John S. Dwight, who wrote over one hundred such reviews for the magazine before its demise in 1849. He received occasional assistance from George W. Curtis, Christopher Pearse Cranch, and William W. Story. At Brook Farm, Dwight's column, "Musical Review," was limited solely to criticism of music. With the magazine's transfer to New York, the column's title was changed to "Art Review" so as to include additional articles by Dana, Ripley, Godwin, and Elam Ives, Jr., on such subjects as the theater, the American Art Union, painters and paintings, and foreign art.

After *The Harbinger*'s demise, Dwight eventually founded and edited *Dwight's Journal of Music* (1852–81). But by 1849 he had established *The Harbinger* as America's leading journal of music criticism, and *The Harbinger,* in its turn, had afforded the Brook Farmer the opportunity to establish himself as the country's foremost music critic. Music criticism, however, as well as the translation of foreign works, poetry, and the book reviews, formed only a part of *The Harbinger*'s contents. Understandably, the bulk of the material that filled the magazine's pages had to do with Associationism; so much so, in fact, that this subject must be treated separately under its own heading.

2

The Harbinger and Associationism

Nicholas V. Riasanovsky observed in his study of Charles Fourier that the Frenchman's writings were characterized by "an obsessive and overwhelming repetitiousness. . . . In a sense, they contain only a single message, a single, almost palpable, formula which, once applied, would magically transform human society and the universe itself." [1] Riasanovsky's observation could apply with equal force to *The Harbinger,* for the magazine's pages were filled almost exclusively with articles promulgating certain of Fourier's doctrines as the chief remedy for eliminating such social evils as pauperism, crime, prostitution, slavery, and the degradation of the laboring classes by a capitalist monied class. This is not to suggest that the attitude embodied in *The Harbinger* was uniformly single-minded. On the contrary, the magazine regularly included such features as book reviews, poetry, and music criticism in its first five volumes. Volumes 6–8 contained, in addition, a weekly gossip column, theatre news, art reviews, and news from Europe. Nevertheless, *The Harbinger*'s *raison d'être* was to advance the cause of Associationism in America, and thus the majority of the magazine's contents concerned that subject. If anything characterized *The Harbinger,* it was the high seriousness with which the magazine discussed the subjects of Associationism and Fourierism, as well as the single-mindedness of purpose with which it proselytized for the acceptance of these utopian socialist programs in the United States.

Among the more cogent articles designed to serve this purpose was one written by Albert Brisbane to the editor of the *Democratic Review* (1837–49)—which was the journal that had absorbed Orestes Brownson's *Boston Quarterly Review* in 1842—that was reprinted in *The Harbinger* in the number for 7 March 1846. Brisbane said that Associationists desired thorough and organic social reform. They wanted to replace the present social mechanism, which was characterized by conflicts, misery, disunion, and servitude, with a new social order, one in which labor would be dignified and made attractive, for industrial reform provided the means to secure universal abundance for all and thereby "banish the scourge of poverty from the world" (2:202). Brisbane noted that the American people already had begun this reform, for they had done away with political oppression in the form of kings, aristocracies, estates, and titles. The most serious anarchy remaining was industrial in nature. The present system of commerce was brutalizing and degrading, pitting, as it did, labor against capital, and thereby creating relentless competition, unequal social opportunities and privileges, domestic servitude, and a system of menial and hireling labor. Associationism was formed to change this situation and thus it was, Brisbane said, the holiest of causes because its chief aim was the elevation of mankind from poverty, ignorance, and degradation to a state of universal abundance, universal intelligence, and universal happiness. The means for achieving such a goal was Association, or the organization of industry according to the guidelines set down by Fourier. Associationists were not interested in establishing a new church, nor did they consider themselves in any sense a new religious sect or new political faction. Their primary concern, it had been noted on an earlier occasion, was simply the doing away with "the antagonisms and jealousy which did [not] fail to spring up whenever the principle of competition [was] permitted to usurp the place of cooperation" (1:90).

In this statement (which Brisbane originally wrote to the *Democratic Review* in rebuttal of that magazine's attack on Eugene Sue and *The Wandering Jew*—see chapter 1, pp. 20–21), Brisbane addressed himself less to the philosophical than to the practical aspects of Associationism. In fairness to Brisbane, *The Harbinger* had covered the former ground on several occasions, notably in an editorial essay by George Ripley on the "Relation of Associationism to Civilization," which appeared in the number for 4 December 1847.

Associationists believed, according to Ripley, that God created the material and spiritual worlds and was their legislator. His laws extended to every human fact and every phenomenon of nature, whether the progress of human history or the movement of planetary spheres. Man's existence on earth, as well as his social, moral, religious, philosophic, aesthetic, and economic progress, was part of a complicated drama, the climax of which was to be universal harmony on earth. This harmony would not be realized until man discovered the already existing order of relations in nature with which he could put himself in perfect unison. That mankind would some day make this discovery, and that society would be part of the universal harmony, was as absolutely certain "as the course of the Sun, from one quarter of the horizon to the other" (6:37). Associationists claimed that gradual progress toward this end could be seen historically, since man had already witnessed the successive stages of what were called Savagism, Patriarchialism, Barbarism, and Civilization. It was the present age, then, which tended more toward universal harmony than any of the others preceding it. Nevertheless, human nature in the present age was still debased, and Associationists were fully aware of "the monstrous evils which characterize the present organization of society" (6:37). These evils—the result of violating divine social laws—would not be eliminated until man perfected himself and discovered and aligned himself with the divine plan.

Fortunately, the essay went on to state, one man had made significant progress in revealing the laws of universal harmony, and that man, of course, was Charles Fourier. The present age, then, only required the application of these laws. And judging by the spirit of the times, the "most active and the most torpid minds" alike had been aroused to an interest in Associationism. Thus Associationists were confident that the truth would soon be revealed to everyone like "the brightness of the noonday sun" (6:37).

Though the Associationist movement, insofar as instituting a thoroughgoing socialist reform in America was concerned, proved to be a failure, nevertheless *The Harbinger* helped to plant seeds that are being harvested today, among them, women's rights, racial equality, and concern for the downtrodden members of society. No other magazine campaigned more vigorously, more seriously, or more thoroughly for the acceptance in the United States of Associationist doctrines. Despite the sudden and unexpected demise of Brook Farm and the eventual transfer of *The Harbinger* in November 1847 to New York, despite ever-present financial difficulties that continually threatened to shut down publishing operations altogether, and despite frequent attacks from usually uninformed and spiteful critics, the editors of the magazine consistently and enthusiastically proselytized for Associationism. From its frequent translations of such French writers as George Sand, Charles Fourier, and Victor Considerant (see pp. 36–37 and below), to its weighty editorial essays on Associationism, to its instrumental role in the establishment of the American Union of Associationists, to its reports on the Wisconsin Phalanx, the North American Phalanx in New Jersey, and the Integral Phalanx in Illinois, to its coverage of the 1848 revolution in France (see below, pp. 44–45), *The Harbinger* virtually bombarded its readers with material pertaining to all aspects of the Associationist movement in Europe and especially in the United States.

Actually, much of the material published in *The Harbinger* was not originally written for the magazine. There was considerable reprinting of material from American journals (see below), but much more from European sources, especially in the form of translations from the leading writers of the French Associationist school. In fact, with one possible exception, all of the translations published in *The Harbinger* derived from the French Associationist school. The one exception was George Sand, who was not an Associationist but whose works often were sympathetic with Associationist aims. That surely had much to do with the magazine's decision to be the first in America to publish her *Consuelo* and *The Countess of Rudolstadt*. The serialization of *Consuelo* appeared in all but one of the magazine's first fifty-five numbers, and *The Countess of Rodolstadt* was serialized in thirty-eight numbers of the third and fourth volumes. These two novels were the only fiction ever published in *The Harbinger*.

In addition, the magazine translated and serialized two of Fourier's works, his *Le Nouveau Monde Industriel* in twenty-three numbers, and his *Cosmogony* in four numbers. Fourier's "Confirmation of the Doctrine of Association, Drawn from the Holy Evangelists" was the first of the Frenchman's writings to be translated for the magazine, and it appeared in the 11 and 18 October 1845 numbers. No other writings by Fourier appeared in *The Harbinger* after 15 August 1846, at which time the magazine published "An Unpublished Fragment of Fourier." Insofar as numbers of translations were concerned, Victor Considerant, then the leader of the French Associationist school, was more popular than Fourier. Three of his books, two of his longer articles, and one of his shorter articles were translated and serialized in *The Harbinger*—namely, *Harmony* in fifteen numbers, *Industrial Organization* in eight numbers, *Architecture* in four numbers, "Studies Upon Several Fundamental Problems of Social Science" in six numbers, "The Doctrine of Redemption, and the Return to the Christianity of Christ" in four numbers, and "Passion" in one number. In addition, *Elementary Notions of the Social Science,* written by an H. Gorsse, a member of the French Associationist school, was serialized in thirteen numbers.

The magazine had two very convenient sources for its translations of articles in *La Démocratie Pacifique* and *La Phalange,* the former a daily paper published by the French Associationist school, the latter a monthly journal conducted by Victor Hannequin, a leading French Associationist. *The Harbinger* frequently translated articles from these publications, especially from *La Démocratie Pacifique,* on a wide variety of subjects, but all pertaining to Associationism.

The Harbinger was not nearly so selective, however, in publishing reprints of articles from American and European journals. To all appearances its only criterion was that an article be concerned with Associationism, a criterion that made for a wide latitude in selection. Articles on the famine in Ireland, the war with Mexico, the workingmen's protective union, and the homestead exemptions, for example, were excerpted from such diverse papers as the Pittsburgh *Journal,* the Chicago *Democrat,* the Milwaukee *Courier,* the New York *Tribune,* the Boston *Chronotype,* the London *Sunday Despatch,* the *People's Journal* (London), the *Liberator* (Massachusetts), and the Edinburgh *Journal.* The editors of *The Harbinger* were remarkably aware of the contents of other journals, and, since only *Godey's Lady's Book* and *Graham's Magazine* copyrighted their material, they ransacked and freely reprinted from those journals. Not infrequently the editors used these reprinted articles as springboards into discussion of Associationist doctrines.

This was not the case with the correspondence published in the magazine, however, for there was really no need for editorial comment on letters that generally praised *The Harbinger,* the Associationist movement, and even, on occasion, such individuals as William Henry Channing, the leader of the

Religious Union of Associationists. The editors of the magazine valued this correspondence, not only because the letters brought approval and encouragement, but because they often contained news of the progress of different Phalanxes as well. This information was especially important to *The Harbinger,* for if the paper was to function effectively as the official organ of the Associationist movement, it had to keep its readers apprised of the developments of such important practical experiments in Associationist living as the Wisconsin Phalanx, the Integral Phalanx (Illinois), and the North American Phalanx (New Jersey).[2] Correspondence enabled the magazine to do this, though, judging from the many letters that filled *The Harbinger*'s last three volumes, at a time when it was failing, the editors began to regard this item more as a convenient filler than as a valuable source of information.

Despite the fact that letters, translations, and reprints comprised the staple of the magazine, the editorial essay was still its principal feature. In these editorials, the editors responded to the attacks of detractors, explained the Associationist position with respect to certain of Fourier's doctrines, expressed optimism on the progress of the cause, campaigned for the establishment of an American Union of Associationists, encouraged friends to circulate *The Harbinger* and other Associationist publications, as well as to establish affiliated Unions in their own communities, and they informed readers of the successes of the American Union's lecturers as they traveled through New England and New York preaching the doctrines of Associationism. Other editorial essays defined and explained the terms, theories, and principles of the Associationist school, as well as its resources and educational and social advantages, while yet others criticized the "false and corrupting" institutions of society, particularly the "antogonistic and competitive arrangements of the present Civilized Order" (4:60). The titles of just a few of these essays are representative: "Progress of the Cause" (1:110); "Civilization: The Isolated Family" (1:251); "Theory of the Human Passions" (2:97); "Affiliated Societies" (3:64); "What Shall We Do?" (3:408); "Social Reorganization" (4:60); "Integral Education" (5:141); "Policy of Associationists" (6:20); "The Idea of a Divine Social Order" (6:121); "The Associative Theory of Property" (7:172); and "Socialism Against the World" (8:92).

A typical way by which the magazine illustrated the "exhibitions of civilized depravity and [the] deterioration" of society was to cite statistics reflecting contemporary social conditions. For example, in the "Fourth Annual Report of the Association for Improving the Conditions of the Poor" (in New York City) it was noted that between 1 November 1846 and 1 November 1847, 25,110 persons in New York City received some form of financial relief (6:68). What this statistic actually meant in terms of New York City's total population was made more specific by *The Harbinger,* quoting the 1847 report of the New York *Journal of Commerce,* which stated that one-fifth of New York City's population were paupers who had to be supported in whole or in part by charity (6:68). Likewise, *The Harbinger* deplored the great crime rate in New York City by citing the *Police Gazette,* which reported a thirty-three-percent increase in all crimes in the last half year over the first half year of 1847. From 1 January to 30 June, 9,438 crimes had been reported; from 1 July to 31 December, that number had risen to 14,381 (6:68). *The Harbinger* elsewhere pointed out that the living conditions of laborers in New York City had not been improving at all: 20,000 laborers were daily unemployed, a fact that no doubt contributed to the crime rate. Of the 300,000 who did have jobs, their wages, when divided among the members of each family, averaged only $1.00 a week for the support of each person (3:305).

Similarly, *The Harbinger* reported that conditions in Europe, specifically in England and Ireland, were just as bad. Quoting from the *National Police Gazette, The Harbinger* noted that in 1844 twenty-one persons in England and twenty in Ireland had been convicted of murder, that England had convicted 108 persons and Ireland ninety-two for manslaughter, that 148 people in England and fifty-two in Ireland had been convicted for rape, or assault with intent to rape, and that 354 persons in England and forty-five in Ireland had been tried and convicted for burglary (3:291). Even worse, the magazine stated, two million people in England were unemployed in 1846, and an equal number in Ireland would die during the twelve-month period 1845–46 because of that country's famine (4:381).

The Harbinger found that these conditions were directly attributable to the inequitable system of industrial organization in these countries, and that social ills such as these statistics suggested could be eliminated in Associationism, for the program would do away with selfishness, the insane devotion to wealth, and the fierce antagonism, discontent, and apathy so characteristic of contemporary society (2:32). It was therefore with a sense of satisfaction that the magazine announced in its 1 April 1848 number that a provisional government with decidedly Fourieristic tendencies had been established in Paris on 22 February 1848, a move that initiated the French Revolution of 1848.

The Harbinger hailed the French Revolution "with nine cheers of delight," and thought it was particularly appropriate that a social revolution on so grand a scale should occur first in France, the birthplace and home of Fourier (6:172). The importance that the magazine attached to the revolution is suggested by the fact that no other event, whether American or European, received nearly so much attention in its pages. From late March 1848, when *The Harbinger* first received news of the revolution, until early October 1848, by which time the provisional government had lost much of its influence, the magazine virtually abandoned such regular features as its musical review, art review, theatre news, and weekly gossip in order to provide space for the many articles dealing with affairs in Paris.

That *The Harbinger* underwent such significant editorial changes during this period is explained by the fact that the paper thought it had been given a "special mission" as a result of the revolution. That mission consisted not only of keeping readers informed of developments in Paris, but, more important, of distinguishing fact from fiction in other journals' reports of what was happening in France. *The Harbinger* was especially annoyed that so many American papers—among them the New York *Herald,* the New York *Express,* the Boston *Atlas,* and the Boston *Transcript*—were identifying communism with Fourierism in respect to the revolution. The New York *Express* claimed, for example, that there was no socialism involved in the revolution; that, rather, it was a belief in communism, the "extremest and most crazy kind of Socialism," that prompted the movement for a new government in Paris (7:20). *The Harbinger,* of course, rejected such charges, and countercharged that the New York *Express,* as well as other American papers that denied the social character of the revolution, were lying. The magazine noted too that "the doctrines of these two sytems [communism and Fourierism] are no more alike than the doctrines of the whigs and democrats" (7:12).[3] *The Harbinger* also stated that it never claimed the revolution was exclusively the work of socialists. It had only said that the "public mind" of France had been prepared for the revolution by the agitation of socialists, especially Associationists (7:20).

The point, however, that ought not to be lost in this exchange, was that the revolution was the logical consequence of what *The Harbinger* had been advocating since its inception, and its editors hoped that the leaders of the world would regard that peaceful rebellion as a "stern and solemn protest against those principles of political economy, which nations have heretofore followed" (7:20).

It is doubtful that regular readers of *The Harbinger* were at all surprised by the magazine's covering the French revolution so extensively. Aside from the obvious importance of the revolution to all Associationists, the paper had on many earlier occasions devoted considerable attention in its editorial essays to the Associationist cause in France, particularly as it was reflected in the French Associationist school. The magazine, for instance, published a series of articles on "The French School of Association" in which aspects of the school, such as its history, its recent progress, its means of action, and its financial stability, were discussed. No doubt *The Harbinger*'s admiration for the French Associationist school was due largely to the fact that it was the "parent" school, for it had been founded while Fourier himself was still alive. Nevertheless, the attention given the French school in the magazine was not a result of intellectual interest only. The fact is, the French Associationist school was financially successful, and was considered a model to the economically troubled American Associationist school (the American Union of Associationists). *The Harbinger* did not fail to inform its readers that the French school regularly collected money from affiliated societies in the form of weekly and monthly dues, and that these dues netted the school an annual income of 105,823 francs ($21,000). Readers were also reminded on more than one occasion that *La Démocratie Pacifique* was so widely supported by French Associationists that the French school was able to publish it on a daily basis. Perhaps *The Harbinger* itself best summarized its real interest in the French Associationist school when in another context it said of the lectures by a French Associationist: "The example of our friends in France will stimulate us in America to fresh devotion" (5:254).

But despite the overall success of the French Associationist school, it was still *The Harbinger*, after all is said and done, that provided the best example of effectiveness to American Associationists. It is therefore appropriate to conclude our discussion of the magazine and Associationism by focusing, however briefly, upon two areas of the Associationist movement in America in which *The Harbinger* was quite involved. One has to do with what might be called the radicalization of women in the Associationist cause; the other, with the development of the American Union of Associationists, the central organization of Associationists in the United States.

The Harbinger was concerned that women were not playing an active enough role in the promulgation of Associationist doctrines. For in the so-called true state of society, or Association, women, of course, would be equal to men in all respects. This was already the practice in the practical associations then in existence (for example, in the so-called Wisconsin, Integral, and North American Phalanxes). In addition, then, to pointing out women's subservient position in American society and to explaining its views that women ought to be equal to men, *The Harbinger* attempted to enlist women to champion the Associationist cause, if only because the Associationist cause was their cause. This effort at enlistment was a determined one. The campaign began on 18 July 1846 with an editorial on "Women's Function in the Associative Movement." The article called upon women to "set a full example to their sex, by putting forth all their energies in the cause of Unitary Reform" (3:95). The magazine specifically asked that women "write tracts on the Rights, Duties and Conditions of Women . . . form Societies of their own, or . . . take an active part in our Societies . . . and circulate our papers and . . . obtain contributions for our funds" (3:95). *The Harbinger* averred that the motivation for such action needed to be no more than a woman's awareness of the extent to which in American society her intellectual energies had been paralyzed, her affections repressed, her usefulness restricted, and her privileges denied.

The magazine followed this article with another two months later in the 26 September 1846 number on the "Influence of Association on Women." This essay discussed the special educational benefits offered to women under the Associationist system that were not available to them elsewhere. In addition, *The Harbinger* championed women's rights by discussing the intellectual disadvantages of being a woman in America:

Woman has been deemed a being of some inferior order, holding a rank in creation several degrees below the autocrats of the Universe, and destined to find her happiness in submission to their authority. Her claims to intellectual culture have not been recognized; her capacity for the loftiest branches of scientific investigation has been more than doubted; her pretensions to any learning beyond the most superficial smattering have been covered with ridicule; and her immense natural superiority to man in the fine, subtler, more delicate exercises of genius . . . has as yet scarcely been suspected. [3:252]

Such disadvantages would not obtain in Association, *The Harbinger* promised, for in it, women would be guaranteed a complete and thorough education, and they therefore would be able to enjoy the "highest intellectual cultivation."

Several months after these appeals, the magazine printed a letter from an unidentified female correspondent who invited women everywhere to attend the first anniversay meeting on 11 May 1847 of the American Union of Associationists in New York. It was time, the correspondent stated, for woman "to shake off the paralysis with which long ages of subjection have benumbed her" (4:351). Though no concrete action was taken on behalf of women at that meeting, decisive steps toward the establishment of a "Woman's Associative Union" were initiated two weeks later at the convention of the Boston Union of Associationists, an affiliate of the American Union. Immediately following the Boston convention, a special session was held for those interested in the collective action of women in the Associationist movement. A circular was drawn up, "To the Women Interested in Association," which announced that the women associated with the Boston Union had appointed a secretary, Anna Q. T. Parsons (who perhaps will be remembered as the recipient of scores of letters written at Brook Farm by Marianne Dwight), and a corresponding committee of five for the purpose of starting a newsletter among the women of all affiliated unions.

It took the women less than six months after their inaugural meeting in Boston to establish the "Woman's Associative Union." In that city on 1 December 1847, fourteen women drew up a constitution that formally established the new society as an affiliate of the American Union of Associationists. Within six months of its inception, the Woman's Union had netted a profit of $169.78 from the sale of domestic articles, books and tracts, and refreshments at its weekly meetings.

The Woman's Associative Union never became a powerful organization, for by the time it was formed, the Associationist movement in America was moribund. The point, however, is that its very existence would have been improbable without the leadership provided by *The Harbinger.*

Just as *The Harbinger* helped to create the Woman's Associative Union, it also helped to create the American Union of Associationists, though its role was somewhat less significant. Just before the paper began to enlist the aid of women in the cause, it began proselytizing for the formation of a central organization that would unite all Associationists in America. According to an editorial entitled "The Associative Movement—Its Present Condition—Practical Measures—Meeting in May of the New England Fourier Society," which was published in *The Harbinger* of 9 May 1846, the editors were quite annoyed by the fact that, apart from the establishment of the New England Fourier Society and an occasional lecture now and then on Associationism and Fourierism, no real organized action had been taken since the Convention of Associationists in New York in 1844:

> No general plan of wise and efficient action has been devised, which should concentrate the strength, that is now scarcely recognized or perhaps wholly lost by diffusion, and give unity, and consequently increased vigor, to the resources which now exist, to a large extent, for the promotion of the Associative cause in the United States. [2:346]

The Harbinger added that, with the quarterly meeting of the New England Fourier Society scheduled for 27 May 1846 in Boston, it was a particularly appropriate time to make suggestions toward establishing a more efficient system for the promulgation of Associationist doctrines. Specifically, the magazine recommended that (1) a central office be established; (2) affiliated societies be formed throughout the United States; (3) a permanent fund for advancing the cause of Associationism be established; (4) provisions to support an extensive program of lecturing be instituted; and (5) funds be provided for increasing and sustaining a system of Associationist publications (2:346).

From the magazine's standpoint, certainly the most important decisions reached at that meeting of the Fourier Society were the ones to create the "American Union of Associationists" and to make *The Harbinger* the official organ of the Union. The paper enthusiastically announced to its readers that Associationists now had an efficient and systematic means for the promotion of their doctrines, and it added that the measures adopted by the Fourier society would surely consolidate the Associationist movement in America. In the following months, however, the expectations voice by *The Harbinger* were disappointed. True, the American Union had emerged as a powerful force for advancing the cause. Among other things, it had established a program of lectures and a system of collecting monthly dues from affiliated unions. But George Ripley thought more was needed. In an editorial essay on the "Conditions and Prospects of the Associative Cause" published about a year after the Union's inception, he complained that the movement had become characterized by "inequality, uncertainty, [and] incoherence" (4:267). These characteristics were attributed to the absence (in America) of a central organization that, like a political party, could wield control over the phalanxes. True, Ripley acknowledged, the dissemination and popularity of Associationist doctrines were owing to the zeal of those individuals promoting the cause, but would such energy and devotion ensure success for the movement in the future? Without a central organization, might not the Associationist movement tend to disintegrate? To promote such a cental organization, Ripley made five proposals, reminiscent of those made a year earlier (see above).

Many other essays in the magazine eventually led the American Union of Associationists to establish a central office in New York; to staff that office with two full-time officers of the Union; to assume financial responsibility for *The Harbinger,* which included payment of weekly salaries to the editors, a luxury not possible when the paper was published at Brook Farm; to improve its program of lectures; and to increase the monthly dues of affiliated societies. But the American Associationist school was never really an integrated organization. It was, rather, a conglomeration of individuals, several thousands of them, to be sure, who subscribed, in varying degrees of enthusiasm, to the doctrines of Associationism. What gave these individuals any sense of unity or collective purpose was *The Harbinger,* even after the American Union of Associationists was formed. Had the magazine not conducted itself in the manner that it did, the so-called Associationist movement in America would have remained considerably more disorganized, confused, and misunderstood. To the extent that that movement enjoyed any success in the United States, *The Harbinger* must be given full credit. If the magazine is remembered in the annals of American history, it is for the leadership it provided in advancing the cause of Associationism and for the dignity with which it represented Associationism at a time when American journals, not to mention the American public, were almost unanimously hostile to the Associationist program for social reform. Above all, *The Harbinger* should be remembered for keeping alive the liberal spirit of compassion for the downtrodden.

3

Social, Political, and Economic Matters in *The Harbinger*

As has been observed, the atmosphere in which *The Harbinger* was published was highly charged with revivalist and reformist fervor. The decade of 1840 in America was nothing if not a time of widespread interest in social, political, economic, and industrial reform, for this was the age of abolitionists, feminists, and socialists, of organizations concerned for the insane and the criminally incarcerated, of diet reform, the water cure, mesmerism and phrenology, of the Democratic and Whig parties, and of the Tenants' League and the Moral Reform League—to mention just a few. It was not inappropriate, of course, for a magazine such as *The Harbinger,* which was devoted to establishing a peaceful and harmonious society by eliminating social evils such as competition, slavery, war, and poverty, to address itself to many of these subjects. But the magazine considered Associationism to be a comprehensive social-reform program that encompassed all specific reform movements, and thus it did not pay as much attention as one might expect to matters such as those cited above.[1] On those occasions, however, when *The Harbinger* did discuss slavery or the Mexican War, for example, it did not hesitate to speak out boldly, despite the fact that many of its ideas must have been considered radical by an American populace that was largely conservative in social and political matters.

The essence of Associationism was industrial reform. It was this subject more than any other which engrossed *The Harbinger,* for the editors of the magazine thought that the organization of industry was "the most important practical [question] which can engage the minds of men" (1:62). Specifically, *The Harbinger* was devoted first to the cause of the "oppressed, the down-trodden, [and] the insulted and injured masses of our fellow men. Every pulsation of our being vibrates in sympathy with the wrongs of the toiling millions, and every wise effort for their speedy enfranchisement will find in us resolute and indomitable advocates" (1:9). To this end, *The Harbinger* proselytized vigorously and continuously for the creation of an order of society in which there would be a union of labor, capital, and skill under a system of joint-stock proprietorship.[2] In addition to translations and reprints of articles dealing with all aspects of industrial relations, the magazine also published several poems that propagandized the cause of the laboring class,[3] as well as many essays that denounced America's commercial system, often by drawing parallels between the plight of the white laborer in the North and the black slave in the South.

For its translations of works dealing with industrial organization, *The Harbinger* turned exclusively to the writings of the French Associationists. The *Démocratie Pacifique* and *La Phalange,* both French Associationist organs, proved valuable sources for pertinent articles, but the works of Charles Fourier, the "father" of Associationism, and Victor Considerant, Fourier's chief French disciple, provided the best discussions on the many problems inherent in industrial reform. Accordingly, the magazine translated and serialized Fourier's *New Industrial World* in twenty-three numbers, and Considerant's *Industrial Organization* in nine numbers and his *Harmony* in eight numbers.

The Harbinger also reprinted numerous articles on labor from a variety of American journals and newspapers, but most noticeably from the New York *Tribune.* For under the editorship of Horace Greeley, himself the president of the American Union of Associationists[4] as well as, generally, the champion of many liberal causes, the *Tribune* frequently published articles on such matters as "Industrial Anarchy," "The Anarchy of Labor," and the "Right of Man to the Soil," articles certainly quite congenial to *The Harbinger.* The longest article that the magazine reprinted from the New York *Tribune* was one on "Labor in New York," which was an examination of the "circumstances, conditions, and rewards" of such areas of employment as printing, bookbinding, clockmaking, dressmaking, millinery, rag-carpet weaving, and shoemaking. This article ran to twenty-six installments in the pages of *The Harbinger.* The *Voice of Industry* (Massachusetts), a magazine devoted to industrial reform and conducted by former Brook Farmer John Allen, was another useful source of material, as were the Boston *Chronotype,* the Cincinnati *Herald,* and *Howitt's Journal* (London). Actually, the source of an article did not matter at all to the editors of *The Harbinger;* if the material propagandized the cause of labor, they reprinted it in their magazine. The titles of a few of these reprinted articles are representative: "Organization of Labor," "Children in Factories," "Children in the Workshops Near Paris," "Co-Operative Leagues," and "Organization of Intellectual Labor."

It is clear from the very inception of the magazine that the editors of *The Harbinger* were particularly worried that the laboring classes in America would become apathetic about their distressing condition, so they spent considerable time in the editorial columns reiterating the need for workingmen to unite. In one early essay on the "Means and Measures" of solidifying the workingmen's movement, for example, the magazine told readers to strengthen "each other in the faith that the day of real freedom is about to dawn; let us gather together; . . . let us unite; let us join hands in fraternal union" (1:78). In another essay on "The Workingmen's Movement," *The Harbinger* said that it would press the subject of the organization of work-ingmen in season and out of season, for "the movement [was] not intended as a benevolent operation to mitigate any immediate distress, but to correct the errors of the prevailing system" (1:267). These and several other calls by *The Harbinger* for organized labor were answered in late 1845 with the formation of the "Workingmen's Protective Union," an organization that would, because of its mass buying power, enable the laborer to procure the necessities of life at greatly reduced prices. While *The Harbinger* may not be given full credit for the establishment of this organization, certainly it must be noted that the magazine played a significant role in its inception, as well as in the creation of the many other "protective unions" that were started in New England at this time. In addition to its frequent complaints that the condition of laborers called loudly for redress, *The Harbinger* spoke often of the "urgent necessity for the producing classes of the land, to unite them-selves together as a band of brothers." No less often readers were admon-ished to take such action "while they have time and power and not supinely wait until they are completely prostrated" (2:15). No doubt, then, the maga-zine was pleased to be able to announce in the number for 1 May 1847 that the Workingmen's Union had saved its members some $26,000 a year in mutually purchased products.

Many of *The Harbinger*'s essays on labor included remarks on slavery, for the magazine thought that labor was a form of slavery rivaled in its inhuman-ity only by chattel slavery, or the ownership of one man by another man. Indeed, *The Harbinger* stated on several occasions that "the question of Slavery is nothing but the question of Labor" (1:205). But while the maga-zine was most often inclined in its editorial remarks on labor to draw paral-lels between the "slavery of capital" and chattel slavery, it did not fail to note too that it was vigorously opposed to all forms of servitude. In fact, in the second number, *The Harbinger* identified nine different forms of slavery, the abolition of which, it stated, would be "one great step in the onward progress [of man] towards a higher Destiny":

1. Corporeal or chattel slavery
2. Slavery of the soil, or serfdom
3. Slavery of Capital, or the servile system of hired labor
4. Domestic servitude
5. Slavery of Caste—Pariahs of India
6. Sale and seclusion of women in Seraglios—common in about one half of the world
7. Military conscriptions and impressments
8. Perpetual monastic vows
9. Indigence, or passive indirect Slavery [1:29–30]

Because *The Harbinger* was the spokesman for the reform movement that would one day enfranchise most of the American masses, it continually called upon Abolitionists in the United States to oppose all forms of slavery in their reform program. The magazine frequently charged Abolitionists with being too parochial by championing the cause only of Negro emancipation: "It is not the chains of the black slave in the South alone that are to be broken, but the chains of all the slaves upon God's earth" (1:30). If nothing else, those involved in the antislavery movement, *The Harbinger* thought, should at least proselytize equally for the cause of the white laborer in the North and the black slave in the South, for their overall social predicaments were quite alike. In some respects, in fact, the plight of the "white slave" was considerably worse than that of the black; Northern labor, for example, was "more heartless and had less direct sympathy with its victims [than did] Southern slavery. [Thus] the laboring classes under the Wages system were subjected to calamities more dreadful than those suffered by personal slaves" (4:407).

The Abolitionist press generally did not subscribe to *The Harbinger*'s notion that the antislavery movement in America was too narrow, and it rejected particularly the magazine's claim that the laboring classes in America were as destitute as the Negro slaves. *The Harbinger,* of course, thought that a primary cause of slavery was competition, for it was this, and the "forced selfishness resulting thence, which makes every man . . . an unnatural tyrant and disregarder of the rights of other men; it is this which establishes the rule of Might makes Right." Given these premises, *The Harbinger* had no difficulty concluding that "the grasping character of northern commerce is as much Slavery in principle, as any slavery in which the same spirit has ultimated itself at the South" (5:330). That the Abolitionist press, however, did not agree with these notions was the cause of several minor disputes between *The Harbinger* and such antislavery papers as the *True American* (Kentucky), *The Liberator* (Boston), and *The National Anti-Slavery Standard* (New York).

The *True American* was conducted by Cassius M. Clay, a devoted Abolitionist who repeatedly denounced chattel slavery in one of its strongholds, namely, Lexington, Kentucky. *The Harbinger,* in turn, praised Clay and his paper on several different occasions in its own columns,[5] mainly because it thought Clay to be an intelligent Abolitionist, one who was ardent, fearless, and impetuous, but not too rash or dogmatic in his plans for Negro emancipation. More important, as a man who possessed a great love of liberty, Clay's protestations against slavery were prompted as much by his concern for the welfare of the white laborer as for the black slave. The magazine was therefore surprised and disappointed to note on 6 December 1845 that an article written by Clay in the *True American* "treated with levity . . . that most momentous of social problems—the Elevation of Labor" (1:415). The magazine said that it always had thought that Clay's ideas on labor reform closely paralleled its own, and it added that it seriously wished

Clay would reconsider his "superficial views" in this matter. On 17 January 1846 *The Harbinger* was pleased to inform its readers that Clay had, in fact, reacted favorably to the magazine's criticism of him and his article, and it expressed certainty that Clay would eventually be "enlisted as a valiant soldier under our banner" (2:95). In any event, there was no more controversy between *The Harbinger* and the *True American*.

On more than one occasion, both *The Liberator* and *The National Anti-Slavery Standard* criticized *The Harbinger* for repeatedly misinterpreting articles from the antislavery press. These papers claimed that the Associationist magazine printed out of context remarks from different antislavery papers that were then hailed as evidences that these same papers had been "convinced at last" of Associationist doctrines. *The Liberator,* for example, was quite annoyed by a report in *The Harbinger* that Wendell Phillips, the prominent Boston Abolitionist, had said in a speech before the Anti-Slavery Society that the question of labor was "paramount to all others." Phillips himself—responding to this remark in an article originally published in *The Liberator,* but reprinted in *The Harbinger*—noted that not only had he made no such statement, but that "the laborers, as a class, are neither wronged nor oppressed; and . . . if they were, they possess ample power to defend themselves by the exercise of their own *acknowledged* rights" (5:87). *The Harbinger* said that it regretted misconstructing Phillips's statements, which in certain respects, it thought were extremely superficial as well as inconsistent with the principles of justice and humanity upon which he had based so much of his public career. The methods he proposed for elevating the laborer in America ("economy, self-denial, temperance, education, and moral and religious character") were certainly little consolation to the hundreds of thousands of haggard factory workers in the United States. In any event, the magazine said that it did not intend to underrate the evils of chattel slavery, but the truth was that all slavery was the "result of a perverted order of society, and [was] accordingly one of the evils which a true social organization would abolish" (5:93).

Like *The Liberator, The National Anti-Slavery Standard* was upset by the fact that *The Harbinger* had informed its readers that a review in *The Standard* of *The Organization of Labor,* authored by the French Associationist, Matthew Briancourt, was a clear indication that the Abolitionist journal finally had become convinced of the truth of Association. Contrary to what one might expect, however, *The Anti-Slavery Standard* did not rebuke *The Harbinger* following this announcement, perhaps because the editorial duties of that magazine were being taken over, at the time, by James Russell Lowell, who himself had earlier contributed two poems to the Associationist journal. Whatever, *The Standard* published a rather conciliatory article on "The Associationists and The Abolitionists," which *The Harbinger* reprinted in its own columns. While this essay detailed the many differences between the two groups of reformers, it nevertheless noted: "We [Abolitionists] have thrown, and we would throw, no obstacles in the way of Association. We are full of hope of the good it may do for humanity" (5:325). Considering the generally placating attitude of this article, it must have come as something of a surprise to *The Harbinger* when, a few months later, *The Anti-Slavery Standard* published another article denigrating the Associationist magazine for adopting an ambiguous position on the issue of slavery. Though it is not actually clear what prompted *The Standard*'s charges, the editors of *The Harbinger* thought that the attack was motivated by some earlier remarks in the Associationist magazine on the failure of Negro emancipation in the West Indies, for in the number for 23 October 1847 it was noted that emancipation in the West Indies had been unsuccessful because the freed slaves could find no work and no homes in which to live. Accordingly, *The Harbinger* had suggested that the Abolitionist movement in America might also fail if it did not develop some plan for the emancipation of the three million slaves in the United States. Though *The Harbinger* did not at this time advocate adoption of the Associationist program, it did reject a proposal by the Liberty League (known also as the Liberty party, this organization was devoted to Negro emancipation in America) which would establish a political party whose members would be individually and publicly pledged to the Abolitionist creed and platform. *The Harbinger* rejected this proposal on the grounds that the new party would be liable to conservatism and lack of flexibility beyond its own creed (5:319).[6]

In any event, *The Harbinger* was annoyed by the nature of *The Anti-Slavery Standard*'s charge, for it protested:

> There has been no more earnest and consistent advocate of the cause of the slave than the *Harbinger*—none that has more strenuously insisted upon the immediate emancipation of man from all forms of bondage— none whose criticisms of oppression have been more extensively copied into the Anti-Slavery organs generally. [6:108]

The magaine added that, while it differed from the Abolitionists on two points—namely, that it did not restrict its criticism to the plight of the Negro only and that it had a practical plan for abolishing all slavery—it had always recognized that chattel slavery was one of the most malignant forms of slavery. *The Harbinger* did not exaggerate its position, for as early as September 1845 the magazine had stated that "the question of Negro Emancipation will ere long command the attention of the South so imperatively that weakness will not be able to shrink from it, or blustering bigotry bully it out of sight" (1:205). Moreover, *The Harbinger* consistently denounced chattel slavery throughout the course of the Mexican War, for the magazine never wavered from the belief that the annexation of Texas had been conducted by the "slave-holding oligarchy" in America. Indeed, even after the Mexican War had ended, *The Harbinger* continued to condemn chattel slavery in essays such as "The Great Political Question," which appeared as late as 5 August 1848.

The "great political question" of the time had to do with whether the United States should allow its newly acquired territories—Texas, New Mexico, and California—to be settled as slaveholding regions. *The Harbinger* was naturally opposed to such settlement, and it criticized the United States government for even considering any such possibility. Slavery, the magazine reiterated, was a despotism; it could not endure any free thought: "Its spirit is stationary, and it tolerates no reform. Wherever it prevails, it is a political, a moral, and a social blight" (7:108). Why should we abolish freedom, *The Harbinger* asked, to make room for a system fraught with the grossest injustice and inequity? If ever there was a question with one side, the magazine said, it was this.

The question would not have arisen, of course, had the United States not become involved in a war with Mexico, a war that *The Harbinger* consistently denounced as immoral, unjust, and unconstitutional. The magazine was quite certain that the annexation of Texas was "a scheme of slaveholders for the avowed end of upholding, perpetuating and diffusing slavery" (2:393); as such, it condemned the United States aggression from beginning to end.

The Harbinger's first extended remarks on the Mexican War appeared on 25 October 1845, a full six months before the United States officially declared war on Mexico. In an essay entitled "Cassius M. Clay's Appeal," the magazine announced that it was vexed that the annexation of Texas had begun, and that it was particularly annoyed with the way in which the annexation was being conducted. The usurpation of a part of Mexico, the editors of *The Harbinger* thought, was a direct violation of the Constitution of the United States by the "slave power" in America: "The faction which has thus usurped the Legislative, Senatorial, and Executive functions, and which there is every reason to comprehend, will command also the Judiciary, is the Slave Power." This slave power consisted of Southern and Northern capitalists whose union had been brought about because of the profit motive, for slavery in the South was simply another form of serfdom in the manufactories of the North: "Money Before Men, has really been the password and the war-cry of this last conquest of the slave-power" (1:318).

On 30 May 1846, just a few weeks after Congress declared war on Mexico, *The Harbinger* published another essay that made unequivocally clear the Associationist position on the Mexican War. In "Peace, the Principle and Policy of Associationists," the magazine informed its readers that it was the duty of Associationists to be "peace-keepers" and "peace-makers" during the present conflict. The Mexican War was an "outbreak of hell with which we can have no concert," and accordingly, Associationists were to give it "no manner of aid, by word, deed, or any feeling of sympathy." In terms of action, *The Harbinger* stated that Associationists should not only not consider enlisting, but if they were drafted for duty, they should refuse to serve. Moreover, they should withhold that portion of their property tax which would be devoted to supporting the war. The United States was guilty of committing an unprovoked, gratuitous, and mean aggression upon a sister republic, and no man with sound moral or legal principles could support such an action:

> The Spirit of this War is the Anglo Saxon lust of conquest stimulated by national vanity and covetousness; its motive was the purpose of indefinitely extending and perpetuating slavery, of seizing new territories, of acquiring ports on the Pacific; its mode has been Executive usurpation, recklessness, and arbitrary disregard of our own Constitutional limitations and of established National Laws. . . . Certainly, if a nation ever on this earth deserved disaster, it is apparently the United States. [2:393]

One of the striking features of this essay is its obvious similarity in certain respects to Henry David Thoreau's "Civil Disobedience," which appeared just three years later in the only issue of Elizabeth Peabody's *Aesthetic Papers* (1849). We will probably never know, of course, whether an essay such as this—or a later one, "The War—Its Poetry and Its Piety"—had any specific influence on Thoreau's famous essay, though certainly it is clear that the sentiments in all three were very similar.

The Harbinger criticized those poems which were romanticizing the Mexican War in its essay on "The War—Its Poetry and Its Piety," which appeared in the number for 5 December 1846. The American people had the singular ability, the magazine stated, of declaiming the wickedness of the war, and protesting against it, but then frowning upon "the recreant American who can be so dead to law and Patriotism as to suggest quiet and conservative resistance to the war." So far as *The Harbinger* was concerned, this ability amounted to no more than the duplicity of the American people, for "they mutter puny indignation against the President, call him King, Dictator, and then tamely comply with his worst requisitions." *The Harbinger* thought that if the American people possessed half the virtue they continually boasted, they would make it unmistakably clear to the President and the United States government that "the body politic is a machine too good to move unless good springs are touched" (3:411). With respect to the Mexican War, however, *The Harbinger* thought that most people were part of that large group of Americans who were weak and tame, and who, while they deplored the war, did nothing to prevent it. These people, the magazine said, should be regarded with contempt, more so even than the Southern moneymakers who would extend slavery under the banner of making Texas a free state, the military men who "would turn the world into a slaughterhouse in order that there be an honorable sphere for them, which there is not in peaceful times," and the ambitious politicans who would plunge a country into war for their own private gain. Associationists and other social reformers were the only Americans, the magazine stated, who were actively proselytizing for the termination of the war. Indeed, Associationists particularly were so opposed to it that they adopted the following proposal, submitted by William Henry Channing at the convention in Boston on 31 December 1846 of the American Union of Associationists:

> RESOLVED, That the present War, in which our nation is engaged,—in the awful waste of men and means, of intellect and character,—in the perversion of popular conscience which it produces,—in the corrupting struggles of party which it engenders,—and finally in its tendency to divert our whole people from the fulfilment of the destiny to which Providence plainly summons us, is a most manifest proof of the disunity and incoherence with which all modern civilized societies are diseased; and that this inhuman condition of professedly Christian and civilized nations loudly calls on us to seek and apply such a radical Social Reform as may substitute peaceful cooperation for inhuman discord in all life's relations; as shall enable every nation to use the powers for creative good which it now throws away in violence and destruction, and shall unite all nations, the earth round, in working together for the universal well-being of Humanity. [4:78]

Still, *The Harbinger* itself, in advancing the cause of Associationism, had met with enough resistance from the American public to know that the efforts of antiwar advocates would be met largely by indifference: "Things will not be righted. The war goes on; the nation sanctions it" (3:412).

It was not until fully six weeks after the treaty had been ratified, on 2 February 1848, between the United States and Mexico that *The Harbinger* published any editorial remarks on the termination of hostilities. The magazine stated in an essay on "Political Affairs," which appeared on 18 March 1848, that it rejoiced at the termination of the war, but that this conclusion did not obscure the gross incongruity between the accomplished end, which presented "so trifling and pitiful a result," and the "vast powers engaged in producing it." The editors of *The Harbinger* thought that it was

> a remarkable fact that we have made no acquisition of soil, nor settled any other points of difference, by this Treaty [between the United States and Mexico] than could have been effected upon terms quite as favorable before the war! So that the war has, indeed, been not only a monstrous violation of every principle of justice and humanity, and a dreadful curse to Mexico, but has brought upon ourselves calamity and desolation, shedding the blood of thousands of our countrymen, some of them the noblest of spirits, filled for the highest achievements in the arts of peace, and a dead loss in the expenditure of untold treasure, drawn from the toil of the masses, the source and the only source of the revenues of nations. What a reflection is this upon the Wisdom of our Rulers. [6:153][7]

The Mexican War, of course, was not the only occasion the magazine had to comment on the wisdom of the politicians who conducted the political affairs of the United States. On many other occasions, it vigorously denounced the leading political lights of the day. Thus, while it could with some justification be charged that *The Harbinger*'s faith in the masses was overly idealistic, such was certainly not the case with respect to the magazine's regard for politicians. Indeed, if anything, *The Harbinger*'s attitude toward them was quite cynical, if not at times despairing. For example the magazine was very surprised at the excessive show of "virtuous horror" and "pious morality" among the Whigs and Democrats after the publication of a book containing many of the private letters of several prominent politicians, including, among others, Martin Van Buren, the eighth President of the United States (1837–41), Benjamin Franklin Butler, a United States attorney for the southern district of New York, and Jesse Hoyt, a prestigious New York lawyer. These letters, according to *The Harbinger,* revealed the "political profligacy, financial corruption, stock-jobbing dishonesty, mock piety, and profanity" in the political dealings of these men. *The Harbinger* said that it could not begin to comprehend why so many people were upset by the discoveries revealed in these letters, for there was abundant proof that "there is nothing more common than selfish and dishonest politicians and unprincipled men." After all, the magazine remarked, both political parties were equally unscrupulous and corrupt, and so far as Van Buren, Butler, and Hoyt were concerned, they certainly were not the first nor would they be the last "distinguished exemplars of the morals of politics" (1:303).

It was precisely because of reasons such as these that *The Harbinger* claimed to have the least interest in politics of all contemporary matters (7:108). The truth is, however, that the magazine devoted considerable attention to political matters; in fact, it even proposed the formation of a third political party before the presidential election of 1848. This suggestion was prompted by *The Harbinger*'s complete disillusionment with both the Democratic and Whig nominees, General Lewis Cass and General Zachary Taylor respectively. Cass, the magazine said on 17 June 1848, represented no principle, unless it was "the principle of slavish subserviency to his own interest, which has been the only end to which he has been steadfast throughout his career." Cass's entire political and economic life, *The Harbinger* continued, had been an embarrassment to the United States: he had become wealthy by speculating in public lands; as the American ambassador to France, he had "beslavered" Louis Phillippe with flattery while he maligned the Republicans; and his career in the Senate had been an everlasting contradiction, for he was at first a decided opponent of slavery, but he later became a sworn adherent of this system. Considering these qualifications, *The Harbinger* said that it could only bemoan the fact that the great Democratic party—the party that had boasted Jefferson and Jackson as its chiefs—had completely collapsed when it nominated so singularly unqualified a man as Cass.

That Zachary Taylor was a militarist and a slaveholder was enough to make *The Harbinger* repudiate him. The magazine thought that the only reason the Whig party had nominated Taylor was because of the notoriety he had gained in the Mexican War as a result of his military exploits. Certainly he had never rendered any service to the Whig party, and Taylor himself had admitted he was ignorant of the merits of the great political questions of the day. Thus, it was obvious that the Whig party was interested only in gaining power, for why else would it nominate a man who had no qualifications other than his popularity? But by nominating him, the magazine stated, the Whigs had made a decision that was "a reckless abandonment of all their high professions—[it was] a voluntary putting aside of character and honesty for the sake of a probable success" (7:52).

This despairing political situation, the editors of *The Harbinger* thought, was sufficient cause to speak freely on a subject that did not normally receive much attention in the pages of the magazine. The recent movements of the Democratic and Whig parties, it was stated, had great meaning, not only because they intimately concerned the cause of Associationists, but because "they show us, in a word, that Politics are dead":

> That politics which thinks it has done its whole duty when it has put up or put down a monstrous Bank, which higgles whether a tariff of duties shall be thirty or fifty per cent., but which refuses to touch nearly all the vital topics of the times—has lost its vitality, has fallen into decrepitude, is stricken with death. [7:52]

It was, then, with a view toward revitalizing the American political system that *The Harbinger* proposed the formation of a third political party. This party—whose motto would advocate no slave territory, freedom of the public lands, rights for states and townships, and organized labor—would be comprised of dissatisfied Whigs, barn-burning Democrats, National Reformers (land), Liberty men (labor), and Associationists. From these groups, *The Harbinger* thought that a third party could be formed that would wield tremendous influence in the affairs of the United States, for among these people there were great and dynamic principles that would form the nucleus of a strong unity. *The Harbinger,* of course, was right, for the Free-Soil party, a political organization formed in 1847–48 and composed principally of Barnburners, antislavery Whigs, and members of the former Liberty party, received, with Martin Van Buren as its presidential candidate, 300,000 votes in the election of 1848.[8] Thus, *The Harbinger's* concern for the welfare of the democratic system in the United States was alleviated immediately, and in a way that would have a lasting effect on the American political process, for in 1854 the Free-Soil party was absorbed by the Republican party.

As a liberal, progressive, and idealistic magazine, *The Harbinger* was democratic in the best sense of that word. It was always independent, equalitarian, and pragmatic, especially in political matters. The magazine itself perhaps best defined its understanding of democracy when, in the "Introductory Notice" that appeared in the very first number of the journal, it stated: "By democracy we do not understand a slavish adherence to 'regular nominations,' nor that malignant mobocracy which would reduce to its own meanness all who aspire to nobler ends than itself" (1:9). Democracy, the notice continued, was an exalting and refining creed that held that the main object of government was to secure for the people the blessings of liberty and order. This object could be achieved by ensuring that every man was guaranteed the right to the full development of his entire nature—moral, intellectual, and physical. That this was not the case in our political democracy was naturally a constant source of frustration to *The Harbinger,* so much so, in fact, that it had occasion to note just a week after the "Introductory Notice" that if democracy in the United States were an individual, it would have it indicted for false pretenses. It continually promised what it never performed. Nothing was less respectable, the magazine stated, than "a puny, lisping, foppish democracy" that talked all day about equality and human rights, but did not mean one word of what it said (1:32).

One group that *The Harbinger* thought was particularly inclined to utter meaningless rhetoric consisted of congressmen, and accordingly, the magazine did not hesitate to criticize them. Like most politicians, *The Harbinger* complained on different occasions, congressmen never discussed any great principles. Worse, when an important issue did arise, legislators typically sat tiredly in Congress, completely unaware of the moment of its importance until it had passed. *The Harbinger's* complete lack of confidence in these men was succinctly summarized in an essay on "The Great Politial Question" (see above), where it was stated that congressmen "are corrupt as they are ignorant," which no doubt was one reason that the magazine also thought that the debates in which they engaged in Congress were but "a slight degree removed from the slavering and maudlin brawls of the pothouse" (7:108). Upon learning, then, that an obscure representative known only by the name of Turner ("from the so very far West as never to have been heard of before") had mockingly denounced in Congress the Fourierist plan for industrial and social reform, *The Harbinger* replied in "Fourierism in Congress" that it was not particularly impressed by the attack, for it was a dubious distinction at best to be abused in Congress. Nevertherless, there was, the magazine admitted, a certain degree of appropriateness in the source of the attack, for "do not the noble men who are congregated there [in Congress] abuse pretty nearly everything they touch, and especially the confidence of their constituents?" (8:76). It was a gross vanity indeed, the magazine remarked, to suppose itself in any way especially complimented by any harsh words from a member of Congress.

What appears to be the overwhelmingly cynical or perhaps realistic nature of *The Harbinger's* remarks on politics and politicians might suggest to the modern reader that the magazine was unable to discuss these matters objectively. To consider this to have been the case, however, is, of course, to obscure the fact that *The Harbinger* was conducted by individuals who were committed to a cause—a utopian one and a good one, if perhaps from hindsight somewhat naïve—and who therefore seized every opportunity to condemn what were to them the corrupting forces of an unnatural and unhealthy social situation. In any event, the fact is that, while no politician was spoken of in *The Harbinger* in unanimously favorable terms, a few at least were the subjects of balanced discussions. One such representative discussion concerned Andrew Jackson, the seventh President of the United States, whose death in 1845 prompted *The Harbinger* to publish an essay on 28 June 1845 that summarized the strengths and weaknesses of the Tennessean during his terms as President.[9]

During his lifetime, Jackson was highly respected as a leading representative of the frontier spirit in America, as well as admired as a vigorous opponent of the aristocratic monied class. Mainly, it was these qualities in him which *The Harbinger* lauded too. The magazine said that there had been few public figures since Thomas Jefferson so deeply imbued with the democratic spirit as Jackson, and it characterized his tenure as President (1829–37) as one of "hostility to everything like public favoritism, to supporting the pretensions of the few against the rights of the many, or to increasing by exclusive legislation the subtle power of the monied interest." One area in which the magazine thought Jackson had been especially effective was in curbing the control of large corporations, which had been formed, *The Harbinger* stated, for the sake of individual profits rather than the welfare of the people. At all times, Jackson had been the unwavering adversary of monopoly and privilege, and no one could ever question his vital faith in the democratic idea.

Nevertheless, while Jackson's presidential triumph in 1829 was hailed as a deathblow to aristocratic pretension, the condition of oppressed people in the United States had not been substantially improved during his terms as the nation's chief executive. The fact was, the magazine said, Jackson had been loyally supported by the working classes in America. It was the enthusiasm of the masses—aroused by the confidence they had in him—that enabled Jackson to be twice elected to the nation's highest office. But Jackson, the magazine charged, had failed his supporters, for the evils that they suffered had not disappeared. On the contrary, "if we look for any vital changes in the condition of the oppressed," *The Harbinger* stated, "any guarantee for the elevation of the laborer to equality with the employer, any preparation for the universal spread of education, riches, and happiness among those who now bear the heaviest burdens of society, we shall look in vain" (1:46). Jackson had failed to establish the prosperity of the masses on any solid foundation and, *The Harbinger* concluded, he had failed to recognize the real source of prevailing social evils. He had put too much emphasis on legislative enactment as a remedy to social problems rather than on integral reform. In short, to put it as *The Harbinger* did, Jackson's main failing as President was his inability, or his unwillingness, to understand the true principles of social science as discovered by Fourier and as they were advocated by Associationists in America and Europe.

It is appropriate to conclude this chapter with a few brief remarks about *The Harbinger* and the feminist movement, for the magazine was one of the earliest and most vocal champions in America of women's rights. It was noted in the last chapter that the magazine made a determined effort to enlist the aid of women in the Associationist movement in America, but it is also important to note that its efforts in this area were not motivated solely by selfish considerations. *The Harbinger* was genuinely interested in seeing women elevated to a social and economic level equal to that enjoyed by men, and while it did publish many articles that enumerated the benefits of Association to women, it also published several others that denounced woman's subservient role in society without proselytizing for Associationism. In one of these articles the magazine remarked that it hoped it would live to see the time when a woman would be allowed to "possess property in her own right; be allowed to form contracts and make a will; [be allowed to] have disposal of the children to which she has given birth; [and] be provided with constant, appropriate, and profitable employment" (4:48). *The Harbinger* did survive long enough to record the fact that the New York State Legislature had passed a law giving married women the sole right of disposing of their own property (7:4), but even if the magazine had survived for several decades more, it would have witnessed few significant advances in the cause of women's rights.

No doubt the writers for *The Harbinger* would have been shocked could they have known that more than a century would pass before the feminist cause would begin to resemble anything like a widespread and unified movement capable of effecting significant changes in the attitudes of the American public. For as early as 1845 the magazine was calling upon women to demonstrate actively for the establishment of their rights, which included, among others, the right to vote, the right to freedom of speech in public, and the right to freedom "from the bonds which do absolutely degrade them from the equal rank which is their right" (1:269). Marriage, *The Harbinger* thought, was the chief leading cause that prevented women from achieving these rights, for once married, a woman legally forfeited all of her rights, even those few she possessed when single. To make matters worse, the nature of society was such that respectability was conferred more often upon those women who were married, and thus many marriages, *The Harbinger* said, were really no more than a form of legalized prostitution. For 6,000 years, the magazine complained in an essay on "Women's Rights," woman had been a dependent of and a slave to man, a fact that *The Harbinger* thought was ironically illustrated at the "Anti-Slavery Fair" in Boston in 1845, where all the women on the roll call were listed by their married names. Those women who advocated the abolition of chattel slavery, the magazine stated in "The Women of the Anti-Slavery Fair," were themselves slaves, for they had allowed themselves to be called by the names of their legal master. Until such time as women came forward and denounced the entire system of female dependence and degradation, *The Harbinger* warned, they would remain slaves and would continue to exist in a state of perpetual minority (1:268).

This admonition was repeated in a review of a book on *The Evils Suffered by American Women and American Children: The Causes and the Remedy* by Catharine E. Beecher (the sister of Harriet Beecher Stowe), in which the author argued that "the office of Woman is the education of children, and that this duty ought so to be arranged and established in society, as to offer an exalted and attractive career [to them]." *The Harbinger* did not denounce this book, for it always welcomed any proposals that might enable women to become more independent, but it did resent the narrowness of Beecher's suggestion. The magazine had complained on other occasions that the great difficulty of being a woman was the fact that the only sphere of interest available to her was marriage; thus it said it felt obligated on the present occasion to dissent from the remarks of Beecher: "The complete truth is that there should be open to woman not one channel alone for the action of a noble and true ambition, but . . . every branch of industry, art, and science, should offer her independence and distinctions" (3:204).

Today, of course, women are beginning to achieve the independence and distinction in industry, art, and science that *The Harbinger* called for well over a century ago. Obviously, it has taken considerable time for this to happen, but women's liberation has finally become a unified, visible, and even militant movement, the ramifications of which have been far-reaching, if long overdue. With respect to *The Harbinger,* the growth of the feminist movement in the twentieth century suggests an important point about the magazine generally. While many of those matters to which *The Harbinger* addressed itself were topical, they were certainly not ephemeral. The women's liberation movement today bears testimony to this fact, although there is ample evidence of it in other areas as well. For example, phrases such as *industrial complex* and *military-industrial establishment,* both of which are relatively recent coinages, have already become a familiar part of Americans' vocabulary. And while the institution of slavery was legally abolished some time ago, racial discrimination continues to manifest itself in such areas as education, employment, and housing. But perhaps worst of all, political disclosures of recent years have made it extremely difficult for many Americans to argue that politicians are any less corrupt and ignorant than *The Harbinger* said they were over a century ago. If nothing else, *The Harbinger* embarrassingly reminds us today that, while more than a century of advanced civilization may have improved the quality of the individual American's life, it has neither eliminated nor substantially alleviated many of those problems which were characteristic of the young, burgeoning American democracy. Standing in the shadows of history, *The Harbinger* reminds Americans today that they have traveled the same road more than once, and they may have to do so again.

4

Literary Criticism in *The Harbinger:*
American and European Authors

In order to assess the literary criticism found in *The Harbinger,* one must keep in mind the brief duration of the magazine as well as the purpose for which it was founded. That *The Harbinger* survived for a period of less than four years is significant in that many of the leading writers of the first half of the nineteenth century could be reviewed in the magazine only once or twice, and sometimes not at all. The kind of literary continuity that characterizes the *North American Review, Graham's Magazine,* and the *Knickerbocker* is not to be found in *The Harbinger.* In short, *The Harbinger* was no literary barometer of the times.

The more important consideration, however, in assessing the literary criticism of the magazine is the purpose of the paper's being founded at all. *The Harbinger* was not primarily intended to be a literary journal. On the contrary, the magazine was the official organ of Associationism in America. Its main purpose was to disseminate Fourier's doctrines on industrial reform, as well as diffuse the aims and ideals of Associationists.[1] Consistent with this purpose was the belief, subscribed to by the editors of *The Harbinger,* that literature should serve a high moral purpose, that it should enlighten and liberate humanity.

It was, then, upon grounds such as these that *The Harbinger*'s reviewers evaluated new books and journals. Charles Dana's review of Anna Cora Mowatt's sentimental romance, *Evelyn; or, A Heart Unmasked* (1845),[2] for example, was decidedly negative because Mowatt was "without taste, without talent, without a sufficient sense either of the great, the good, or the beautiful" (1:107). Likewise, Dana's review of *The Poetical Works of Percy Bysshe Shelley* (1845) seems not to have been prompted so much by an admiration for Shelley's poetical abilities as by the fact that George G. Foster, the editor of the edition, had made the assertion that Shelley's "system" was identical to that of Fourier, thereby giving Dana an occasion to discuss *The Harbinger*'s avowed patron. Similarly, the fact that *The Harbinger* devoted one of its longest and most adulatory reviews to L. Maria Child's *Letters from New York* (1845) is not properly appreciated until one remembers that Child was a good friend of the Brook Farmers, as well as an author who, according to John Dwight, was "full of a great faith in the principle of Universal Unity" (1:42).

But while it is true that a good many of the reviews in *The Harbinger* were prompted by a desire to proselytize, it is no less true that the reviewers themselves were men,[3] in most cases, with no small endowment of literary ability and talent. George Ripley, who wrote sixty-four of the 356 literary reviews that appeared in the magazine, had begun editing his fourteen-volume *Specimens of Foreign Standard Literature* in 1838; John Dwight, who contributed sixty-one such reviews, had been translating German poetry for Ripley's collection; and Charles Dana, who provided 120 literary reviews, served his literary apprenticeship on *The Harbinger* and later gained some celebrity as editor of the New York *Sun*. Additionally, such men as Parke Godwin, who had been a contributor to William Henry Channing's *The Present* (1843–44) and Albert Brisbane's *The Phalanx* (1843–45) before the inception *The Harbinger*,[4] Francis G. Shaw, who provided the magazine with his own copyrighted translations of George Sand's *Consuelo* and *The Countess of Rudolstadt,* and William Henry Channing, who, in addition to editing *The Present* and *The Spirit of the Age* (1849–50), wrote a *Memoir of William Ellery Channing* (1848), reviewed numerous books for *The Harbinger*.[5] In short, the magazine did not want for men with literary taste and talent.

Thus, despite the fact that the majority of the literary reviews in *The Harbinger* were characterized by the dedication with which the reviewers proselytized for Associationism, that dedication was offset by such a command of knowledge and such a degree of sophistication in literary matters that the end result was often penetrating criticism. If nothing else, the reviews were vigorous, lively, and high-minded. Moreover, the reviewers themselves generally chose to discuss books about which they had something to say, and they commended books that in their judgment were sound with as much praise as they condemned poor ones.

American Authors[6]

In the third number of *The Harbinger,* George Ripley, then the editor, announced in a column entitled "Books from Our Friends" that the Brook Farmers had received several books from friends who were "continuing nobly in the study and confession of Truth." Ripley said that the Brook Farmers had long felt a duty to review some of these works, and now the publication of *The Harbinger* afforded him this opportunity. Presumably, Ripley intended to devote a separate column of reviews to works written by friends of the "cause," for in the third number he stated: "With delight we shall name over some of the beautiful books which have been sent us by our friends, and of which we mean to make a series of reviews" (1:30). For whatever reasons, Ripley's idea never materialized. This did not prevent the magazine, however, from occasionally reviewing works by individuals whom it would have considered "friends," among them, Christopher Pearse Cranch, Margaret Fuller, Theodore Parker, Ralph Waldo Emerson, and Lydia Maria Child.

Actually, Christopher Pearse Cranch (1813–92) was the only one among this group of "Friends" ever to contribute any original material to the pages of *The Harbinger*. For the first volume of the Associationist journal he provided one review for his friend John Dwight's column, "Musical Review" (1:59), and he also sent along two poems, "A Glimpse of Light" (1:108) and "Autumn" (1:147), as well as a translation of "The Minstrel's Curse" (1:172) by the German poet, Johann Ludwig Uhland. Cranch then provided one poem for the second volume—"Athanasia" (2:29)—and two for the third, "The Music World" (3:89) and "Sonnet on the Mexican War" (3:89), the latter two appearing in the same number, for 18 July 1846.

Cranch, of course, had been in close contact with most of the leading figures associated with New England Transcendentalism ever since his graduation from the Harvard Divinity School in 1835. His real interests, however, soon proved to be less in the ministry and more in the world of literature, painting, and music. He had contributed verse to *The Western Messenger* (1835–41)—a journal that Cranch had helped to edit for a time— and to the *Dial* (1840–44), and, in 1844, many of his earlier poems were collected and published as *Poems*. It was, in fact, the appearance of this work that provided the occasion for the only literary review of Cranch to appear in *The Harbinger*.

John Dwight wrote the review of *Poems,* and it appeared in the number for 12 July 1845, which was only a few weeks after publication of the very first issue of *The Harbinger*. Dwight's review—it may be stated immediately— was anything but objective. Cranch was a friend of the Brook Farmers, and he would be treated accordingly. Dwight even admitted that he did not have time on the present occasion to undertake a "critical or profound analysis" of his friend's verse, a circumstance that did not prevent him, however, from providing enough general remarks about Cranch himself to fill four and a half columns. The "review" remains one of the lengthiest to be published in the Associationist journal.

It will likely never be clear just why Dwight spent so much time discussing Cranch rather than his poetry. Possibly it was because the latter was supportive of the Associationist program for the reform of society; or perhaps it was simply because the two men were such good friends. Probably the motivation had something to do with both those possibilities. Dwight did remark, for example, that he thought Cranch was inspired by the recognition that there was unity throughout nature; the poet saw the intimate correspondence between man's soul and nature. The Brook Farmer also invoked

Charles Fourier's division of boys and girls into "Little Hordes" and "Little Bands" in his effort to characterize Cranch. The "little hordes," Dwight said, would consist of two-thirds boys and one-third girls, who, full of energy and industry, would seek the beautiful through the good. The "little bands," on the other hand, would consist of two-thirds girls and one-third boys, who, full of a sense of taste and beauty, would seek the good by way of the beautiful.

Cranch, of course, would belong to the second group. His was a delicate and refined nature. He was a man who would rather "court the shade, than *claim* regard." He was sensitive, spiritual, and contemplative, and these were qualities reflected in his verse. What was most genuine and unmistakable about his poetry, however, were these things: "The fine perceptions of a deep pure love, the genial glow of a refined humanity, the generosity, the candor, the humble confidence of a self-cherished youthfulness, and at the same time a quiet manliness" (1:106). Dwight then concluded the review of Cranch's *Poems* by reprinting "Enosis" (he had also included "The Field-Notes" earlier in his remarks), and he stated that he was prepared "to say that Mr. Cranch's Transcendentalism, or whatever you may choose to call it, has given us some of the most perfect little gems of poetry which have yet been mined in America" (1:107).

Margaret Fuller (1810–50) was perhaps the most brilliant and erudite of all the American Transcendentalists. She reportedly once told Emerson: "I know all the people worth knowing in America, and I find no intellect comparable to my own." Of this statement Perry Miller has since remarked that Fuller "was indeed speaking the sober truth."[7] Not known so much for her creative talent as for her critical ability, Fuller was one of the young geniuses who in the early 1840s recognized the importance of establishing judicious standards of criticism. To this end she and others contributed a number of important articles to the *Dial* (1840–44), articles that resulted in making that magazine "a landmark in our intellectual history" because it "endeavored to set up catholic standards of 'poetic' criticism."[8]

Papers on Literature and Art (1846), the only work of Fuller's reviewed in *The Harbinger*, reprinted most of her articles from the *Dial*, as well as a composite of a number of her critical notices written for Horace Greeley's New York *Tribune* during 1844–46. In his review of *Papers* for *The Harbinger*, John Dwight used the occasion both to continue the discussion initiated in the *Dial* and to praise Fuller for laying the foundation for sound literary criticism in America.[9] He began his review by discussing the difficulty of being a critic:

For one who is by nature a critic to be willing to be that, and wear the character actively, sincerely, and courageously, involves a degree of self-sacrifice. For the character is naturally unprepossessing. We are not apt to love it; by its seeming excess of consciousness it separates itself from us; by its coldness it discourages our enthusiasm; by its regard of more than one thing at a time always, it seems never to abandon itself to anything with that entire devotion which we esteem beautiful. [2:249]

Despite all this, Fuller, Dwight thought, had accepted the character of critic unquestioningly, and because this was so, she had erected for criticism "a very high and important place, if not one absolutely central in our literature."

Of the many reviews reprinted in *Papers,* Fuller's essay on "American Literature" was perhaps the most important. Perry Miller has described it as "one of the boldest and most courageous utterances of the era."[10] Dwight's reaction to this essay was enthusiastic, though not so adulatory as Miller's: "'American Literature' tells many plain truths, and deals out liberal justice on all hands." He agreed with Fuller that both Longfellow and Lowell had been overly praised, though he was not willing to go so far as Fuller in labeling Lowell an inferior poet. Actually, he thought Lowell—who had, it will be remembered, married in 1844 Maria White, herself something of a Transcendentalist—to be a true and "noble bard."

Dwight's only criticism of Fuller concerned her style. Dwight said that Fuller was a gifted conversationalist but unfortunately, he added, her writings were marked by that hurriedness that characterized her conversation. The result was that the reader often had to weigh her sentences singly, much as one would weigh a mathematical proposition. Furthermore, Dwight said, her grandiloquence suggested that she regarded herself as an Olympian god pontificating to the mundane world below. Nevertheless, it was, paradoxically, this stylistic weakness, Dwight noted, which gave her strength as a critic, for without this preponderance of intellect she would have been unable to survey the entire field of literature and art, a task she performed remarkably well. Few critics "have surveyed so large a portion of the whole field [as Fuller had in *Papers*]; perhaps no other American; and few are so able to point inquiring minds to what is best and most significant in literature and art" (2:249). Indeed, *Papers on Literature and Art,* Dwight concluded, contained more original and independent thought in it than could be found in collected volumes of America's most respected reviews.

Theodore Parker (1810–60) was, like Fuller, a frequent and welcome visitor during the several years that Brook Farm survived. Charles Crowe has noted, for example, that the practical jokes of Parker and George Ripley were a constant source of amusement to members of the community.[11] Unlike Margaret Fuller, however, Parker ultimately dedicated his prodigious intellectual abilities to almost every major reform movement: for example, he championed women's rights, the abolition of slavery and capital punishment, and rehabilitative programs in penal institutions. It was therefore only natural that *The Harbinger* devoted a good deal of space to the author of *A Discourse on the Transient and Permanent in Christianity,* for not only were many of Parker's social sympathies identical to those of the

Brook Farmers, but several of his most vitriolic and sensational sermons were published during the period of the magazine's existence.

Between February 1846 and January 1848, *The Harbinger* published five reviews of Parker's sermons, two by Charles Dana and three by George Ripley. Additionally, the paper also noticed the publication in 1848 of the German edition of Parker's most important book, *A Discourse on Matters Pertaining to Religion* (1842).

That Parker was a good friend of many of the Brook Farmers, and that he was an energetic social reformer, did not prevent the often acidulous Charles Dana from criticizing him in his reviews of *The Idea of a Christian Church* (1846) and *A Sermon of War* (1846). However, the main object of Dana's criticism in his review of *The Idea of a Christian Church* was the Christian Church itself. In terms reminiscent of earlier Transcendentalists who had in the 1830s criticized the Unitarian Church, Dana said that the Christian Church had failed, among other things, to eliminate social ills such as pauperism and slavery: "Why is it that after eighteen hundred years of Christianity, there is in the most enlightened and Christianized countries, an amount of human misery and degradation, such as no history records?" (2:158). Espousing socialism as a solution to social wrongs, Dana stated that there would be no peace or harmony in society until competition in industry was replaced by a "system of brotherly cooperation." Equally perplexing, Dana said, was the fact that the Christian Church, as well as clergymen such as Parker, had not taken a sufficiently active role in social-reform movements that would elevate the financial status of the laborer. Indirectly praising the Brook Farm community, Dana concluded the review by noting—quite unfairly when one recalls what a tireless preacher Parker was—that it was one thing to identify social evils (which he admitted Parker had done) but quite another thing to work actively for the elimination of those evils.

This same call for action was repeated in Dana's review of *A Sermon of War*. Empty rhetoric, it was stated, would not extirpate social evils. The important question, as Dana saw it, was: How was the idea of social, political, and individual freedom to be made real in the United States? Parker, and men like him, Dana said, had not answered this question. There were many men who sincerely believed in social and individual freedom "but who never so much as think of the path which leads from the conception to the fact." Dana admitted that Parker's sermon had shown that war was an "infernal evil," but he concluded his review by remarking that it was foolish to cry out with indignation against the war with Mexico while remaining quiet about the warfare of competitive labor that so characterized contemporary society.

Although Dana never directly said it in his reviews, there is little doubt that his lack of enthusiasm for Parker's sermons was due to his belief that the minister of the Twenty-eighth Congregational Society had offered no concrete remedies for existing social ills. However, Perry Miller has noted:

"It has been the fashion in some quarters to hold against Parker the fact that he could propose no more realistic remedy for social evils than moral regeneration. Considering the ethos of the time, this charge need not be weighed too heavily."[12] Whether or not it was due to his own ministerial background, one of the things that distinguished George Ripley's three reviews of Parker from those by Dana was precisely this: the former's recognition that Dana's implied charge "need not be weighed too heavily." On the contrary, Ripley recognized the need for an individual who was not afraid to identify the falseness and corruption of society, for as he noted (in rhetoric that must certainly have appealed to the Brook Farmers): "We need the rough ploughshare to break through the stiffened crust of prevailing prejudice and error, before the sower can cast the precious seed into a receptive soil, or the reaper exult in the yellow sheaves of a ripened harvest" (3:363).

Ripley reviewed three of Parker's sermons for *The Harbinger: A Sermon of the Perishing Classes in Boston* (1846); *A Sermon of Merchants* (1847); *A Sermon of the Dangerous Classes in Society* (1847). Ripley's reviews were noteworthy for two reasons. First, despite the fact that Parker had been ostracized by respectable Boston after he delivered his sensational sermon on *The Transient and Permanent in Christianity* (1841), and despite the fact that each of the three sermons reviewed by Ripley caused a great commotion in the Boston community, *The Harbinger* editor never compromised his beliefs about the reform minister; he recognized the importance of an individual who was willing to address himself not only to a critique of American society, but to a critique of the American businessman as well. As he said in his review of *A Sermon of Merchants,* Parker was a man who had "no taste for fictions, common places, or awful sounds without sense; his sharp, lancet-like wit is a terror to all pretension; and the evident strength of his own convictions arms his words with an authority that cannot be lightly resisted" (4:137).

Second, in his reviews of Parker's sermons on the perishing classes and the merchants, Ripley, employing satire, mounted perhaps his own most vigorous attack (in *The Harbinger*) on the Christian Church. He stated in his review of the perishing classes that instead of being first, contemporary theologians were the last persons on earth to whom an appeal could be made regarding the most vital interests of humanity. Ripley was convinced that Emerson's admonition eight years earlier in the "Divinity School Address" had not been heeded:

> Peering sharply through their [theologians'] spectacles into the letter of the Bible, spending days and nights in the discussion of the meaning of an insignificant phrase in a dead language, wrangling with the fury of prize fighters for some thin subtlety that not one in a hundred can comprehend, and scattering loads of learned dust in the eyes of those who look to them for guidance, they are as cold and torpid in view of the monstrous outrages which every where stare them in the face, as if the throbbings of a heart of

flesh had given place to turning over the leaves of a mouldy volume. [3:361–62]

Indeed, it was almost incomprehensible to Ripley that the "snow-white Pharisees," the "ponderous doctors of divinity," the "sleak and studious Scribes" could remain silent in the midst of the innumerable oppressions and evils that existed in contemporary society. Tongue-in-cheek, Ripley admitted that, strictly speaking, Theodore Parker was no theologian and *A Sermon of Merchants* was no sermon, for Parker repudiated Original Sin, the Devil, and the Trinity, and his sermons lacked a text and violated "Congregational usage." What, then, Ripley asked, was Parker?

> We say, one of the bravest, noblest, most sincere, and most effectual speakers that now hold the public ear, in the pulpit or out of it. He was never able to write anything that has the air of a sermon, any more that [*sic*] he could find a place in his brain for the dusty dogmas of the church; but he deals in words that are like polished steel, which charm and dazzle while they cut to the bone. His surpassing eloquence is founded on his massive common sense, kindled by the fire of noble passion which always burns in his heart. He is one of the great teachers of the day; his earnestness will always attract earnest men; his knowledge of the world gives him access to the shrewdest heads; he looks directly in to the centre of the subject which he handles; and at his potent touch the cobwebs which have been accumulating for ages disappear. [3:362]

Here Ripley pinpointed some of the qualities that made Parker one of the most important spokesmen for Transcendentalism in America. Only Emerson (1803–82)—and in the world of action some would argue not even Emerson—had such a direct hand in the shaping of this philosophy which flourished in New England during the decades 1830 and 1840. Ripley and his associates were especially aware of Emerson's importance, and initially they believed that the success or failure of Brook Farm depended, to some extent, on his participation in their socialistic enterprise. Emerson, of course, refused to join the community,[13] certainly because of his commitment to absolute individualism. He believed that social progress was an illusion; the only fundamental reform was the reform of one's self. In his often-quoted journal entry at the time of Ripley's request to join the community, Emerson noted:

> I have not yet conquered my own house. . . . Shall I raise the siege of this hen coop [Brook Farm] and march baffled away to a pretended siege of Babylon? It seems to me that to do so were to dodge the problem . . . and hide my impotency in the thick of a crowd.[14]

Emerson's refusal to join the experiment in communalism brought to the foreground the basic difference between his social philosophy and that of the Brook Farmers. Unlike Emerson, who preached the gospel of self-reliance as an end in itself, the Brook Farmers believed that self-reliance was important only as a means to a higher end, namely, the economic, social, and political betterment of mankind. However frequent and congenial were Emerson's visits to the West Roxbury community, the Brook Farmers never reconciled their philosophical difference with him. Nevertheless, even the writers for *The Harbinger* could not deny Emerson's intellectual brilliance, though John Dwight was more anxious than any of his colleagues to qualify his praise of the Concord sage. In his review of *Poems* (1847), Dwight said that he thought Emerson was a true poet, capable of beauty, majesty of thought, and originality, for he celebrated the mystical, exceptional, and transcendental side of life. Dwight added, however, that he could not give much praise to a man whose life had been "one ever-lasting non-committal." The fact was, Dwight said, Emerson did not write for humanity. His verse, like Emerson himself, was cold and distant; his poems "counsel lonliness, and call that true life" (4:93).

After Emerson delivered his seventh and final lecture on "Representative Men" at the Boston Lyceum, George G. Foster reviewed them for *The Harbinger*. Though his discussion was primarily a reiteration of Emerson's comments on Plato, Swedenborg, Montaigne, Napoleon, Shakespeare, and Goethe, it did contain some interesting remarks, not the least of which had to do with Emerson's reputation among his fellow citizens in early 1846:

> Gradually the belief with which persons of one deaf ear inoculated others of two long ones, that all his metaphysics tended to nothing and had scarcely a plank between it and the awful deeps of insanity, has exploded, and during this course of lectures, all denominations and classes of persons, from cooks to clergymen, sat entranced by the music of his voice and the beauty of his thought. He has become the fashion, or rather the fashion has become him. His admirers have gradually become the public. [2:143]

Thus it really did not matter, Foster added, that there might be "chaff in his [Emerson's] brain; [or] that his system be only partly true, or that he has no system." For what was certain, Foster said, was that "a man stands behind his words, and that he is never idle in his speech, but sincere and strong."

It was because of the nature of Emerson's remarks on Swedenborg in the "Representative Men" lectures that Charles Dana had the occasion to review *Professor Bush's Reply to Ralph Waldo Emerson on Swedenborg* (1846) in the 4 April 1846 number of *The Harbinger*. Dana said that Bush's defense of certain of Swedenborg's doctrines from the assaults of Emerson was adequate so far as it went. However, "we desired to see the primary errors of Emerson's speculative thinking called into court and convicted." As it was, Bush had failed to settle important matters pertaining to Swedenborg's religious philosophy, and consequently, these matters were left to "wander homeless in the misty unrealities which Mr. Emerson and his school teach as transcendental philosophy."[15] Nevertheless, Dana did add that Bush's unsuccessfulness in seizing the point behind Emerson's expressions was not entirely his fault: "He might perhaps as well have grasped at the Aurora Borealis as to have attempted with the uninitiated understanding to apprehend the nimble ideas of that gentleman's beautiful and poetic rhetoric" (2:268).

John Dwight may have thought that Emerson did not write for humanity, but this was certainly not the case with Lydia Maria Child (1802–80), whose *Letters from New York. Second Series* (1845) and *Fact and Fiction: A Collection of Stories* (1847) he reviewed for *The Harbinger*. In his review of *Letters,* Dwight readily admitted that his primary interest in this work was the author's conviction that contemporary society demanded radical change. Of course, Mrs. Child's faith in Fourier's doctrines as the best means to affect such change interested Dwight more than a little. He was obviously glad to note that the author possessed "a most undaunted faith in the speedy triumph of Truth and Beauty over the wrongs and wretchedness of the Past," and he was surely no less pleased to encounter a work that embodied such great faith in the principle and science of universal unity. Accordingly, he praised Mrs. Child: "No one will deny the name of an artist to the author of Philothea" (1:43).

If Dwight's review of *Letters* was enthusiastic, his review of *Fact and Fiction* was embarrassingly extravagant. Dwight himself admitted his difficulty in discussing this work in qualified terms, for no other collection of stories, he said, delighted *The Harbinger* more than *Fact and Fiction*. He added that he would call "The Children of Mount Ida" (the first story in the volume) the "most exquisite piece of classic fiction we ever read" if he did not know the danger of superlatives! Ironically enough, very few reviews in *The Harbinger* employed so many superlatives:

> She [Mrs. Child] is generally acknowledged to be one of the most genial, buoyant, versatile, impetuous, playful, earnest, humane and unpretendingly, informally religious writers of the times,—a sincere, generous, great woman, to whom no conventional sham or folly by any possibility can cleave,—and a poet, in whom the faculty of seeing beauty in every thing and sympathizing with it, and recreating it in forms of art, seems never suspended, never blunt or wearied. [4:57]

There is little doubt, of course, that these reviews, particularly of Fuller, Parker, and Emerson, were inspired to some extent by the fact that there were substantive ideological differences between them and the Brook Farmers. The simple fact is—and it was an important one to the members of the West Roxbury community—that these three important individuals had refused to be regularly involved with or committed to Brook Farm. Men such as Ripley, Dwight, and Dana were not able to forget this. At the same time, one must be nevertheless impressed by the overall accuracy of *The Harbinger*'s criticism of these individuals, thus suggesting a very important point about the editors of this journal, as well as, indeed, much of the literary criticism in the magazine itself: friends or not, ideological considerations or not, the high-mindedness and intellectual honesty of men such as Ripley, Dwight, and Dana typically lead to judicious criticism and a lively and vigorous discussion of ideas. This fact is perhaps nowhere more evident than in the magazine's reviews of contemporary American poets, which included Fitz-Greene Halleck, Edgar Allan Poe, Henry Wadsworth Longfellow, Oliver Wendell Holmes, James Russell Lowell, and John Greenleaf Whittier.

Possibly the most interesting thing about *The Harbinger*'s reaction to the American poets it reviewed was the generally unenthusiastic reception it gave them. At a time when America's literati had an almost obsessive concern for the establishment of an indigenous national literature that would not only rival but be superior to the European models upon which so much of the country's earlier writings had been based, *The Harbinger* showed remarkable critical balance. This is not to say that the magazine did not do its fair share of puffing of delicate lady novelists and genteel provincial essayists; but its enthusiasm was generated more by a desire to proselytize for Associationism and Fourierism than by any wish to propagandize for a still nascent American literature. The fact is, *The Harbinger* did seem to recognize the need for careful critical discrimination. This was evident, for example, in Parke Godwin's review of *The Poems of Fitz-Greene Halleck* (1847).

Fitz-Greene Halleck (1790–1867) had been a leading member of the Knickerbocker group, of which Washington Irving, James Kirke Paulding, Joseph Rodman Drake, and John Howard Payne, the actor and dramatist, were also members. Halleck was one of those individuals who, according to Robert Spiller, helped "in making literature an accredited profession in America."[16] Godwin, in fact, recognized this too, and he noted that Halleck had "taken his place among the earlier literary celebrities of the republic, and his name [was] familiarly associated with that illustrious quartette [Irving, Cooper, Paulding, Halleck] which, once and for a long time, constituted the galaxy of the new world." Recalling his own youth, Godwin rather neatly summarized the earlier American attitude toward its few "established" writers, as well as the all but negligible state of American literary criticism only a few years earlier:

> Irving, Cooper, Paulding and Halleck, in our school-boy days, were the accredited luminaries that every American was expected to swear by, while, in the indiscriminating enthusiasm of that period, they were assigned a sort of indefinite position among the greatest of the great ones. How far they excelled Shakespeare, Cervantes, Scott, etc. was not precisely determined, but certain it was that every patriotic body felt sure that their place was somewhere in the very brightest region. [6:39]

Godwin then rendered his critical judgment (and perhaps the twentieth century's as well) on the four writers, a judgment that was particularly noteworthy since it was made in 1847, a time when Edgar Allan Poe and Margaret Fuller were the major professional critics in America, and a time when Irving (1783–1859), Cooper (1789–1851), Paulding (1778–1860), and Halleck, all still alive, continued to be revered by the American reading public:

> At this day, these stars shine with a somewhat diminished lustre. Irving alone still radiates a mild splendor from the distant horizon; Paulding seems to have gone out altogether; Cooper is fast trying to bury what light he had originally in the red vapors of a pugnacious self-conceit; while Halleck, having been behind a cloud for many years, manages to twinkle briefly in a new shining face [in the present volume under review], and will then retire to his favorite shades.
> In other words, . . . it must be confessed that our early writings have been greatly over-rated. [6:39][17]

Godwin's recognition that these earlier writers had been unduly overestimated was, in addition to being accurate, an encouraging indication that American literary criticism had at least developed to the point where it could make such forthright remarks about highly regarded American writers.

Charles Dana's remarks about Edgar Allan Poe (1809–49) were also forthright, but the tone in his review of *Tales* (1845) was considerably different from that of Godwin's in *The Poems of Fitz-Greene Halleck*. Dana attempted to criticize Poe by the use of satire. Employing excerpts from the tales themselves, he satirized what he considered to be Poe's melodramatic tone in the volume:

> When we come to "the general burst of terrific grandeur," which makes our countenances "cadaverously wan" with "an intensity of intolerable awe," as "a flood of intense rays rolls throughout and bathes the whole in ghastly and inappropriate splendor," we begin to be "oppressed by an excess of nervous" agitation; "but when we have fairly heard the "one long, loud, and continuous scream, utterly anomalous and inhuman,—a howl,—a wailing shriek, half of horror and half of triumph, such as might have arisen out of hell, conjointly from the throats of the damned in their agony, and of the demons that exult in the damnation," . . . we now say . . . to the public, that Mr. Poe's *Tales* are absolutely overwhelming. [1:73]

Dana concluded that Poe's tales were "clumsily contrived, unnatural, and every way in bad taste." They were "like the vagaries of an opium eater," he said, and although they possessed a kind of power, it was the "power of disease."

John Dwight also reviewed Poe for *The Harbinger,* but his discussion of *The Raven and Other Poems* (1845) was not nearly so acidulous as was Dana's of *Tales*. Perhaps the most interesting thing about the review was Dwight's remarks pertaining to the reputation Poe was beginning to earn as a result of his feuds with certain New York and New England publishers and critics. At the time of Dwight's review (December 1845) several of the numerous literary battles in which Poe had been for some time embroiled were about to culminate in his downfall as a critic, for 1845 and 1846 were, according to Sidney P. Moss, "the period of Poe's crack-up, a crack-up from which he never fully recovered and in the throes of which he behaved quite unfortunately, when not irresponsibly."[18]

Dwight began his review by giving what was, in Moss's opinion at least, only a slightly exaggerated summary of Poe's reputation in late 1845:

> Mr. Poe has earned some fame by various tales and poems, which of late has become notoriety through a certain blackguard warfare which he has been waging against the poets and newspaper critics of New England, and which it would be most charitable to impute to insanity. Judging from the tone of his late articles in the Broadway Journal he seems to think that the whole literary South and West are doing anxious battle in his person against the time-honored tyrant of the North. But what have North or South to do with affairs only apropos to Poe! . . . Edgar Poe, acting the constabulary part of a spy in detecting plagiarisms in favorite authors, insulting a Boston audience, inditing coarse editorials against respectable editresses, and getting singed himself the meanwhile, is nothing less than the hero of a grand mystic conflict of the elements. [1:410]

Dwight said that he would have avoided making any remarks about Poe's personal life had the present volume under consideration been free of this controversy, but

> the motive of the publication [of *The Raven* volume] is too apparent; it contains the famous Boston poem [*Al Aaraaf*] together with other juvenilities, which, he says, "private reasons—some of which have reference to the sin of plagiarism, and others to the date of Tennyson's first poems"—have induced him to republish. Does he mean to intimate that he is suspected of copying Tennyson? In vain we have searched the poems for a shadow of resemblance. Does he think to convict Tennyson of copying *him?* [1:410–11]

Dwight's review of *The Raven* volume was less than adulatory. In one respect, at least, this was quite natural, for *The Harbinger* reviewer believed, like so many of his contemporaries, that divine inspiration represented the best explanation of the creative process. Poe, of course, was the first American to insist upon the conscious creation. Nevertheless, Dwight did recognize the importance of effect in Poe's literary aesthetic, not an imperceptive observation considering that "The Philosophy of Composition" (1846) was published after Dwight's review: "The impression of a very *studied* effect," Dwight noted, "is always uppermost after reading him."

Mainly, however, Dwight criticized Poe on grounds similar to those on which he had criticized Emerson, that of "morbid egotism." It was this in Poe, Dwight thought, that resulted in the cold and passionless quality that so often characterized his verse. And this led Dwight to conclude that the beauty about which Poe wrote did not spring from any real feeling, a curious conclusion indeed from a critic who thought that "The Raven" contained "the true grief of a lover, an imagination of a brokenheartedness enough to prove a lover in earnest, a power of strange, sad melody, which there is no resisting."

In the final analysis, of course, Dwight could not be too enthusiastic about Poe, if for no other reason than his belief that the author of "The Raven" did not write for humanity, an important critical criterion in *The Harbinger*, as was earlier seen in reviews of Emerson and L. Maria Child. Nevertheless, Dwight acknowledged Poe's uniqueness as a poet in mid-nineteenth-century America:

> He certainly has struck out a remarkable course: the style and imagery of his earliest poems mark a very singular culture, a judgment most severe for a young writer, and a familiarity with the less hacknied [sic] portions of classic lore and nomenclature. He seems to have had an idea of working out his forms from pure white marble. [1:411][19]

Poe, of course, was identified mainly with the South, whereas *The Harbinger* devoted much of its critical attention to its New England neighbors. At least until the Civil War, and probably for most of the nineteenth century, New England was considered by some the cultural capital of the United States, and Boston, the cultural capital of New England. Orestes Brownson, for example, who was one of the most outspoken of the Transcendentalists before his conversion to Catholicism in 1844, recalled with pride that he had been trained in Boston, the " 'Hub of the Universe' at a time when it was really the focus of all sorts of modern ideas," and he wondered, "What have any of you to teach one who participated in the Boston intellectual movement from 1830 to 1844? We Bostonians were a generation ahead of you."[20] There was, of course, good reason for someone such as Brownson to feel this way. Here was located the greatest American university; here, led by men such as Emerson, Ripley, and Brownson himself, was the scene of a most important cultural-philosophical revolt; here was one of the major centers of publishing; and here was the social and cultural mileau that favored the kind of poetry written by such men as Henry Wadsworth Longfellow, Oliver Wendell Holmes, and James Russell Lowell, the literary trio of Boston Brahmins.

The Harbinger's critical response to these three men was balanced, especially when one considers that Longfellow, Holmes, and Whittier were among the most highly regarded poets in America at this time. Indeed, only recently has there been critical consensus that the Boston Brahmins were not poets of major rank, a fact that Charles Dana recognized some time ago, insofar at least as Longfellow was concerned. Longfellow (1807–82) was considered one of the big frogs in what Poe, sneering at Boston, had called "Frogpondium," but this did not prevent Dana from writing an unusually candid review of his *The Belfry of Bruges and Other Poems* (1846) for the second volume of *The Harbinger*. Dana accurately identified many of those features for which Longfellow, today, has been criticized and even denigrated. He thought that, above all, the Boston poet had been the subject of much unfortunate and injudicious praise. It would have been to his advantage, Dana said, had he been criticized with less admiration, for more severe judgments might have imparted "a real manliness" to his verse. But as it stood, Longfellow was "undoubtedly the most elegant sentimentalist that the literature of New England has produced." As a literary technician, Dana thought Longfellow to be highly accomplished, for his verse was consistently marked by melodiousness. As a poet of ideas, however, *The Harbinger* reviewer said Longfellow was not at all original: " as a thinker and creative artist his rank cannot be marked by any high figure." Quite simply, his poems were the production of a "belles-lettres scholar of extensive reading and good taste, who transfuses into his silken rhymes what others have discovered by soul-racking experiences" (2:173). Longfellow had not "breathed any original inspiration into the public heart"; his popularity was due to the fact that his verse often repeated thoughts about which the heart had already become excited. In fact, his poems could be likened to sugar candy—they were pleasant in small quantities. Dana added that he would have been less inclined to criticize them if they "were not [so] inflated with that dilettantism which is a leading characteristic of the Cambridge school of writers." Although Longfellow's poems did contain some noble and beautiful sentiments, "we soon weary of them and lay them down with . . . no great anxiety ever to see them again."

One person who did not agree with this assessment of Longfellow's poetry was Dana's colleague, John Dwight, whose review of *Evangeline: A Tale of Acadie* (1847) was the only other one of the Boston Brahmin to appear in *The Harbinger*. *Evangeline* would have naturally appealed to an Associationist such as Dwight, for it was a poem about a "simple rural population [who lived] together in Acadie, on the shores of France, in innocence, . . . industry, and peace" until the arrival of several armed English ships that forced the peaceful villagers to emigrate to America. Although the review was heavily padded with lengthy excerpts from the 1,500-line poem, and it offered little, if any, penetrating criticism, Dwight did say that he thought *Evangeline* was Longfellow's best effort to date, for in it he managed to create a "true marriage between form and spirit." Not only were his unrhymed hexameters "unspeakably richer . . . than the jingling rhymes of our stiff English measures," but they were reminiscent of the hexameter of Homer and Virgil because they were so grand. In terms of its content, Dwight said that the poem belonged in a class with Goethe's *Hermann and Dorothea,* although Longfellow's poem possessed "a far deeper spiritual beauty than the German poem." Dwight concluded his review by thanking Mr. Longfellow for providing some hours of "living tranquility . . . amid the anxious cares and interruptions of this wearisome transition from the ages of discord to the unity and harmony of reconciled, redeemed Humanity" [6:14].

Longfellow was, of course, the most popular poet of the Boston group (indeed, the most popular poet in America), but Oliver Wendell Holmes (1809–94) was certainly the epitome of refined Boston culture. Teacher, lecturer, physician, scientist, and writer, Holmes wrote with the facility and polish that befitted that "harmless, untitled, inoffensive aristocracy" to which he gave the title of Boston Brahmins. Perhaps because he dispersed his energies in so many directions, Holmes never became a great writer. His poetry was mostly light society verse, entertaining, if often ephemeral. Holmes's *Urania: A Rhymed Lesson* (1846) and *Poems* (1848) were the two works of his reviewed by *The Harbinger*. In their respective reviews, both John Dwight and an unnamed reviewer evaluated Holmes for what he was: a writer of pleasing and convivial verse. Neither reviewer claimed he was a profound or intellectually engaging poet; on the contrary, Dwight noted in his review of *Urania*, for example, that Holmes's verse was not the sort that was "wrung out by deep experience," and the unidentified reviewer likewise remarked in his discussion of *Poems* that Holmes not only did not "live in any sense, beyond his times," but that there were deeper wells of poetry from which he never drew.

Rarely, however, did *The Harbinger* publish a review that did not contain some good word about the writer or his work, and these reviews of Holmes were no exception. Dwight remarked, for example, that Holmes was a "sparkling lyric poet" who effectively versified his patriotic, didactic, or witty thoughts, and he added that in *Urania*, each thought was perfectly expressed, each image was finished and distinct, and each couplet was a "luscious, swelling contour" (4:10). The anonymous reviewer also praised Holmes for both his "facile perfectness of form" and his spontaneous rhythm, and he said that single stanzas and couplets possessed the complete "beauty and soft, unspeakable lustre of diamonds." *Poems* did not serve any humanitarian end, the reviewed added (it did not espouse the cause of the slave or the "proletary"), but this was no reason to repudiate the book; on the contrary, "the most that all reformers seek . . . is that society shall be conformed to the Divine Law of harmony. . . . The poet who will make us natural for a moment, who will restore a fresh sensation, who will give us one good laugh, or one true thrill of beauty or of joy, does so far put us on the track" (8:71).

James Russell Lowell (1819–91), the youngest of this literary trio of Boston Brahmins, was the most versatile writer among them. Most of Lowell's important writing was done before his thirtieth birthday. In 1848, as *The Harbinger* entered its third year of publication, Lowell published the works that established him as a leading poet, critic, and political satirist: *Poems . . . Second Series* (1848); *A Fable for Critics* (1848); the first series of *Biglow Papers* (1848); and *The Vision of Sir Launfal* (1848). *The Harbinger* re-

viewed all but the last of these works, and its reception of the young Democrat and Abolitionist was consistently enthusiastic.

John Dwight's review of *Poems . . . Second Series* was more a citicism of
modern society than of Lowell's poems. Dwight said he felt perfectly
justified in using the occasion to condemn contemporary society, for he
thought that the humanitarian tendencies of the poet's works formed the
central life both of Lowell specifically and of all true poetry generally. In a
society in which money rules everything, in which the vultures of slavery,
war, and poverty fed on the vitals of civilization, and in which selfish competition was the prime motivating force in man's life, only the poets, earnest
reformers, and artists could be trusted to proclaim the truth and state the
real facts of life. Man lived in a society in which his leaders and his great
national oracles could not be trusted, and this at a time when statesmen,
preachers, the newspaper press, and literature had "grown faithless to humanity . . . or [were] frightened into smooth words by the threats of [a] great
lawless money power." Fortunately, there were poets such as Lowell,
Dwight stated, whose poems were "strong, glowing, humane, [and] truth-
ful." As such, they were "part of the healthy, recuperative life of this degen-
erate age." Lowell's poems were motivated by the "idea of true liberty, true
greatness and true manliness, fearless trust in Truth, the sentiment of Justice, and the thought of Universal Brotherhood."

Dwight's review of *Poems* was a perfect illustration of *The Harbinger*'s
penchant for using the occasion of the literary review to proselytize for
Associationism. Dwight even went so far in this particular instance as to
draw a parallel between Columbus's voyage to America, dramatized in a
poem by Lowell, and Charles Fourier, himself a discoverer who had steered
his ship across "uncertain seas of social chaos and illusive speculations of
political economy . . . to a whole new continent of thought" (6:102). Was it
not really Fourier, Dwight rather absurdly asked, who inspired many of the
lines in Lowell's "Columbus"?

Dwight may have appeared puzzled about Lowell's sources for this poem,
but surely no one associated with contemporary literature could have seriously doubted the identities of those individuals who inspired *A Fable for
Critics,* which was briefly reviewed in *The Harbinger* eleven months after
the review of *Poems.* The anonymous reviewer thought that the caricatures
of Emerson, Bronson Alcott, Whittier, and Hawthorne were well done, but
he regretted that Lowell treated "Miranda" (Margaret Fuller) so harshly
because she was, after all, a woman! But apart from any individual charac-
terizations, the reviewer said that *A Fable* was a "humorous satire" that was
"rippling" and "sparkling" throughout. It was full of invention, quaintness,
felicitous expression, and skilled versification (8:55). He also stated that *A
Fable* was decidedly not a dull work, though he himself preferred *The Biglow Papers* (which he reviewed for *The Harbinger* a week later),[21] presumably because it addressed itself to a more serious matter. The more serious

matter was the Mexican War, which occasioned the writing of *The Biglow Papers*. Although the review of this work was padded with lengthy excerpts, the reviewer did make some interesting remarks about the character of Reverend Homer Wilbur (ostensibly the editor of the book), who was "the soul of the book, the meaning underneath the didlery." Although many readers of *The Biglow Papers* considered Wilbur to be a long-winded, pompous ass, this reviewer thought him to be

> a poet; his intervention makes a poem of the book, fusing the doggerel papers into a whole with a soul to it. The conception of the parson's character is a poetic conception; it is as life-like a character as you will find in the best play or novel written by a genius. [8:62]

Mainly, however, the reviewer's enthusiasm for *The Biglow Papers* was prompted by the poem's antiwar, antislavery attitude. It was noted that the "papers, " when they first appeared separately in different newspapers, had had more than a little influence "in bringing Massachusetts and the North upon their feet, to take the moral ground, amid wicked political party issues." That Lowell did not hesitate to "subject our national inconsistencies, [and] our hypocritical commercial Christianity, to the commentary of rude, simple common sense" led the reviewer to state that it had been years since so rich and genial a book as *The Biglow Papers* had appeared, and he concluded his review by listing some other American poets who, like Lowell, had refused to accept "base compromise": Bryant, Dana, Emerson, and Whittier.

John Greenleaf Whittier (1807–92), as a young man at least, was an ardent Abolitionist. The New England Quaker spoke frequently at antislavery meetings, was an editor of the *National Era* (1847–60), an antislavery journal, and wrote antislavery tracts and verse collected in *Poems Written During the Progress of the Aboliton Question* (1838) and *Voices of Freedom* (1846). Although *The Harbinger* reviewed him three times, today's reader of the magazine finds relatively little information about Whittier's contemporary reputation as a poet.

If Whittier is remembered today for anything, certainly it is not for *The Stranger in Lowell* (1845) and *The Supernaturalism of New England* (1847), two of the three works of his noticed in *The Harbinger*. Charles Dana briefly reviewed *The Stranger* for the paper, but he was far more interested in what we might call the "Associationist overtones" of the work than in anything else. Although *The Stranger* was "not enlightened by the philosophy of Universal Unity," it was, he said, not too far removed from it. At least it did possess a "gentle yet deep humanity," for its author had profound sympathy for man. It was clear too that Whittier loved the beauties of the external world, though he did not consider nature complete "without the life of the human affections" (1:90). Dana concluded the review by saying that he sincerely welcomed this volume, and he recommended the work to *The Harbinger*'s friends.

The Supernaturalism of New England was somewhat different from the usual Whittier fare in that it was mainly a prose narrative about the extent to which faith in a supernatural world still existed in New England. The book consisted of stories about ghosts, magic, and witchcraft, and John Dwight, the reviewer, said that he thought it was written "from no other motive but a poet's mere love of the romantic and the marvellous." He added that the work did not even have the completeness of a historical essay; it was more like "a prolonged winter evening's chat about old superstitions" (4:204).

The third work of Whittier's reviewed in *The Harbinger* was *Poems* (1849), a brief discussion of which appeared two weeks before the magazine's demise. For the most part, the review was general and summary, perhaps because the magazine's editors were, at this time, more concerned with *The Harbinger*'s immediate future than with the writing of literary criticism. The uncharacteristic opening paragraph of the review suggests the superficial tone of the discussion:

> Those who feel any pride in poetry which is American in the best sense, are under obligations to both publisher and artist for this truly elegant edition of our honored Whittier. Externally it is one of the most elegant and tempting volumes which has offered itself among the candidates for the honor of being given away at Christmas and New Year; while, unlike most of its gaudy brethren, it contains a living treasure. An excellent likeness of the Poet forms the frontispiece, and scattered through the book are eight pictorial designs by Billings, which display real genius, simple as they are, and a fine sympathy with his subject. They are truly *designs*— creations of an artist's brain, and satisfy both sight and soul. Especially have we admired the deep and tender beauty, and the lovely grouping of that picture of the women on the Mexican battle field, illustrative of the poem called the "Angels of Buena Vista." [8:102]

Somewhat more to the point, the anonymous reviewer stated that "Bridal of Pennacook" and "Meg Megone" reflected a fidelity to nature "hardly excelled by Bryant"; that "Norsemen," "Cassandre Southwick," and "Exiles" effectively illustrated the poet's respect for tradition and his reverence for the past; and that the pervading tone of the "Miscellaneous" and "Memorial" poems was one of cheerfulness, piety, and love. The reviewer added that *Poems* contained the best of Whittier to date, for it included not only poems that were stirring appeals to the conscience of humanity, but poems that were gentle, deep, and meditative as well. Only when a complete collection such as the present edition was considered are we able to appreciate "the variety, the breadth and depth and delicacy, as well as [the] strength and heroism of the man." As far as Whittier himself was concerned, he was, the reviewer concluded, a poet of humanity as well as a poet of progress, for in him, the love of country, nature, and freedom was always strong.

That *The Harbinger* had a great deal to say, relatively speaking, about American poets, is understandable. For one thing, there were many publishing. For another, verse continued to be regarded as the most effective means of expression in a country whose literary tradition included few significant achievements in the novel or the short story. Moreover, verse had the added benefit of being, historically, the longest established and most widely respected literary means of communication. Certainly this was one reason that, in the late 1840s, there were so few prose-fiction writers in America who received the public's admiration to the extent that a Longfellow or Bryant did. In fact, perhaps only Washington Irving and James Fenimore Cooper were so widely admired. Considering this, then, and the fact that *The Harbinger* itself existed for a period of less than four years, it was quite natural that the magazine reviewed only a few American fiction writers. In fact, Cooper (1789–1851), Hawthorne (1804–64), and Melville (1819–91) were the only prose-fiction writers of note to receive any attention in *The Harbinger*.

During *The Harbinger* years, 1845–49, six of James Fenimore Cooper's thirty-two novels were published. Of the six, the magazine reviewed the three novels that comprised the trilogy known as the "Littlepage Manuscripts": *Satanstoe* (1845); *The Chainbearer* (1845); and *The Redskins* (1846). *The Harbinger*'s decision to review these three novels, but not *The Oak Openings* (1848) or *Jack Tier* (1848), was hardly an indiscriminate one, for Cooper's trilogy dealt with the difficulties between the propertied and propertyless classes in New York in the early 1840's.[22] It was this aspect of the trilogy that most interested *The Harbinger*. Charles Dana himself admitted as much in his review of *Satanstoe*, which appeared in the number for 2 August 1845. In fact, this was the only interesting thing in any of Cooper's recent books, Dana said, for every one of his works since *The Monikins* (1835) had been "unspeakably dull." Dana also said, however, that he had attempted to evaluate the three novels in this trilogy by common standards of art, but he was unable to detect any merit in the works. *Satanstoe* was a flawed novel because it contained, among other things, the same stereotyped characters and incidents so typical of Cooper's earlier romances. And he thought this same lack of inventiveness was evidenced in *The Chainbearer*, where the characters were "the work of a journeyman and not a master." *The Redskins*, too, suffered from a number of problems, problems that Dana, in his not uncharacteristically acidulous manner, did not hesitate to list in the 1 August 1846 number of *The Harbinger*:

> First, it [the Redskins] professes to be a novel; second, it is a treatise on morals; third, it teaches what kind of manners are proper for a gentleman; fourth, it is an essay on spelling and pronunciation; and fifth, it is a more or less violent eructation of Mr. Cooper's sentiments, convictions and opinions on a variety of subjects; and in all of these aspects it is equally a bore. [3:123]

Mainly, then, the three reviews of the "Littlepage Manuscripts," all of which were written by Dana, were occasions in which Dana took issue with Cooper's conservative and aristocratic attitude regarding property. The antirent question was only one aspect of a larger problem very important to the Brook Farmers: the conflict between the wealthy and the poor. Dana said in his review of *Satanstoe* that he did not condone the "rebellious movements of the anti-renters" or "their lawless invasion of the rights of property." In fact, Cooper's defense of the "rights of property in *The Chainbearer* was eloquent and sensible" (1:411). Still, Dana thought that Cooper had failed to consider the "rights of man." His attitude throughout the three novels was narrow and provincial, for he was unable to consider more than a single aspect of a principle. If the truth were known, man would realize that land should not be held by individuals but by *"communities, in joint stock proprietorship"* (the system employed at Brook Farm). If the landholder and tenant would recognize this fact and unite their interests, all the violence and hatred that had resulted from the conflict between the propertied and propertyless classes would vanish. Dana concluded his remarks by saying that Cooper's novels had not shed any new light on this important problem. So long as his works served as vehicles for his own moral, philosophical, and political ideas, "we fear . . . little profit will be derived from them in any quarter" (3:123).[23]

There were many ways, of course, in which Nathaniel Hawthorne was different from such fellow American writers as Cooper, but certainly the one that would have obviously appealed to the editors of *The Harbinger* was the fact that he had been an original shareholder as well as one of the first residents of Brook Farm. *The Harbinger* reviewed him only once, however, for *Mosses from an Old Manse* (1846) was the only work of his published in the years during which the magazine survived. Nevertheless, William Henry Channing's review of this work is noteworthy for the fact that it was one of the most perceptive reviews ever published in the magazine.

Four years before Herman Melville's adulatory review of "Hawthorne and His Mosses" in *The Literary World* (17 and 24 August 1850), Channing recognized that Hawthorne was more than a "man who means no meanings." If Melville was correct in stating that Hawthorne was "a man as yet almost utterly mistaken among men," then Channing is to be all the more praised for his insight in 1846 into Hawthorne. Channing believed that, more than any other American writer, Hawthorne "had been baptized in the deep waters of *Tragedy*." What Melville was later to call Hawthorne's "great power of blackness," Channing here described as his "serene brightness," the kind of brightness that seldom cheered us because it was like "dusky twilight." Indeed, the light on Hawthorne's pages, Channing noted, was never clear or brilliant; rather, it resembled the light of evening deepening into night, or the light of noontime obliquely piercing through the heavy shadows of the forest. In Hawthorne's fiction, sadness was never occasional or transient; it pervaded all the pages of his works. Despite the gloom, however, Hawthorne never allowed this sadness to overcome him; he was neither morbid nor extravagant, for one of the extraordinary things about him was the fact that, given his ability to penetrate appearances and detect awful realities, he had become neither cynical about life nor comfortable in his awareness of life's superficialities:

> He has been endowed with a truly awful power of insight. No masks deceive him. And most plainly, the mockeries of life have cost him sleepless nights and lonely days. His feet have been blistered on the wide sand deserts which human crime has swept over the Eden of primeval innocence. He has wandered long and far to find an Adam, an Eve. But he has been learning all the while not to hate but to love, not to despise but to revere, not to despair but to confide, to look forward and not back. [3:44]

Charles Dana's review of Herman Melville's *Typee* (1846) was not nearly so penetrating as Channing's was of Hawthorne. This may be explained largely by the fact that Melville's novel had to do with the remarkably harmonious social state of the cannibalistic Typee natives, and it therefore afforded Dana an opportunity to proselytize about the benefits of Associationism in America. Dana's review of *Typee,* then, was mainly a criticism of contemporary society in America.

What most impressed Dana about the Typee natives was the high degree of harmony that existed in their society, amazingly so, since they had no judicial system, no municipal police, and no legal provisions through which an individual could secure redress against another member of the community. How was it, Dana asked, that in a

> mere state of nature they [the Typee natives] can live together in a degree of social harmony and freedom from vice, which all our jails, and scaffolds, and courts of justice, and police officers, and philosophers, and immense politicians, and moral codes, and steam engines, material and spiritual, cannot procure for us? [2:265]

Dana, of course, had the answer to his question at hand: in the Typee society there was universal abundance for everyone, whereas in American society there was none. This was a lesson, he thought, that the legislators, philosophers, clergy, and leaders of nineteenth-century America had to learn from the Typee natives. There should be a social system in America "which will produce and distribute to every member of society a complete abundance" in return for honest labor, "and not a niggardly, starving pittance to nineteen-twentieths of the population as the return for slavish and debasing toil, and enormous wealth to the other one-twentieth as the fruit of grasping cunning." As it was, he added, American society did not supply the wants of its people because its social and political institutions were merely forms of "organized selfishness" in which all things were subjected to greedy and fraudulent commerce, and in which "slavery in some one of its disgusting and inhuman forms" was a "necessary and constant fact." Dana added that just as the cause of this deplorable social condition was clear, so too were the means of producing significant abundance for all Americans. The means was a reorganization of industry and a distribution of its products

> according to principles of exact justice. . . . Let associated, cooperative labor once take the place of the drudgery of our gloomy manufactories, the dulness [*sic*] of our agriculture, and the poverty of our cities, and the word *want* will be banished from our language forever. [2:266].

Dana devoted very little attention to any aesthetic considerations of *Typee*. He did say that he suspected Melville of romantically embellishing the narrative facts of the novel. Very possibly, *Typee* was "only an amusing fiction." Considering the nature of his review, however, Dana had no other choice but to conclude that *Typee* did indeed have verisimilitude, for it was upon this belief that he launched his attack on the social order devoted to the "hopeless and miserable existence [of] so large a majority of human creatures."

In addition to its reviews of American writers, *The Harbinger* also noticed and reviewed a number of contemporary American magazines. Three such journals that received treatment in *The Harbinger* were *The Massachusetts Quarterly Review; Hunt's Merchants' Magazine and Commercial Review;* and *The American Whig Review.*

The Harbinger twice reviewed *The Massachusetts Quarterly Review* (1847–50), a magazine considered by some to have been the successor of the *Dial.* In fact, it originally intended to be, according to Theodore Parker, one of its editors and its chief contributor, "the *Dial* with a beard," though T. W. Higginson later characterized it as "the beard without the *Dial.*"[24] But whether or not it was in any respect the successor of the *Dial,* it was certainly very different from that publication. Frank Luther Mott has noted, for example, that the *Massachusetts Quarterly Review* "was more practical, more reformatory, more political, [and] harder hitting" than the *Dial.*[25] Under the joint editorship of Parker and J. Elliot Cabot from December 1847 to September 1848, and of Parker alone from December 1848 to September 1850, the magazine was a philosophical, literary, and humanitarian journal that addressed itself to such matters as slavery, politics, and natural science.[26]

As has already been noted,[27] George Ripley had had only good things to say about his friend Parker when he reviewed three of the theologian's sermons for *The Harbinger,* so it was not unusual that he had mostly positive things to say about the *Massachusetts Quarterly Review* when he reviewed the second and fourth numbers of that magazine's first volume. Ripley even stated in his review of the fourth number that he thought the *Massachusetts Quarterly Review* owed its principal attraction to Parker, whose writings were always "spontaneous" and "picturesque," combining "a gravity and seriousness of tone . . . with a vein of subtle humor" that never failed to beguile his readers. Representative in the fourth number of the *Massachusetts Quarterly Review* was Parker's article on Dr. William Ellery Channing, which deserved "to be classed among the most admirable compositions of its versatile author."

When he reviewed the second number Ripley warned that the reader would be disappointed if he expected the *Massachusetts Quarterly Review* to contain the mysticism, impiety, and radicalism of what had been "absurdly enough called 'Boston Transcendentalism,'" for the character of the Massachusetts periodical was more akin to the judicious composure of the *North American Review* (6:151). It was always conducted with "diligent investigation, extensive learning, and literary integrity." Ripley elaborated on this point somewhat when he reviewed the fourth number of the *Massachusetts Quarterly Review,* in the course of which he summarized *The Harbinger*'s opinion of four other important contemporary periodicals:

> If it [the *Massachusetts Quarterly Review*] does not exhibit the talent of pleasing, gossipy discussion of literary common-places, which distinguishes the ancient *North American,*—or the well-bred, scholarlike dignity with which the courteous *Christian Examiner* treats the gravest subjects in the light of a smooth and inoffensive theology,—or the salient freshness and delightful audacity which give such a charm to the intrepid assertions of *Brownson's Quarterly,*—or the naive subjectivity and Orphic mysticism which gathered a crowd of youthful idolators around the oracle of the illuminated *Dial,*—it is still a bold, earnest, original publication, and is entitled to a high rank in the periodical literature of Massachusetts. [7:150]

Hunt's Merchants' Magazine (1839–70) was so different in character from the *Massachusetts Quarterly Review* that one would expect *The Harbinger* to have been somewhat critical of a magazine devoted to mercantile interests. That it was not is perhaps best explained by the fact that it was conducted by Freeman Hunt, a man who, according to George Ripley at least, had great "faith in the highest ideas of the age," as well as a love of humanity (6:151). Ripley reviewed Hunt's magazine four times for *The Harbinger,* and with only one exception gave it high praise because it was among other things, "not blind to the evils of the present commercial system." The one exception had to do with a remark made by one of Hunt's correspondents to the effect that Egypt, a country "sunk in barbarism," possessed thirty-eight war ships. Hunt himself responded to the statement in his magazine (August 1846) by saying that he did not think "a navy [was] any *very* decisive indication of true Christian Civilization"; to which Ripley sarcastically replied that the editor must be a "blind fanatic" if he believed that men could love one another without guns, or modern commerce could prosper without "red-hot shot," for surely he realized that all the most learned teachers advocated the notion that "blood [was] the only seal for the covenant of our freedom" (3:160).

Mainly, however, Ripley did think that Hunt was genuinely concerned with the welfare of humanity; his magazine was not a "blind apologist" for the present system of trade, for it defended the "great improvement that would result from a more systematic organization of business." He also said that the magazine was "indispensable" to anyone aspiring to be a well-educated merchant. It contained vast amounts of statistical, commercial, and financial information, which was always presented in a readable and attractive manner. In fact, Ripley thought there were few periodicals so "uniformly sustained" as Hunt's, and he said that he was glad to learn the periodical had such a wide circulation, for its intrinsic merits warranted a large patronage.[28]

Interestingly enough, *The Harbinger* remained generally free from the literary feuds which not infrequently characterized the world of nineteenth-century American magazines. Only on two occasions was it drawn into anything resembling a literary battle, and in both these instances the exchange of words was quite tame when compared, for instance, to the literary battles conducted by Poe in the *Broadway Journal.* One of the magazines that engaged *The Harbinger* was the *Democratic Review,* and the circumstances surrounding the "feud" between these two journals have already been discussed (see chapter 1, pp. 21–22). The other magazine was the *American Review* (1845–52), a political journal devoted to setting forth and defending "the doctrines held by the United Whig Party of the Union."[29] In May 1847 the *American Review* published a scathing article on the "Religious Union of Associationists," a Fourierist-inspired religious organization headed by William Henry Channing, which was supported by such men as Ripley, Dwight, and Brisbane. Exactly what prompted this article is not clear. It is possible, of course, that the Religious Union of Associationists and *The Harbinger* represented everything to which the *American Review* was opposed. Politically and socially, the *American Review* was very conservative, whereas *The Harbinger* was, of course, extremely liberal. It seems more likely, however, that the *Review* was overreacting to *The Harbinger's* critical treatment of it, for Charles Dana had reviewed the Whig journal three times between late 1845 and mid-1846, and his treatment of it was generally adverse. For example, for the December 1845 number, Dana noted that the *American Review* contained, among other things, a story by Poe, which seemed to have been written "mainly to disgust their readers"; a "harmless contrivance" that William Gilmore Simms "supposed to be [a] poem"; an article on "Heraldry," the chief merit of which was that it covered only four pages; and a ten-page article on "The Figures and Figuratives of Tobacco," which was "wholly unfit for a place in a publication which aims to 'diffuse through the land a higher order of taste in letters and the arts'" (2:27). But Dana then somewhat qualified his criticism by acknowledging that this number contained an excellent article on the antirent movement in New York; an interesting "Chapter on Chatham"; and one of the finest pieces of historical narrative he had ever seen. Nevertheless, he concluded his remarks by stating that the journal did not do justice to the Whig party; that its political articles were dull and unreadable; that its philosophy was neither lucid nor instructive (although he did remark satirically that it was profound); and that its literary features were nothing to boast about.

Dana's second review (of the March 1846 number) was no less adverse than his first, although his tone was more satirical and whimsical. He first complained that the present number arrived a month late at *The Harbinger*'s offices, but he added that he still thought the *Review* "pretty fair" for a political monthly, at least he presumed it to be, for, he said, he did not really read it very carefully, except for the poetry. With respect to the poetry, William Wallace was the "great gun" for the *American Review;* a tremendous gun, too, Dana said, "to judge his discharges, which are somewhat of the longest and smoke like,—we don't presume to say what." But there was, at least, a good critique of the modern French novelists, written by a man who had some comprehension of things in general but no "very astounding insight into every thing in particular." What most characterized the article was its admirable sense of propriety—indeed, its "veritable prudery"—a quality that, Dana said, occasionally had been attributed to "old maids," but one that, he added, he had never before seen in a monthly review. But just as he was admiring the "exquisite delicacy" of the article, he found a passage excerpted from a book entitled *Over the Ocean,* a passage he thought rather piquant to have been written by a lady, but one that, "after the moral lessons of the *Review,*" would absolutely have made him blush if anyone else had been around. *The Harbinger,* he concluded, hoped that the *Review* would not be guilty of this kind of inconsistency again.

Dana opened his third review (of the July 1846 number) by noting that *The Harbinger* had not received its exchange copy. "One day," he remarked, "ah day unlucky! we criticized it, and have not seen it since, until yesterday, when we got sight of it at second hand" (3 : 107). And despite this apparent oversight, Dana said that he still had some positive things to say about the July number: it contained an article of "great ability" on the Mexican War and also a poem entitled "Rain," the faults of which were more than redeemed by a fine play of sentiment and a real naturalness. Overall, Dana admitted that the *Review* had made some improvement, but this, of course, did not prevent him from noting some of the weaknesses in the present number, not the least of which were some verses by W. T. Bacon—"of which the less said the better"—and a seventeen-page article on American and European civilization that, while containing many good thoughts, lacked "a clear knowledge of what Civilization is." Of course, it was not necessary for a magazine to understand the subject about which it wrote, Dana sarcastically added, as long as it knew how to write " 'about it and about it.' " Dana noted that the capacities for a magazine were boundless, but that only the smallest number of American monthlies had so far combined the "ideal and the actual" in their pages. The *American Review* was not one of them.

Obviously, Dana's criticism of the *American Review* was hardly flattering, but whether he motivated its attack on the Religious Union of Associationists remains uncertain. One thing, however, was certain: *The Harbinger* considered the essay "a most elaborate and cynical attack upon the doctrines, services and motives of the Religious Union of Associationists" (5:28), and it deeply resented the *Review*'s charges that William H. Channing, the principal speaker and conductor of the organization's services, was hypocritical, ambitious, and even insane.

John Dwight was assigned the task of refuting the article, and he did so in four consecutive numbers of *The Harbinger*.[30] It is not necessary here to follow Dwight's refutation, for it was, predictably enough, a defense of the aims and ideals of Associationists. Instead, the point to be made here is that, while *The Harbinger* frequently used the occasion of the literary review to propagandize for a cause—and that is very much in the American tradition—the magazine's judgments of those contemporary American writers whom it reviewed are remarkably consistent with modern critical assessments of them. In short, *The Harbinger*'s dedication to the cause of Associationism and its belief that literature should serve humanitarian ends did not prevent it on many occasions from writing penetrating literary criticism.

European Authors

Swedenborg

It seems best to begin a discussion of *The Harbinger*'s attitude toward foreign authors with Emanuel Swedenborg (1688–1772), for no other author, whether European or American, received nearly so much attention in its pages. *The Harbinger* published seventeen literary reviews of works written by or about or involving the Swedish theologian, scientist, and philosopher, a number that does not include the numerous editorial discussions of the man.

Swedenborg, of course, had been no stranger to the New England Transcendentalists right from the beginning of the movement. In fact, throughout the important decades of the 1820s, 1830s, and 1840s, he exerted a pervasive influence on the Transcendentalists that was, according to Perry Miller, as fundamental as that exerted by Samuel Coleridge and Thomas Carlyle.[31] The principal figure who represented Swedenborg to the young "infidels"—to use the word that the 'hard-headed Unitarian Pope' Andrews Norton did—was a man named Sampson Reed. Reed had come to Harvard with the intention of becoming a Unitarian minister, but shortly after receiving his baccalaureate degree in 1818, he was converted to Swedenborgianism and thus was personally compelled to withdraw from the Harvard Divinity School. He stayed on at Harvard, however, where he received his M.A. degree in 1821. At the commencement ceremonies that year, Reed delivered his famous "Oration on Genius," an address that was inspired in no small way by his reading of Emanuel Swedenborg. At least one graduating senior who heard those remarks that day was profoundly impressed by them, for shortly afterward, Ralph Waldo Emerson borrowed the address from Reed in order to make a copy of it.

Reed followed the "Oration" a few years later with the publication of his *Observations on the Growth of the Mind* (1826), a small, thinly-veiled pamphlet on Swedenborg that would, in the years following its publication, have anything but a small effect on individuals such as Emerson, Ripley, Hedge, Clarke, and the younger Channings. Thanks, then, largely to Reed's influence, men such as these began to read Swedenborg themselves. The interest, of course, could not have been more worthwhile. Not only did the Transcendentalists derive from him an important "theory of correspondence," but the Swede provided them with the basis for their aesthetic theory as well[32]—a theory that has sometimes been referred to as "organicism," or the "organic theory of art."

Emerson, for one, would eventually find it necessary to repudiate Reed (the victim of "this immense arrogancy and subtle bigotry of his [Swedenborg's] church"),[33] though it would take many years before he would be able to do so. He did not have to do the same with Swedenborg, however, if only because he was never able completely to embrace Swedenborgian doctrine in the first place. This should not suggest, though, that Emerson was not greatly attracted to the Swede. He and Bronson Alcott would often spend hours, for example, discussing the Swedish theologian. Moreover, Emerson's published writings, as well as his journals and correspondence, are punctuated by references to Swedenborg. And though it is true that his lecture on "Swedenborg, or the Mystic"—first delivered in the Boston Odeon in 1845 and published, in 1850, in *Representative Men*— was by no means unqualifiedly enthusiastic, it did offer more praise than criticism of the Swedish philosopher. Of Swedenborg's followers, Emerson had already remarked earlier in a letter to Thomas Carlyle, dated 20 November 1834: "They are to me however deeply interesting as a sect which I think must contribute more than all other sects to the new faith which must arise from out of all."[34]

Finally, though, Emerson was never a man to be compromised. He had never been comfortable with dogmatisms of any kind, and his own philosophy—eclectic in nature as it was—was evidence of that distrust. The problem with a figure such as Swedenborg—as, indeed, it was with some one such as Fourier, too—was one of loss. To the extent that one allied himself with the specific views of any single person or institution was one's individuality necessarily diminished. Unfortunately, in the case of Swedenborg, the matter of acceptance or rejection was not a simple one. As Marguerite Beck Block has remarked in her study of the New Church of America: "The

character of the man [Swedenborg], his comprehensive scientific knowledge, and his idealistic philosophy, appealed to Emerson strongly,—but the
theology of Swedenborg repelled him. The problem, therefore, was how
logically to accept him as a philosopher and a scientist, but reject him as the
prophet of a new religion."[35]

Block goes on to argue that Emerson did manage to resolve the problem—
not, however, by willy-nilly rejecting Swedenborgian notions, and certainly
not by accepting them wholesale. Instead, Emerson, according to Block,
began increasingly to emphasize the mystical side of Swedenborg, for "it
[was] possible to pay transcendental respect and reverence to a mystic without understanding his doctrines."[36] Whatever the case may in fact have
been, Emerson himself would recollect Swedenborg many years later, in his
one hundreth address before the Concord Lyceum in 1880, as "a man of
prodigious mind, though as I think tainted with a certain suspicion of insanity, and therefore generally disowned, but exerting a singular power over an
important intellectual class."[37]

In devoting the considerable space that it did to Swedenborg, *The Har-
binger* was simply continuing a practice established in the days of Albert
Brisbane's *The Phalanx*. Nevertheless, there were other reasons for *The
Harbinger*'s lively interest in Swedenborg. For one thing, several of *The
Harbinger*'s contributors were members of the New Church (which was
founded by the Scandinavian's disciples and organized on his scientific and
philosophical principles), chief among them, James J. G. Wilkinson and
Henry James, Sr. For another, the reading of Swedenborg's works was not
an infrequent activity at Brook Farm on Sunday afternoons,[38] and William
Henry Channing in 1845 even proposed using "the Swedenborgian ritual or
book of worship" at the community's religious services.[39] Thus, it was no
coincidence that the watchword of the magazine—"All things at the present
day, stand provided and prepared, and await the light"—came from Swedenborg.[40] Indeed, so far as the editors of *The Harbinger* were concerned,
Charles Fourier was indeed the authority on the "laws and conditions of
harmony in the outward or material" world, but Emanuel Swedenborg was
the discoverer of "the true order of degrees and the true relation of the
outward to the inward life." Or, to put it as John Dwight did in a review of
the *New Jerusalem Magazine* (the leading Swedenborg journal in America):
"There is a most remarkable, although unconscious correspondence, between the leading views of Swedenborg and those of Fourier, respecting the
true form and destiny of human society" (3:393).

This drawing of a parallel between Fourier and Swedenborg was not un-
common in the pages of *The Harbinger*: it occurred frequently, whether in
the editorial essays on Fourier or in the literary reviews of Swedenborg. For
example, in an announcement of the impending publication of Parke Godwin's *The Teachers of the Nineteenth Century* (1846), the magazine took
time to note that "the chief characteristic of this epoch is its tendency, every

where apparent, to Unity in Universality, and the men in whom this tendency is most fully expressed are Swedenborg [and] Fourier" (1:400). In publishing the prospectus of the London Swedenborgian Association, *The Harbinger* again pointed out: "It is quite proper to say that however much Swedenborg and Fourier differ both in the character of their minds, and the immediate end of their studies, the method they adopted was fundamentally the same" (2:351).

While the Swedenborg-Fourier parallel sometimes appeared in editorial notes, it occurred most frequently in the literary reviews of the scientist-philosopher. Regarding Swedenborg's scientific writings, for example, Charles Dana stated: "We say without hesitation, that, with the exception of the writings of Fourier, no publications of the last fifty years, are, in our opinion, to be compared with them in importance" (3:72). Earlier he had remarked in his review of *The Memorabilia of Swedenborg: Or, Memorable Relations of Heaven and Hell* (1835): "Inferior perhaps to Fourier in grandeur and comprehensive sweep of mind, less mathematical and exact in his forms of expression, he [Swedenborg] carries into his studies a deep Scandinavian reverence, a poetic and religious sentiment with which Fourier was not endowed" (1:377–78). And John Dwight wrote:

> Deeper foundations for science have not been touched by any sounding line as yet, than these same philosophical principles of Swedenborg. Fourier has not gone deeper; but he has shed *more* light on these deep foundations, taken their measurement with a more bold precision, and reared a no insignificant portion of the everlasting superstructure. But in their ground they are both one. Taken together they are the highest expression of the tendency of human thought to universal unity; of the demand for unitary science, in which the soul of man shall feel all sciences co-ordinated to its own living springs of action. [5:6]

Of the seventeen literary reviews published by *The Harbinger* that directly concerned Swedenborg, seven were critiques of his works; and in all seven instances, the magazine gave unqualified praise to Swedenborg's writings generally and to his scientific writings specifically.

The attitude expressed by Dana in his review of Swedenborg's *The Apocalypse Explained* (1846) was characteristic:

> No man of sincere and unsophisticated mind can read Swedenborg without feeling his life elevated into a higher plane, and his intellect excited into new and more reverent action on some of the sublimest questions which the human mind can approach. Whatever may be thought of the doctrines of Swedenborg or of his visions, the spirit which breathes from his works, of which the present is generally regarded as one of the most valuable, is pure and heavenly. [2:315]

For *The Harbinger* regarded Swedenborg's "mission" to be of the highest importance to the human family. Associationists, Dana added, study "him continually for the light he sheds on so many problems of human destiny," and consider him to be a "great poet and high priest" whose doctrines are "profound, living, and electric."

Swedenborg's scientific writings *The Harbinger* considered to be "invaluable" and "indispensable." They provided for a "True Science"—that is, a science "which explains man to himself, and all things in their correspondence with him." In the judgment of the editors of *The Harbinger*, no scientific publications of the last fifty years compared in importance with these works of Swedenborg. Indeed, Fourier's works excepted, "there are no writings on scientific subjects in existence . . . which evince so deep and broad an insight into the nature and laws of the Universe." For, as seen by Associationists, Swedenborg's science was an endeavor to unfold the "supreme laws of Universal Harmony," laws that, if applied, would lead to a "New Social Order."

As *The Harbinger*'s high esteem of Swedenborg was not universally shared, the magazine took every opportunity to defend Swedenborg, and inevitably itself, against detractors. When, for instance, *The Perfectionist*, a theological newspaper published in Putney, Vermont, derided *The Harbinger* for "the deference paid Swedenborg," Dwight replied:

Swedenborg we reverence for the greatness and profundity of his thoughts. We study him continually for the light he sheds on so many problems of human destiny, and more especially for the remarkable correspondence, as of inner with outer, which his revelations present with the discoveries of Fourier concerning social organizations, or the outward forms of life. [2:94]

Another such defense was made by George Ripley in a review of Enoch Pond's *Swedenborgianism Reviewed* (1846) and Leonard Wood's *Lectures on Swedenborgianism* (1846). Ripley cited examples of the "false reasoning" employed by these "most eminent professors of theology at Calvinistic seminaries" in order to arrive at absurd conclusions regarding Swedenborg. "Their reasonings," Ripley said, "remind us of the mathematician trying to make out what is proved by the 'Paradise Lost' " (4:217).

Though *The Harbinger* often defended Swedenborg, it did not always defend all his doctrines, nor the New Church. Even in its first volume, Charles Dana qualified the Associationists' position on Swedenborg. He announced that though Associationists in general had profound respect for Swedenborg's views,

we are far from pledging the members of the Associative School to his doctrines, or to the so-called New Church as a special body. In fact we do not think that the New Church has yet fully comprehended those doctrines which in our opinion can be understood only by the help of Fourier's theory of General Destinies. [1:378]

By the third volume these views of Dana were expressed more forcefully. In reviewing the *New Jerusalem Magazine,* John Dwight criticized the Swedenborgians because they were "quietists" and "exclusivists." Though they recognized the unity of man with man, of man with nature, and of man with God, "they [did] not lend themselves to any . . . schemes of social reorganization with a view to the speedy fulfillment of this unity" (3:393). Instead of engaging actively in social reform, as the Associationists were doing, the Swedenborgians were concerned too exclusively with reformation of the individual. And, as the Associationists saw the situation, individual reform was atomistic. General reform of the entire society of individuals was their dream, and the means to effect this dream was through reformation of society itself.

In spite of its criticism of Swedenborgians, *The Harbinger* had only the deepest reverence for Swedenborg himself. That he was mentioned favorably in the context of Fourier is surely an indication of the importance that the magazine attached to his principles, though, to be sure, the influence Swedenborg exerted on the views of *The Harbinger* needs still to be more thoroughly assessed. Fourier thus far has been regarded as the sole social light of the magazine, but the fact is that *The Harbinger*'s doctrine of man's need for a "unitary science" was influenced principally by Swedenborg's scientific writings.

German Writers

Swedenborg was the only Scandinavian whom *The Harbinger* discussed, though the magazine, of course, recognized important writers from other countries. Germany was one such country, for *The Harbinger* thought its literature to be "the deepest, richest, and heartiest literature of the world" (5:72) and its writers men of "profound thought, subtle speculation, massive learning and genial temper" (4:150). Given this view, it is remarkable that so little attention, relatively speaking, was devoted to the Germans in the magazine. It is true that there were five notices of Goethe, but there was only one notice each for Schiller, Schlegel, and Fichte, and two of Heinrich Zschokke, a German tale writer. Perhaps the reason for this is that George Ripley, one of the editors of *The Harbinger,* had become increasingly disillusioned with German idealism. Even in a generally favorable review of his friend Frederic H. Hedge's *Prose Writers of Germany* (1848), Ripley questioned the value of German thought: "We have here the ultimate results of what philosophical speculation and literary culture have been able to accomplish among the best minds of the nineteenth century, and to what does it amount?"[41] (4:150-51).

Ripley's attitude is explained by the fact that his own views were engendered largely by French idealism, and that he seems to have lost interest at this time in Transcendental metaphysics. Ripley, for instance, wrote a letter to Theordore Parker, dated 31 January 1852, in which he explained why he refused to publish his translation of Schliermacher: no one would read the work and he had lost all "immediate interest in that line of speculation."[42] Despite Ripley, and however truistic the observation, those German works which exhibited values and beliefs shared by the Associationists were the works that received high praise in *The Harbinger*. Thus, Goethe and Fichte were more enthusiastically received than Schiller and Schlegel, for reasons discussed later in this chapter.

Viewed chronologically, *The Harbinger*'s attitude toward Goethe (1749–1832) developed from indifference in its first volume (the first notice) to great admiration and respect in the fifth volume (the last review). The first mention of Goethe was a mere notice of his *Essays on Art* (1845). The second notice, which appeared only a week later, in the 21 June 1845 number, was a fairly long and mixed review of the first volume of the *Correspondence Between Schiller and Goethe from 1794 to 1805* (1845). John Dwight described the work as "tame and prosy," and he questioned the extent of which its contents were of interest to the reading public. In his judgment, the correspondence between two editors of a literary journal was hardly the kind of material the public would regard as stimulating reading. Despite this, Dwight himself thought Goethe a "master in numerous departments of art," an "artist in language" whose profundity often startled the reader, and a writer of "sound, clear mind" who worked "away at his problems—making Art its own end." Nevertheless, Dwight said that he had "no sympathy with such as set up Goethe as a god, or even as the beau-ideal of a man. . . . Let him [Goethe] be weighed in an even balance—we wish not to apologize for the selfishness we discover in his character, nor to deny that we think him better than most men of his condition in that country and at that time" (1:25).

By September of that year, however, Goethe's value to the Associationists had become evident. In the number for 27 September 1845, Dwight wrote an extended review of *Essays of Art* (1845), though only three months earlier he had devoted a mere two paragraphs to it. In this second review, Dwight discussed the nature of the artist and the value of art for social man. He said that a philosophy of art was really a philosophy of life because there could not be art without a belief in the future. In spite of the artist's isolation from mankind, he was nevertheless thoroughly wedded to humanity, since humanity supplied the material from which art was made. Although the artist seldom regarded himself as a politician, Dwight thought he was, at least unconsciously, a "social architect." While the artist may not be theological (so far as church and creed were concerned), yet "are his work and world most deeply religious, more reverent, harmonious, and full of love" (1:250).

As to art itself, Dwight pointed out its value to Associationists. The primary goal of Associationism was to marry the spiritual and material worlds within social man, worlds which, because of the present structure of society, remained antagonistic to each other. Art, along with the reformation of society, of course, was one means of accomplishing this because it wedded form and idea, the actual and the ideal, and the outward and the inward. Dwight believed that Goethe's essays reflected these principles and he therefore stated unequivocally:

> We believe there have been no profounder criticisms on Art than these of Goethe. No man has better seized the spirit, comprehended the aim and methods, classed the styles and tendencies of Art, than he. [1:250]

With this critique, Goethe began to receive only the highest praise in *The Harbinger*. In a review of *The Autobiography of Goethe* (1846), which limited itself to parts 1 and 2, Goethe was described as a "poetical genius of the first order" whose autobiography was the "wisest, richest, truest, most romantic and most fascinating piece of biography extant in any language" (4:9). And in a subsequent review of parts 3 and 4, Goethe was hailed as "the great German Poet, in the calm mirror of whose works the whole spirit of the nineteenth century is reflected as in no other" (5:71).

Fichte (1762–1814), too, received praise similar to that accorded Goethe, although the *Memoir of Johann Gottlieb Fichte* (1846) was his only work reviewed in *The Harbinger*. The fact that Fichte's philosophy concerned itself not only with man's progress, but with the depths of man's soul (his "instinctive sense of justice, duty, universal harmony, and unity") was bound to be appealing to the Associationist magazine. In his review, George Ripley summed up those qualities in Fichte that made him, in Ripley's judgment, the most distinguished of the German writers:

> Filled with the deepest reverence for Divine things, he was accused by his contemporaries of Atheism; fired with an enthusiastic zeal for the elevation of humanity, he was stigmatized by the conservatives of his day as a demagogue and a democrat; and swayed by a burning soul, he was denounced by those who were unworthy to sit at his feet, as a reckless innovator. [2:197]

As was suggested earlier, the magazine's high regard for Goethe and Fichte was not extended to Friedrich von Schiller (1759–1805) or August Wilhelm von Schlegel (1767–1845). Schiller's *History of the Thirty Years' War* (1846), for example, received merely a notice, and the only substantial remarks on the poet and playwright appeared in Dwight's review of the *Correspondence Between Schiller and Goethe,* discussed earlier. In that review, Dwight noted that, compared to Goethe, Schiller was simply an "aspiring Telemachus." Goethe's sound, clear mind and his steadfast devotion to art were "the more beautiful when contrasted with the idleness and morbid feeling of his distinguished friend." The hope was nevertheless expressed that Schiller would, under the guidance of his mentor, "walk more and strut less," a curious remark indeed since Schiller had died in 1805. Be that as it may, Dwight said that his "pedantic stiffness and oratorical affection is what often disturbs us in reading Schiller's works." Thus, though he praised the simplicity that was sometimes evident in his ballads and poems and acknowledged his qualities as a historian, Dwight nevertheless thought that Schiller was "often inflated, proud, stiff, and diseasedly self-conscious."

Schlegel, on the other hand, in the opinion of Parke Godwin, was perhaps better adapted to the "present intellectual development of this country, than other Germans who possess a richer and more original vein." Although the subject treated in *The Philosophy of Life, and the Philosophy of Language* (1845) was a most important one to Associationists because it concerned the aims and ends of life, Godwin felt Schlegel treated matters too conventionally:

> There are a great many fine things said of Man's duties, &c., but we are not conscious of having met with anything new, and in laying down the work, we did not feel inspired with any new determinations for the present, or any new hopes for the future. [6:47]

But if the reviewers in *The Harbinger* were unexcited by Schiller and Schlegel, they were certainly not so with Heinrich Zschokke. In his initial review of *Tales from the German of Heinrich Zschokke* (1845), Charles Dana attributed his very positive reaction to Zschokke to his having wearied his brain with Fichte, Schelling, and Novalis. Zschokke's tales, he felt, brought relief to the reader of German literature because they made one realize that we were "not machines for thought and imagination merely, but that it is 'the human heart by which we live.'" In addition to gay humor (which threw "one oftentimes into the healthiest laughter"), Zschokke's satire, which was never motivated by personal spite, generally hit the mark at which it was directed. Zschokke was an authentic artist; in "truth, delicacy, elevation and pathos, he [had] few superiors." It was for these qualities that Zschokke was considered next to Goethe one of *The Harbinger*'s favorite German writers (2:217).

English Writers

English authors and their works formed the basis for a great many critical discussions found in the magazine, so many, in fact, that one is forced to be selective. Thus, representative English writers will be discussed here under three general headings: poets, nonfiction writers, and novelists.

English Poets

The Harbinger's critical treatment of Percy Bysshe Shelley, Thomas Hood, and Alfred Lord Tennyson illustrates again, as is to be expected, the magazine's tendency to use the literary review as an occasion to proselytize for Associationism and Fourierism.

Shelley (1792–1822) would probably have been noticed in *The Harbinger* even if George G. Foster, editor of *The Poetical Works of Percy Bysshe Shelley* (1845), had not asserted in his introductory remarks to this volume that the English poet's "system" and Fourier's were identical. The fact that Shelley had a zeal for freedom and progress would have been reason enough to devote a few columns to the English poet. Nevertheless, only one review of Shelley appeared in *The Harbinger*.

Charles Dana, who reviewed the Foster edition, reacted with considerable surprise to Foster's assertion that Shelley's instincts led him "to the same great and eternal scheme of practical social redemption" as that reached by Fourier (2:74).[43] Between Fourier and Shelley, Dana pointed out, there was no intellectual agreement. Fourier's faith in God, as well as his insight into the destiny of man and the harmony of the universe, was in direct contrast to Shelley's "wandering in the mazes of the ideal philosophy in search of a wisdom it never contained." To establish his assertion, Dana quoted Parke Godwin, who, in Dana's estimation, wrote the "best analysis of Shelley that has yet been written": "It is evident he [Shelley] had not yet settled, to the perfect satisfaction of his mind, the theories of the Universe, Man and God, which perplex and disturb all thoughtful persons." Foster's assertion, therefore, according to Dana, was the result of "a too eager wish to find an agreement where none exists." Dana added that *The Harbinger* could not allow a wrong impression of so broad a nature to pass uncorrected.

In spite of the apparent imperfections in Shelley's philosophy, Dana regarded the poet with both admiration and affection. Any man whose soul exhibited an "all containing love of Humanity, great sincerity, and a heroic devotion to the search for truth," was bound to receive the sympathy of *The Harbinger*. Shelley was such a man—a man who had "long been with us [*The Harbinger*] a select and sacred name. . . . We believe too, that he was a prophet, though certainly not the highest prophet, that has been given to this age."

Thomas Hood (1799–1845) was not ranked among the highest prophets given to the age either, but very few writers, native or foreign, were esteemed so highly by *The Harbinger* as was the author of *The Song of the Shirt*. In fact, John Dwight thought him to be "perhaps the greatest of living authors." In partial defense of this attitude, Dwight noted that Hood's humor was healthier and "less contracted than that of Charles Lamb," and it was more imaginative than that of Dickens. With respect to originality and imaginative power, Dwight classed Hood with Keats and Tennyson. His "Hero and Leander" was "worthy of the best mythological dreams of Keats," and his "Lycus the Centaur" contained "a theme for which no other imagination but Tennyson's . . . could be equal" (2:360). This parallel between Hood and Tennyson was significant, as *The Harbinger* believed that Tennyson was "*the* English poet of the day" (6:158). Indeed, the magazine took pride in the fact that, years before Tennyson received any widespread recognition in America, they were "martyrs . . . to our admiration of [his] earlier poetry" (6:158).

Specifically, George G. Foster regarded Hood as a spokesman for all the downtrodden and persecuted members of the human race in that he waged uncompromising war with "Evils, abuses, corruption,—the gigantic shadows which stalk the world" (1:113). In addition to one notice and two lengthy reviews, Hood received the unusual distinction of a front-page obituary notice that extended to eight columns (1:113). Foster, who wrote this notice, said that Hood was "a man for all the world to love, to twine their hearts around," and he added that *The Harbinger* admired Hood for his wit, for his great capacity to love, and for the tenderness and pity he extended to oppressed women. Hood did not shy away from the evils of the world: wherever there was suffering, hunger, or misery, there, too, was Hood, "exuding the golden nectar of sympathy."

In spite of its boast concerning Tennyson (1809–92), *The Harbinger* reviewed only one of his works, *The Princess: A Medley* (1848). John Dwight praised him for his poetic individuality, his attempts at rendering Swedenborgian correspondences, and his interest in the relationship between thought and form and the ideal and the actual. The reviewer stated that Tennyson's poetry reflected a poet whose nature was pure. This was especially important, Dwight said, since we live in times "of unnatural conventions, soul-destroying mal-education, hypocritical moralizing and dogmatizing, thorough worldliness, money-worship, and universal competition" (6:158). It was refreshing to see "any single nature unfolding according to its own law, and continuing in some sense *itself.*"

Dwight did think, however, that Tennyson never managed to wed fully the ideal with the actual. It was true, he remarked, that none of Tennyson's earlier poetry contained a deeper meaning than that found in that most "mystical of poems," *The Lady of Shalott.* However, the poem, in his judgment, was excessive in the "direction of mere beauty"; it was too exclusively ideal and select. Reiterating ideas on the nature and function of art similar to those found in his review of Goethe's *Essays on Art,* Dwight said that it was not enough for art to exist on an abstract level. Poetic abstractions were never nearly so meaningful as when "airy, fairy Lilians," "imperial Eleanores," and "lady Psyches" were taken and made into

> flesh and blood existences in true functions of life, where, by a just *organization of labor,* according to that natural law which lifts its every detail to a level with the fine arts, the individual man and woman shall contribute to the vital harmony and symetry of the Grand Man, which is Humanity. [6:158]

Dwight concluded the review by stating that Tennyson's desire for a new social world, as seen especially in "The Princess," was a noble one. Dwight asked, however, if Tennyson's poetic visions of society would "become any the less poetry, by becoming social *science?*" Undoubtedly, Tennyson's purely "creative . . . imagination," and his effective use of "symbolic disguises . . . in . . . artistic forms," would be all the more valuable if the poet fully realized that "Poetry must pass into life."

English Nonfiction Writers

In addition to these three English poets, the works of many of Great Britain's literary critics, historians, journalists, and essayists—among them, William Hazlitt, Leigh Hunt, and Thomas Carlyle—were reviewed in *The Harbinger*. Generally, the reviews of these three individuals were significant for two reasons: first, they represented one of the rare occasions in *The Harbinger* when brief evaluative comments on the contemporary state of literature were offered; and second, the reviews were not occasions for proselytizing for Associationism.

The Harbinger's reviewers were as critical of historians and literary critics as they were of any other group of writers. John Dwight's reviews of Carlyle and Hazlitt, however, did enable him to bemoan the fact that "nearly all literature now is swallowed up in history and criticism" (2:56). Specifically, in his reviews of Carlyle's *Oliver Cromwell's Letters and Speeches: With Elucidations* (1845) and Hazlitt's *The Spirit of the Age: Or Contemporary Portraits* (1846), Dwight complained that literature in general had become too reflective. In addition to the fact that poetry had become too critical, Dwight also stated in his review of Carlyle that "pure creation, as well as the simpler thing, confession of one's experience, [was] becoming more and more banished into the sphere of the Fine Arts" (2:56). All the best writers, Dwight thought, were reviewers. They spent the majority of their time writing critical essays on the works of others writers, and in the process, they expended all their intellectual energy. As a result, Dwight remarked in his review of Hazlitt, "poets and romancers are for the most part only critics in the dress of rhyme or parable." The age was "absorbed entirely in the study of itself," and Dwight thought it comprehended "itself apparently about as little as the unconscious shepherds and hunters of Abraham's and Esau's time" (3:298).

In spite of these reservations, Dwight generally gave high praise to Hazlitt and Carlyle. He considered Hazlitt one of the most penetrating and erudite of the early romantic critics, as well as one of the greatest masters of English prose. These facts were evident, he thought, in such works as *Table Talk: Opinions on Books, Men, and Things* (Second Series, 1845) and *The Spirit of the Age* (1846), the two works by Hazlitt reviewed in *The Harbinger* by Charles Dana and John Dwight, respectively.

In his review of *The Spirit of the Age*, Dwight characterized Hazlitt's style as vigorous, clear, and concrete, never vague or abstract: "Each . . . sentence . . . contains a thought, a point, an image, something that arrests you as you glance over the page." Hazlitt's style was further enhanced by his use of illustrations, always "new and timely," and by his wit: "He says terribly severe things in the best humor imaginable" (3:299).

Charles Dana was less enthusiastic than Dwight because his standards of judgment were different. He commented in his review of *Table Talk* that "the lover of Humanity who seeks in an author for . . . a wide-reaching and deep-rooted faith in Providence and hope in man, will find no inspiration in his [Hazlitt's] pages" (2:249). Nevertheless, both Dana and Dwight agreed that as a critic, Hazlitt was sharp, genial, and appreciative. Shakespeare, Dwight stated, was "better known to us by his criticism," and "Artists [held] his essays upon painting to be inestimable." Yet he was not so original as Carlyle, Dwight added, nor so effective in organizing materials as Macaulay. He was "never intense and never cold, but always human, always strong, and always ready with something well worth saying" (3:299). In short, as Dana put it, Hazlitt's merit as a critic was "eminent and indisputable after all deductions" (2:249).

Leigh Hunt received far less praise in *The Harbinger* than did Hazlitt, though he was noticed once and reviewed twice. In fact, his *Stories from the Italian Poets* (1846) was the subject of one of the more bitter critical pieces to appear in the magazine. Contrary to principle, for most of the literary criticism in *The Harbinger* was based on the notion that "no criticism [was] legitimate which [was] not of the positive kind," the anonymous reviewer found nothing good to say about Hunt's book. For example, he thought that Hunt could have taken the romance by Ariosto and given it "a homespun English dress" that would "gratify the voracious appetite of superficial readers" without "laying unholy hands on what is most holy in poetry." Moreover, Hunt had "wounded afresh the bleeding heart of Tasso" by his gossiping and flippant life of him. The section on Tasso he found devoid of any deep sentiment or real perception of the genius of the Italian author. But the most serious weakness in this edition of Italian poets had to do with Hunt's treatment of Dante. The reviewer said that the weaknesses he had identified were, however serious, forgivable; but "to break the unity of Dante's divine genius . . . is a crime for which no adequate punishment has yet been invented, and in one who styles himself and is acknowledged to be a poet of no mean order, high treason against the majesty of genius, before which he should kneel and humbly veil his face." Without a doubt, the reviewer concluded, *The Harbinger* had never encountered biographies "of more puritanic bareness, or systematic, unimaginative dryness." Certainly Hunt "must be accorded the credit of . . . [clothing] the inspirations of the loftiest poetry in the most prosaic and unmitigated prose" (2:233).

While the anonymous reviewer could not detect any merit in *Stories from the Italian Poets*, John Dwight was not so severe in his criticism of Hunt's edition of *Wit and Humor, Selected from the English Poets: With an Illustrative Essay and Critical Comments* (1846). Acknowledging that *Wit and*

Humor was "a well ordered mass of witty and humorous selections" from such English poets as Chaucer, Shakespeare, and Pope, and that the author's critical notices were just, lively, and discriminating, Dwight nevertheless questioned Hunt's method of collecting material for a book, a method that Dwight called "curious." Dwight said that Hunt, with the entire field of English poetical literature before him, took one particular theme (for example, "Imagination and Fancy," "Wit and Humor," "Action and Passion") and ransacked the English poets for examples to illustrate the theme in question (3:393). This accomplished, Hunt then published his findings as a book. Thus the fact that *Wit and Humor* received more praise than *Italian Poets* was indeed no great praise at all.

Remarks of a literary nature by or about Thomas Carlyle appeared four times in *The Harbinger*. One was a lengthy review of *Cromwell;* two were shorter reviews of *On Heroes, Hero Worship, and the Heroic in History* (revised ed., 1846) and *The French Revolution* (1846); and the fourth was a letter by Carlyle to his cousin Alexander, reprinted from the New York *Tribune* (4:200). George Ripley devoted so much attention to the author of *Sartor Resartus* because, in addition to the Scotsman's explosive attacks on sham, hypocrisy, and excessive materialism, Carlyle had profoundly influenced him as early as the mid-1830s. At a time when Carlyle had already gathered a wide circle of American devotees, Ripley was especially attracted to the Scottish writer because he saw in him a spiritual ally. As Charles Crowe has pointed out, "When Carlyle struck at the cheap money gods, the miseries of the mill town, and the dead English conservatism, the American [Ripley] felt that each of these blows staggered his own enemies."[44] Indeed Ripley was so moved by Carlyle's writings that he wrote a letter to him on 1 June 1835 in which he communicated his "sympathy" with Carlyle's "revelations." Among other things, Ripley told Carlyle: "I have communed with your spirit in the utterance of its deep wisdom, and when I have felt the significance of your mystic saying, my heart has leaped up with the response, 'This unknown being is my brother.' "[45]

Perhaps because Carlyle responded coolly to Ripley's letter, or because Ripley was simply embarrassed, the American Associationist waited a year before writing again to Carlyle.[46] Although Ripley's second letter repeated his admiration for the sage of Chelsea, the tone was somewhat apologetic:

> I was rejoiced to find that you understood me; and forgave me what, certainly, seems on reflection, to have been an utterance that one might have regarded as extravagant or too free. But I felt it all to the very marrow of my bones; and I could not help saying so in articulate words. You can, probably, form but a faint conception . . . of the earnestness with which a true voice is welcome here, . . . the greater, as such voices are seldom heard among us,—the din of business and politics well nigh drowning all sounds. . . . There are not a few, however, who are watching and longing for a new light, who hope for a new birth of philosophy, religion,

. . . literature, . . . social progress, . . . Christianity, . . . and the universal church. We cannot but hail you as a brother in this patient waiting.[47]

Ripley's second letter was never answered, and although years later, after the founding of Brook Farm, Carlyle scornfully described Ripley as one of the "Socinian preachers [who] quit their pulpits in Yankeeland, saying, 'Friends, this is all gone to colored cobweb, we regret to say,' and retire into the fields to cultivate onion-beds,"[48] Ripley's admiration for Carlyle seems not to have lessened during *The Harbinger* years, as evidenced by his review of Carlyle.[49]

The occasion for Ripley's review of *On Heroes* was the American publication of the revised edition of the book in 1846. Carlyle had written an imprimatur to Wiley and Putnam of New York, authorizing that "they and they only . . . had the right to print and vend the same [*On Heroes*] in the United States" (3:267). Ripley thought that *On Heroes* was "more Carlyleish than anything he has written," and believed that those of Carlyle's writings originally written as lectures were more remarkable than his other writings. The lectures were characterized, Ripley said, by their boldness, their originality, their strength, and their startling illustrations. Indeed, Carlyle's talk was "the outpouring of lava-flood, which has swept away in its fiery descent, gold, jewels, precious stones, and all things rich and rare, in promiscuous magnificence" (2:267).

John Dwight, who reviewed *Cromwell* and *The French Revolution*, agreed with Ripley on the whole. Dwight believed Carlyle to be "the chief of historian-critics," and his influence "the most vital . . . now felt in literature." *The French Revolution*, he stated, was "the most brilliant and impressive history ever written" (4:10). Dwight, however, did not give unqualified praise to Carlyle: he criticized him because he loved "heroism too much for its own sake." This "hero-worship," Dwight observed, was only another version of "Might makes Right," as Carlyle failed to realize that the power of one man over others was not necessarily a token of God's presence in that powerful individual. Carlyle was a "ready worshipper" of all powerful men, for he never questioned the quality of a man's strength, only the quality of strength possessed by an individual. Dwight concluded by stating that the characteristic weakness in *Cromwell*—and in so much of Carlyle's thought generally—was that the Scot made "one or two great virtues stand for all." On the whole, however, Carlyle was regarded as Hazlitt had been: both men were considered to be sensitive critics and extraordinary historians.

English Novelists

Though *The Harbinger* devoted much space to reviews of works by England's literary critics, historians, and essayists, as well as her poets, it devoted far less space to her novelists. Apart from the fact that *The Har-*

binger survived for less than four years, the magazine was published at a time when poets, historians, literary critics, and essayists comprised England's literary strength. Still, there were certainly novelists in England who emerged between 1845 and the beginning of 1849, among them, Bulwer-Lytton, Charles Dickens, William Thackeray, and Charlotte and Emily Bronte, and the magazine did notice some of them and reviewed others.

Bulwer-Lytton was somewhat appreciated by *The Harbinger* because George Ripley thought that his novels embodied a keen awareness of the existing evils in England's social institutions. "No writer," Ripley said in his review of *Lucretia; or, The Children of Night*(1847), "has shown up, in more vivid colors, the frivolity and heartlessness of her fashionable circles, the sordid vulgarity of her monied interest, and the luxuriance of crime in the midst of her bristling legal technicalities" (4:41). Yet, in spite of Bulwer-Lytton's recognition of England's social corruption, Ripley felt that he criticized more in the tone of a cynic than with the hope of a philanthropist. Because he had no insight into the "harmony of a true social order," the reader of his works was left "despairing of the present, and hopeless of the future." Such was the case with *Lucretia*, a novel that Ripley regarded as an "atrocious insult to humanity." In addition to its weak execution, its awkward and complicated story, and its comparatively lifeless descriptions, the novel was judged to be one that offered no clue to man's future well-being because its author had "no perception of the laws of social progress."

The Harbinger also published reviews of *Jane Eyre* (1848) and *Wuthering Heights* (1848) in the mistaken assumption that both books were by Currer Bell, the pseudonym of Charlotte Brontë. Perhaps the most interesting thing about these brief reviews was the note of surprise that both books could have been written by the same individual, for much as *Jane Eyre* was praised, *Wuthering Heights* was denigrated. Charles Dana, for example, remarked that *Jane Eyre*

> has a freshness and originality, a manly vigor of style, a penetration into the secrets of human character and a vividness in the deliniation [*sic*] of the same together with a dramatic power and directness in the action of its story which fully justify the high and unanimous praise it has received from the British press. Such books preserve romance writing in its legitimate dignity as an art and have a share in the progress of society. [6:95]

The Harbinger also published a short piece on *Jane Eyre* by an individual who identified himself only by the initial "U." It seems clear that the magazine requested the piece because the characteristic "For the Harbinger" appeared at the head of the article. His verdict was that "the author [of *Jane Eyre*] will take rank at once with the best of our domestic novelists."

In reviewing *Wuthering Heights* four months after this brief discussion of *Jane Eyre*, Parke Godwin expressed some doubt as to whether Currer Bell did in fact write *Wuthering Heights*. He described the novel as an "unmitigated atrocity. . . . It is true, the work is full of power, but it is the power of a devil; all the characters seem to us to be demoniacs, and we cannot find a single redeeming trait in any part of the volume" (6:206).

The magazine's reviewers had no such problems with the works of Charles Dickens, however, except, that is, for *American Notes* (1842). American sensibilities were smarting from this work, which advocated the abolition of slavery and the establishment of international copyright laws, and *The Harbinger* proved no exception. Charles Dana described the book as being "as shallow as it was pretentious," adding that as a traveler and political dabbler, Dickens's observations resembled the gossip "a sketchy gentleman or lady might compose without difficulty after dinner" (2:234). But about Dickens as a novelist or humorist, Dana, who tended to be the most acidulous reviewer in *The Harbinger,* found little to criticize. In fact, Dickens received a good word in each of the three notices and two reviews devoted to him.[50] Mainly, the high regard accorded Dickens was based on the novelist's "sympathy with the great masses of our common Humanity." That his works illustrated the iniquities and inequities of the London environment, as well as the selfish and subversive nature of humanity under the present economic system, was the great appeal to the reviewers of *The Harbinger.*

Dwight's review of Dickens's *Pictures from Italy* (1846) was representative of the magazine's attitude toward the English novelist. To Dwight, the real significance of *Pictures* was that it contrasted "imagined" Italy—the land of cathedrals, "ideal creations of art," and of romantic historical associations—with "actual" Italy—a land of poverty, miserable social conditions, and moral decay. What Dickens saw with his "talking eyes" were

> the miserable condition of the people, the universal duplicity and fraud, the poor God-forsaken mummery of the Romish worship and the whole pontifical estate, [and] the armies of beggars, cripples, and deformed human monstrosities which lurk near every splendid church and every pillar and portal of every palace. [3:27]

The moral of *Pictures* was obvious to Dwight: there would never be a "Divine Social Order" until man eliminated destructive passions from society and replaced them with economic and social justice for all men.

French Writers

The treatment in *The Harbinger* of French authors, especially of novelists, was perhaps the most interesting of all its reviews. As George Joyaux has pointed out in "George Sand, Eugene Sue and *The Harbinger,*" at a time when "American critical journals were almost unanimously hostile to French fiction in general, *The Harbinger* [stood] out in the forties as the staunchest defender of [the] French novel . . . and in particular of George

Sand, who was by far the most controversial French literary figure of the time."[51]

The Harbinger's defense of George Sand against the critical attacks of other contemporary periodicals[52] was very likely motivated by the fact that she was sympathetic with Fourieristic doctrines. Indeed, The Harbinger was so sympathetic with the social attitudes permeating her works that it serialized two of her novels, Consuelo and The Countess of Rudolstadt. These two novels, translated by Francis G. Shaw, were the only two pieces of fiction to appear in The Harbinger. Despite its sympathy for her social views, The Harbinger reviewers recognized Sand's literary weaknesses as well as her strengths. In a review of Jacques (1847), for example, John Dwight stated that that novel was not to be compared to Consuelo as a work of art: "It is a story without variety; a mere record of the play of feelings, involving themselves in the inevitable meshes of false relations." All of the characters were "unreal"; "there are some violations of delicacy, some things hasty and imprudent in it, and . . . it was written when indignant impulse . . . had not been tempered and subdued" (4:121). George Ripley was no less critical than Dwight when he reviewed Sand's The Journeyman Joiner (1847). Ripley did not predict for this work the success that other of Sand's novels had achieved. The reason, he thought, was that the novel had an "air of being composed for a didactic purpose . . . and is too destitute of scenes of tumultuous passion for those who seek for a certain intellectual intoxication from the creations of this glowing author" (5:298).

Yet The Harbinger's overall defense of George Sand placed the magazine in a unique position in the 1840s. Its courage in publishing two of her novels, besides several excerpts from her other works, and in giving her high praise in its reviews, is all the more noteworthy when one remembers, first, that some American reviewers generally based their criticisms of Sand upon her alleged immorality, and second, as Howard Mumford Jones has noted:

> anything like a fair or unbiased evaluation in these years was impossible. To begin with, she was French; and in the period of moral reaction, all things French were under the suspicion of being immoral, unless proved otherwise. In the next place, she was a woman. . . . The age was inclined to think that home, church, children and good works were sufficient occupation for the feminine mind. In the third place, she was usually associated with French romanticism, and French romanticism was not viewed with favor in these United States. Finally, the attacks on marriage in the earlier novels of this author shocked a public still uneasily afraid that novel reading itself was a sin.[53]

Despite all this, John Dwight regarded the French novelist as "one who has sacrificed reputation to truth, and loved mankind too well to court its transient applause." She was "the advocate of every heart that . . . impotently frets against the chains of civilized duplicity and tyranny" (4:121), as well as "one of the purest and most eloquent reformers of the age, inspired with the humanity sentiment, as few have ever been" (5:296).

Eugene Sue's initial reception in America was far more favorable than that accorded Sand, though one might not get that impression from *The Harbinger*'s treatment of the French novelist. It has been shown earlier (see pp. 20–21) how *The Harbinger* came to Sue's defense on two separate occasions, once after the magazine learned of William Herbert's attack on him, and again after the *Democratic Review* published a denigrating review of Sue's novel, *The Wandering Jew* (1845). The fact is, *The Harbinger* considered Sue more important for his interest in Fourierism and Associationism than for his abilities as a novelist, and thus it felt the need to defend this powerful ally from attacks by other individuals and magazines. As early as the second number, *The Harbinger* reprinted from the New York *Herald* a letter by Albert Brisbane defending Associationist doctrines from the repeated assaults of James G. Bennett, the editor of the *Herald*. In the course of his remarks, Brisbane noted:

> In Literature this great problem [of social reform] has found in France some powerful allies and advocates; one of its noblest champions is Eugene Sue. It was under the inspiration of this new social idea [of Associationism] that he wrote the *Mysteries of Paris* . . . as well as . . . *The Wandering Jew,* in which the ideas of Association, the organization of labor, and of social reform . . . show how broad a field the grand conceptions of a more just and fortunate order of things and a higher and happier destiny for man on earth throws open to literature. [1:21]

Just how effectively Sue utilized these social ideas as a basis for his fiction was made clearer some months later when John Dwight wrote a laudatory article entitled "Eugene Sue," which appeared in two parts in the numbers for 15 and 22 November 1845. Specifically, Dwight hailed *The Wandering Jew* as "the most remarkable novel of the day," and he added that "in the magnificence of its plot, it dwarfs all other works of fiction" (1:365). Significantly, only one other of Sue's novels was ever commented upon in *The Harbinger,* and all that Charles Dana had to say about *Martin the Foundling* (1846) was that the English translation of this work was "wretched" (3:188).

Perhaps George Joyaux best summarized the relationship between *The Harbinger,* and George Sand and Eugene Sue when he stated:

> Their literary talents were considered to be of secondary importance; what mattered to *The Harbinger* was essentially their social thought, and in those terms the editors evaluated their works. When they defended George Sand and Eugene Sue against their American detractors—they were merely defending their own beliefs in the Principles of Association, the *raison d'être* of Brook Farm.[54]

Joyaux, of course, is right, though his explanation, it ought to be added, does not fully account for the fact—and it is an important one—that *The Harbinger* was the first in America to publish translated versions of Sand's *Consuelo* and *The Countess of Rudolstadt*. Indeed, perhaps the easiest mistake that can be made in assessing the literary criticism published in *The Harbinger* is to think that the reviews were merely occasions to proselytize for Associationism and Fourierism. Extraliterary considerations of this sort were important, to be sure, but they certainly did not form the only criteria for evaluating books. On the contrary, if this were indeed the case, then there would not have been such dispassionate and penetrating reviews as John Dwight's of Poe and Carlyle, Parke Godwin's of Halleck, Charles Dana's of Longfellow, William Henry Channing's of Hawthorne, and George Ripley's of Sand.

5

Poetry in *The Harbinger*

In his early study of *The Periodicals of American Transcendentalism* (1931), Clarence Gohdes noted that the so-called poetical department of *The Harbinger* must have been one of the most difficult to provide for, since so many of the poems that filled its pages were reprints from other sources.[1] To be sure, Professor Gohdes was certainly correct. Exclusive of the poetry printed for illustrative purposes in literary reviews, *The Harbinger* published over 440 poems during its four-year existence. Of that number, only ninety-one bear the characteristic "For the Harbinger," thus indicating that less than one-fourth—or only about twenty percent—of the magazine's poetry was original. With the exception of approximately nineteen additonal poems translated exclusively for *The Harbinger,* all other verse published in the magazine was reprinted from a wide variety of sources.

That *The Harbinger* did indeed have difficulty filling the half-columns that its weighty prose articles had an uneconomical habit of leaving blank is suggested by these extracts from a letter by Charles Dana written to John Greenleaf Whittier. The letter was dated 3 July 1845, which was just three weeks after the first number of *The Harbinger* was published:

> Friend Whittier:
> I received your letter today, but the book has not reached me. . . . I am glad that you like *The Harbinger.* The testimony of a person like yourself not pledged to its special doctrines, is an evidence that we are not wrong in the manner of setting forth our views. . . . Will it be too much to ask of you an occasional contribution to our pages whether of prose or verse? You will see in this week's paper a little piece of yours which, I fear, by the way, the paper from which we copied it, did not print correctly.
> Our poetical department is not an easy one to fill. The *New Spirit* has hardly yet made its way among the gentler Muses, though when the *Poet* has once comprehended the destiny of Man, such strains will burst from his lips as the world has never yet echoed with.[2]

Whittier may indeed have "liked" *The Harbinger,* but, despite Dana's request, he contributed only one poem to its pages: "To My Friend on the Death of His Sister" (1:108) appeared in the number for 19 July 1845. This

111

did not prevent *The Harbinger*, however, from subsequently reprinting seven of his poems from other sources.

Predictably, the magazine relied on the already taxed talents of Charles A. Dana and John S. Dwight for original contributions: Dana eventually contributed five poems, and Dwight provided seven. James Russell Lowell, possibly because Dwight had contributed to his own short-lived magazine, *The Pioneer* (1843), supplied two poems—"To a Pine Tree," which appeared in the first volume, and "Si Descendero in Infernum, Ades," which was printed in the fourth volume. Thomas Wentworth Higginson, who was just then beginning his literary career, contributed nine original poems (which thereby ranked him first among those supplying original verse to *The Harbinger*), and William W. Story, who would later be the subject of a biography by Henry James (2 vols., 1903), sent along eight. Using the initials "E.Y.T.," George H. Calvert—who would later author a Fourierist-inspired *Introduction to Social Science* (1856)—contributed seven poems, and Augustine J. H. Duganne, a popular American writer of the time of poetry and dime novels, sent along six. Christopher Pearse Cranch, who had a few years earlier helped to edit *The Western Messenger*—to which he then contributed a considerable amount of verse—and George W. Curtis, the noted writer, social reformer, and editor, supplied six and five poems respectively, all of which appeared in the first four volumes (both Cranch and Curtis left for Europe in 1846). From the muse of William Ellery Channing, Henry Thoreau's close friend and the nephew of the great Unitarian divine of the same name, the magazine received just one poem, which was printed in the third volume. In addition, several notable individuals contributed single poems, among them the scholarly Frederic Henry Hedge, Parke Godwin, who eventually took over the editorial duties of *The Harbinger* after the magazine's transfer in 1847 from Brook Farm to New York City, and Edgar Poe's friend, Frances S. Osgood.

For whatever reasons, a number of contributors preferred to remain anonymous. Thus, a few of the poems written "For the Harbinger" were signed with such curious pseudonyms as "Portia" and "One of the Steps," while others simply bore initials, such as "X.," "R.H.B.," and "E.B.B." Even more cryptic than the pseudonyms, however, were these designations, which followed no less than seven different poems that appeared originally in the magazine: $*$, $*_**$, and $*_**$. *The Harbinger* also relied on a few of its contributors for translations of European poets, especially the German poets, Johann von Goethe and Johann Ludwig Uhland. Dana and Dwight, for example, translated a total of thirteen such poems exclusively for the magazine; Calvert translated four; and Cranch and Higginson each translated one.

As was already noted, however, the bulk of the poetry appearing in *The Harbinger* consisted of reprinted poems from a wide variety of sources. This is not surprising, of course, when one realizes that the group of regular contributors to which the editors could appeal for verse was small indeed. In fact, after the first four volumes, in which just about half of the published verse was original, the editors of *The Harbinger* appear to have had to rely almost exclusively on reprints. In volume 5, for example, thirty-six of forty-one poems were reprinted. Volume 6 contained ninety-five poems, of which eighty-six were not original. Of the seventy-two poems published in volume 7, only nine were orginal. In the incompleted eighth volume, for which there were only fifteen numbers instead of the usual twenty-six, twenty-three of the twenty-seven poems were reprints.

All this would logically suggest that the editors of *The Harbinger* simply reprinted poems indiscriminately, but this was not, in fact, entirely the case. The content of a poem, as we shall see, was important, and so was the individual author of the particular poem. In this regard, James Russell Lowell was certainly the most popular, for sixteen of his poems were reprinted in the pages of *The Harbinger*. Next in popularity was a Goodwin Barmby, eight of whose reprinted poems appeared in the magazine. He was followed by John Greenleaf Whittier and Augustine Duganne, each of whom had seven of their poems reprinted in the Associationist journal. Six poems by William Cullen Bryant and five by Henry Wadsworth Longfellow were reprinted in the magazine, though only two by Ralph Waldo Emerson were, possibly because the Sage of Concord had refused an earlier request by Dwight for a line or two for *The Harbinger,* or possibly because Emerson's popularity as a poet was not especially noteworthy at the time.[3]

Among the English poets whose verse appeared most frequently in *The Harbinger* were Thomas Hood and Charles Mackay, each of whom had thirteen of their poems reprinted, while seven pieces by William Blake were reprinted in the journal. Of the many women poets whose verse was reprinted in the magazine, the most popular were Anne C. Lynch, with seven reprinted poems; Alice Carey and Mrs. Southey, with four each; and Frances S. Osgood, three of whose poems the editors reprinted.

In addition to these people, the editors of *The Harbinger* reprinted poems by more than one hundred other individuals. Generally, either the author or the original source of the reprinted poem was identified. Only twenty-four poems in the journal appeared without reference to the author or to the source from which it was excerpted. Ninety-five poems are completely identified both by the author's name and the source from which it was reprinted, whereas 144 poems cite the author but not the source, and forty-six identify the source but not the author. Among the journals from which the editors most often reprinted poems were the *National Era* (Washington, D.C.), *Graham's Magazine* (Philadelphia), the New York *Tribune,* and the Irish paper, *Dublin Nation.*

On the average, each of the 197 issues of *The Harbinger* contained only two poems, a number that is certainly not insignificant, but one that hardly ranked the magazine as a major outlet for contemporary poetry in America in the late 1840s. Of course, *The Harbinger* was never intended to be a poetry review. It was to be obviously a thoroughgoing Associationist journal, and it would trumpet that cause proudly and enthusiastically. Poetry, then, would be important chiefly as a means of enhancing the magazine's appeal, of making it more attractive to a public that might not be naturally inclined to listen only to the Associationist message. In addition to the fact that poetry could be used to offset the consistent and unrestrained tone of seriousness that characterized all of the other features in the journal, it had the advantage, too, of providing a convenient filler for the half-columns left empty by the heady editorials on Associationism and Fourierism.

To presume from all this, however, that poetry in *The Harbinger* was therefore unimportant would be to miscalculate completely the extent to which the individuals who conducted the journal were committed to the cause of Associationism. If anything characterized that magazine—especially the first five volumes—it was the care with which it was written and printed each week under the direction of men such as George Ripley, John Dwight, and Charles Dana. This quality of carefulness extended as well to the matter of selecting the verse to be published in each number. The simple fact is that it was the rare item indeed—be it prose or verse, original or reprint—that coincidentally found its way into the pages of *The Harbinger*.

Perhaps the most obvious thing to note about the more than 400 poems printed in *The Harbinger* is that they fall roughly into four or five broad poetic categories. Most of the poems printed in the journal could be described as being essentially either thematic, didactic, religious, or lyrical in nature.[4] In addition, there were quite a few elegies and sonnets. The elegies might most appropriately be discussed with the religious verse; the sonnets will be treated briefly as a separate group of poems.

Of the numerous poems in *The Harbinger* that seem to treat a particular theme, a significant number—approximately thirty-five—deal with nature, mainly the seasons or natural scenery. The editors of the magazine seem to have had the least difficulty soliciting original verse of this kind, for about twelve of the thirty-five or so poems having to do with nature appeared originally in the Associationist journal. James Russell Lowell, Christopher Pearse Cranch, William Ellery Channing, and George W. Curtis each contributed one poem about nature; William W. Story sent along three; and Thomas Wentworth Higginson contributed two.

Much of the nature poetry printed in *The Harbinger* concerned the seasons, specifically summer and winter. The general attitude in these poems was that summer was the best season and winter the worst, an attitude that likely was inspired to some extent by the fact that most of *The Harbinger* readers would have been familiar with the cold and frequently harsh New England winter. Even the poems not specifically addressed to summer, such as "Autumn" (1:360) by Alfred, Lord Tennyson, "Autumn Song" (1:263) by George W. Curtis, "The Coming of Winter" (3:390) by an anonymous poet, "Spring is Coming" (2:189) by an anonymous German poet, and "Longings" (4:25) by William W. Story praised the beauty of nature in summer and mourned its loss with the changing of the seasons. Whereas autumn was regarded as a sad time of the year because it marked the end of summer—and therefore the death of the beauty of nature—spring was viewed as a joyous time because its nightingales were the harbingers of summer. None of the poems about the seasons had anything positive to say about winter, though Curtis's "Autumn Song" suggested that it did at least make one more appreciative of nature's beauty in the summer.

Of the poems about the seasons that used nature emblematically, "Autumn" (1:348) by Cranch and "Song" (1:134) by William Cullen Bryant are the most successful. Cranch's poem was written "For the Harbinger" and is a tribute to the beauty of autumn, though it yielded in the last stanza to the philosophical thought that, like the season, the poet's life was passing. The narrator concluded that he hoped that his death would be as peaceful as the "glide of Autumn." Bryant's poem, reprinted from *Graham's Magazine,* used a running stream to symbolize the "stream of life." The stream, "forever fresh and full," was ever replenished with water from punctual spring rains. Man's life, however, was like "one brief summer"; "where thy glittering waters ran, the dust alone remains."

A number of the nature poems praised natural scenery and the beauty of the individual elements that comprised nature. Some of the titles, for example, are suggestive: "On Entering a Wood"; "To the Moon"; "Pines"; "Mountain Stream"; "Hymn to the Sun"; "The Ice Ravine"; "The Coral." A majority of the poems revered nature for its strength and mystery, as well as for the independence and freedom that it represented, and a few emphasized the harmony of the diverse elements in nature. Others depicted individuals who were happy because they had developed a harmonious relationship with nature as a whole. In "The Backwoodsman" (2:296), for example, a poet identified only by the initials "E.B.W." suggested that a particular family's happiness had derived solely from their harmonious relationship with nature. Even more idyllic than "The Backwoodsman" was the reprinted poem "Rural Winter Sketch" (4:153), by a Reverend R. Hoyt, in which a rural family one morning awakened to find newly fallen snow on their farm. All was peaceful and tranquil, and the family, the poem informed the reader, went about the job of living, seemingly without a care in the world. In "The Landscape Monopolist" (5:313), reprinted from the *London Morning Chronicle,* the reader was presented to one Baron Braeman, who, though he owned vast expanses of land, refused to let anyone see or use them. The narrator interrupts the poem at the end to condemn Braeman, and to remind the reader that no one can own or control nature.

Not surprisingly, labor was another of the main themes, or subjects, treated in the poetry printed in *The Harbinger,* just as it was the focus of so many of the other items appearing in the magazine. The reader was regularly reminded in these poems that labor was dignified and even noble. Thus the laborer should stand erect and be proud of his work, for the future of America depended on his efforts. A few poets, such as T. B. Read in his poem "Labor" (4:196), even went so far as to suggest that God had a special love for the laborer. Was it not true, the poem asked, that God Himself labored six days in creating the world? At the very least, Edward Youl stated in "Labor-Worship" (5:164), labor was one of the most religious acts man could perform, for just as God created ever anew, to be like Him, man must work.

Often, the life of the laborer was portrayed in romantic or idyllic terms, and there are plenty of poems in *The Harbinger* that describe him as possessing iron arms, that applaud him as "God's high priest," and that remind him that honest labor inevitably brings rewards. Just as often, however, the editors printed poems in which the life of the laborer was depicted in realistic terms, which prompts one to remember that, while George Ripley and his fellow Brook Farmers may have been idealistic in their social and economic views and expectations, they were thoroughgoing realists when it came to recognizing the difficulty of putting into practice the reforms they espoused. They knew, after all, from firsthand experience that life in their own West Roxbury community was not—as Emerson had earlier referred to it in an uncharitable moment—a transcendental picnic. It was this sense of realtiy that lead the editors of *The Harbinger* regularly to select poetry that exhorted the laborer. A representative example of this kind of verse is "Earth-Sharing," by Augustine Duganne, which appeared—not coincidentally, one feels certain—in the number that was issued the day before Independence Day in 1847. Though the poem was reprinted from the *National Era,* it clearly indicates why Duganne was bound to be among the most popular contributors of verse to *The Harbinger.*

> Listen, workers! listen!
> Ye who all your lives are toiling,
> In the field and workshop moiling—
> Lo! your serpent wrongs are coiling
>   Closer round you. Listen!
>
> Ponder, workers! ponder!
> While ye poise your iron sledges,
> While ye fix your rending wedges—
> Lo! your strength and skill are pledges
>   Of your manhood. Ponder!
>
> Listen, workers! Listen!
> Sledges may crush else than matter—
> Wedges may your curses scatter—
> Toilers once again may batter
>   Moral Bastiles. Listen!

Ponder, workers! ponder!
God gave equal earth to mortals,
Ere they left fair Eden's portals—
Where's the ancient law that foretells
     Mortal slavery? Ponder!

Answer, workers! answer!
Have the woes which you are sharing,
Have the chains your limbs are wearing,
Palsied all the hope and daring
     Of your spirits? Answer!

Listen, workers! listen!
Earth is yours—the broad, wide guerdon
Given to man with life's first burden—
God hath set his seal and word on
     Man's true title. Listen!

Ponder, workers! ponder!
Hold this truth within your keeping,
Till the harvest you are reaping—
God is landlord, and unsleeping
     Watcher o'er you. Ponder!

                                        [5:52]

It followed, of course, that if man worked now, he would secure for himself a better future. Much of the verse printed in *The Harbinger* emphasized the importance of the present on the future. There was almost unanimous agreement that the future would bring unity and harmony among men, the likes of which mankind had never known. Little attention was given to the past, for it was, after all, the past, and nothing could be done about it. In "The Three Preachers" (3:169), a poem excerpted from an Irish paper called the *Newrin Examiner,* an anonymous poet presented in the characters of three preachers what might fairly be described as *The Harbinger*'s attitude toward the past, present, and future. In the poem, one preacher, representative of the past, is old and "backward"; a second, representing the present, is mild and pleasant, but not amenable to change; and the third, representative of the future, is young and brilliant—a figure over whom crowds rejoice. In addition to this poem, the titles of several others also make the point directly: "Dream No More" (4:43); "A Hymn of the Day That Is Dawning" (4:130); "Patience" (3:150); "Progress" (4:19); "Look Aloft, Look Abroad" (2:363).

Poems such as these are different from the kind cited above on labor in the respect that they are less specifically thematically bound. Actually, a good many of the poems published in *The Harbinger*—indeed, more than one hundred—are considerably more generalized than, say, Augustine Duganne's on the workers, though these other poems do, in fact, have at least one thing in common, and that is their tendency to attempt to inculcate a lesson or to draw a moral from the subject under consideration. Thus it would probably be more precise to categorize and briefly mention this substantial group of didactic poems separately from those on nature, or those on labor and the laborer.

In addition to several didactic poems on the past, present, and future, others dealt with poverty and its effects, primarily those of starvation and suffering. Some of these poems treat those individuals who have been crushed by the "will of the stronger": the destitute woman and her baby who starve to death, the peasant girl who owns nothing in life, and the laborer who toils endlessly in the fields, only to confront famine at his proverbial doorstep. One reprinted poem, "Conferences" (5:328), by Edward Youl, presents a man, a woman, a boy, and a girl, who, because they are starving, are separately thinking of suicide. A policeman, presumably representative of society's indifference to these people, confronts each and tells them to "move on." Other poems, such as Ernest Jones's "A Song of the Starving" (5:99), and an anonymous poet's "The Famine" (5:58), admonished starving people to unite and demand what rightfully belonged to them.

When all is said and done, however, what finally is perhaps most interesting about the didactic verse is the tendency of the poems almost invariably to end on a positive note. All but a few of the poems that cant and rant against the ills or injustices of society end hopefully. In almost all of the didactic poems, the message to the reader was unqualifiedly encouraging. No matter how difficult times may be, the importance of such virtues as patience, humility, and perseverence must never be forgotten. There would never be peace, harmony, or unity in society until man learned to love his fellowmen. Moreover, while progress was often slow, the future was nevertheless promising. Man must be patient, and he should work, love his fellowman, and trust in God, for God was, in the final accounting, a just being who would reward the downtrodden and punish the tyrant.

Actually, it may well come as something of a surprise to today's reader of *The Harbinger* to learn that it did not print a great deal of what might be called "religious verse." It was not so much that religion was unimportant to George Ripley and his fellow Associationists; indeed, it could be marshaled as yet another means of addressing the pressing social problems that surrounded man. But religion was, after all, abstract in nature. To alleviate man's lot in life, more concrete solutions were needed than those offered by 2,000 years of institutionalized Christianity. Moreover, Associationists were, religiously speaking, a mixed group of individuals. As Ripley had noted at the end of the first volume: "Under our banner are to be found men of almost all denominations" (1:351).

The first thing to say about the religious poetry that appeared in *The Harbinger* is that it was not markedly doctrinal or controversial but rather devotional and exhortatory. Only a few biblical incidents were versified. And though the technical execution of the religious verse was generally smooth, there is throughout a lack of intensity. Very few of the religious poems were written "For the Harbinger"; most were reprints from other magazines.

Not surprisingly, several of the religious poems exhort the reader to reject the sordid materialism of this world and put faith and trust in God. In "Lines: Suggested by Osgood's Head of the Saviour" (7:177), by someone identified only as "Margaret H.," the speaker admitted that she had not been true to God; indeed, she denied Him everyday. She realized, however, that she had pursued "false and fleeting dreams" and so asked God to "waste away" the material idols of this world. Anne C. Lynch, in "Christ Betrayed" (4:172), admonished the reader not to sell himself for gold or comfort. We should be Christ-fearing and remember that "the Christ-Spirit strives with thee." In "Holiness Unto the Lord" (3:28), Thomas Wentworth Higginson appealled to youth to rise above the sordidness of the crowd and show the atheist world that virtue still lived.

Another popular theme of the religious verse was the devotional belief that true peace and comfort would be found with God, if only we would have faith. In poems such as "Prayer of a Desponding Heart" (2:52), by a Mrs. C. M. Sawyer, "Ad Arma" (1:27), by Charles Dana,[5] and "Never Fear" (3:214), by Goodwin Barmby, we are reminded that, despite the work, cares, and responsibilities of this world, our rest will come in the afterlife. There is nothing to fear, for God is always with us. Mrs. Southey even told her readers in "A Fair Place and Pleasant" (3:333) that God assigned angels to watch over them, and an anonymous poet, in "The Unknown Friend" (3:12), asked readers to remember that their "Holiest Friend" was always in their midst.

Still other poems endowed nature with a kind of spirituality, though, to be accurate, probably less often in a religious than in a Transcendental sense. At least that seems to be the thrust of two such poems that appeared originally in *The Harbinger,* one by Charles Dana called "Erotis" (2:139), and the other by Frederic Henry Hedge, titled "The Hanging Moss" (3:219). Dana's poem emphasized the medicinal benefits and regenerative qualities that nature made available to man. It urged man to strive for a complete union with nature. Hedge's poem—the only one that he contributed to *The Harbinger,* and apparently one of only two poems that he ever wrote[6]—used nature emblematically, viewing it as the embodiment of God. The narrator said that he wished he could be a hanging moss, for then he would be a part of nature whole, "Godhead's own."

Finally, the editors of *The Harbinger* included in the pages of the journal a number of religious poems that dealt with the inevitable subject of death. These may be divided into two groups: those which used the occasion of death to moralize and to preach to the living, and those which simply mourned the loss of a loved one, though not necessarily in a didactic or heavy-handed way. These later poems would be most accurately described as elegies.

The moralistic religious poems treating the subject of death typically expressed what might be called the wisdom of Providence: "She died but is not dead"; "She is at peace; God's love watches over her." Actually, this kind of religious verse was almost exclusively optimistic in the sense that the speaker had little doubt that he would be reunited with his lost loved one in the life hereafter. There was in almost all these poems an unquestioned faith in the belief that the departed was at peace because he or she was with God. None of the poems expressed anger; the speaker in each was consoled by the certainty that his soul and the soul of his loved one would eventually meet again. Representative of this kind of verse is a short poem by George G. Foster on the death of a child, which was titled "A Baby's Epitaph." It was published originally in *The Harbinger* in the number for 24 January 1846:

> Pale flower, whose perfume, loved of Heaven
> To the sweet skies has fled away,
> Embalmed within our hearts, 'tis given
> To keep thine image from decay.
> O deeply loved! O wildly mourned!
> How strong thy tender tendrils lay
> Around our hearts! To darkness turned
> The bright world as thou passed away.
> Yet o'er the blue sea of the sky
> Like mingling clouds at break of day,
> Our souls shall meet in rosy bliss,
> No more to part or fade away.
>
> [2:99]

The elegiac poems printed in *The Harbinger*—of which only four of the more than thirty printed were original—were optimistic and hopeful, and they embodied, almost uniformly, the attitude that "our souls will be reunited in Heaven." This is not to say that these poems completely denied the pain of living without a loved one; rather, the speaker concluded—as was usually the case, we just noted, in the moralistic religious poems—that he was confident that his soul and that of his loved one would meet again in death. *The Harbinger* printed elegies addressed to departed wives, husbands, children, and even, on one occasion, an unknown woman. Most of the elegies, however, were prompted by the death of a wife. There was also an elegy to Thomas Hood, of whom Associationists generally were very fond (see, for example, the chapter on "Literary Criticism in *The Harbinger*," pp. 100–1), and an elegy by John Greenleaf Whittier, "To My Friend: On the Death of his Sister" (1:108), cited earlier in this chapter.

In substance, the elegies generally were sincere and honest, if not very profound. Rarely did the reader find any unusual or sophisticated techniques employed, though one reprinted elegy, "Little Nell" (2:283) by Kate Cleaveland, did use nature emblematically—if not very originally—by paralleling the brief life of a young girl to the four seasons. The most popular theme in the elegies was, of course, the transience of life. However, though the speaker was saddened by the fact of the brevity of life, he was never pessimistic. On the contrary, he usually derived a special comfort recalling pledges made with youthful friends, or the special moments shared with a loved one. More than a few of these reminiscences were overly sentimental, and at least one, "Our Bessie" by William H. Burleigh, was embarrassingly maudlin and simplistic:

> Our Bessie was as sweet a girl
>   As ever happy mother kissed.
> And when our Father called her home
>   How sadly was she missed.
> For, grave or gay, or well or ill,
>   She had her thousand winning ways,
> And mingled youthful innocence
>   With all her tasks and plays.
>
> How softly beamed her happy smile,
>   Which played around the sweetest mouth
> That ever fashioned infant words;
>   The sunshine of the South,
> Mellowed and soft, was in her eye,
>   And brightened through her golden hair;
> And all that lived and loved, I ween,
>   Did her affection share.
>
> With reverent voice she breathed her prayer,
>   With gentlest tones she sung her hymn;
> And when she talked of heaven, our eyes
>   With tears of joy were dim.
> Yet in our selfish grief we wept,
>   When last her lips upon us smiled;
> Oh! could we when our Father called,
>   Detain the happy child?
>
> Our home is poor, and cold our clime,
>   And misery mingles with our mirth;
> 'Twas meet our Bessie should depart
>   From such a weary earth.
> Oh! she is safe—no cloud can dim
>   The brightness of her ransomed soul;
> Nor trials vex or tempter lure
>   Her spirit from its goal.
>
> We wrapt her in her snow-white shroud,
>   And crossed, with sadly tender care,
> Her little hands upon her breast,
>   And smoothed her sunny hair.
>
> We kissed her cheek, and kissed her brow,
>   And if aright we read the smile
> That lingered on the dear one's lips,
>   It told of heaven the while!

[5:267]

Elegies, of course, were the one verse form in America that had something resembling a tradition behind them. The Puritans, after all, had regularly written elegies throughout the seventeenth century, a fact that Roy Harvey Pearce has nicely elaborated in his important study, *The Continuity of American Poetry* (1961).[7] Quite the opposite was the case, however, with sonnet writing. In his book, *The Sonnet in American Literature* (1930), Lewis G. Sterner noted that the first sonnet in America—authored by a Colonel David Humphreys—was not written before 1776, and was not published until after 1800. By 1802, only forty-four sonnets had been written, and these, according to Sterner, by only six men. In fact, it would be "extremely difficult," Sterner stated in his "Introduction," to point to a single American sonnet written before 1820 of more than ordinary merit."[8]

The issue of merit notwithstanding, the Transcendentalists themselves were generally no strangers to the challenge of sonnet writing. While he was helping to edit *The Western Messenger,* Christopher Pearse Cranch, for example, supplied that journal with seventeen sonnets, which was only a few less than the approximately twenty-four that the spiritual Jones Very provided. Unfortunately for the editors of *The Harbinger,* they had no such singularly prolific contributor of sonnets—or of any kind of verse, for that matter. Still, no fewer than twenty sonnets eventually appeared in the magazine, of which about one third—six, to be precise—were original. Cranch himself contributed only one ("On the Mexican War," 3:89), though Thomas Wentworth Higginson sent along four, and a contributor identified only as "R.W.B." provided one.

To be sure, the quality of the sonnets published in *The Harbinger* does support Sterner's contention that America was late in sonnet production, for the majority are very irregular in form, and are generally monotonous, trite, and uninspired in content. Mechanically, these verses deserve to be called sonnets only because they are fourteen lines in length and employ no more than five rhymes, though in many of them—to be accurate—the latter point is questionable. Although there seems to have been some attempt to approximate the rhyme scheme of an Italian, English, or Spenserian sonnet, there was, in fact, no "pure" Italian, English, or Spenserian sonnet published in *The Harbinger.* Actually, it is only with some generosity that we can say that most of the sonnets published in the magazine are variant or compromise forms of the three types just mentioned.

In content, the sonnets echo many of the ideas already seen in the other categories: the death of a loved one; unrequited love; nature as a rehabilitative agent for man's spirit; the need for man to be socially active; and the need for faith and trust in God. In addition, a few of the sonnets were dedicated to different individuals, such as Alfred, Lord Tennyson's to Buonaparte ("Madman! . . . We taught him; late he learned humility," 3:169); Mrs. Butler's to Pope Pius IX (he who has lifted "that stone . . . from the heart of a whole nation," 5:38); an anonymous poet's to Raphael ("thou wert chosen by a lot divine," 7:49); and Anne C. Lynch's to Christ ("The incarnation of profoundest love," 5:306).

Far more popular in *The Harbinger* than sonnets were lyrics: that is, poetic compliments and tributes, and the poetry expressive of moods. Over forty poems of this nature were published in the magazine, of which approximately one-fourth were original, provided by such regular contributors as Dwight, Dana, Story, Higginson, Foster, and Curtis. *The Harbinger* also published its usual fare of reprints from the pens of obscure authors, as well as those from more notable figures such as Bryant, Lowell, and Hood.

Poetic compliments and tributes were among the most popular lyrics in the pages of *The Harbinger*. The subjects for these tributes were diverse, ranging from E. M. Sidney's homage to Pittsburgh, "the city of a dream," to Phillip Pendleton Cooke's "To My Daughter Lily," to Charles Dana's translation of one of Heinrich Heine's poems praising a woman's beauty, to W. A. Butler's adulatory tribute to the German poet Johann Ludwig Uhland. Most often, however, the poetic tribute was addressed to a well-known figure. For example, from the *Home Journal, The Harbinger* reprinted a valentine addressed to its close friend and the president of the American Union of Associationists, Horace Greeley, that "great nature" whose "honest heart" and brave spirit made him the champion of "freedom and reform" (4:228). It also published tributes by George G. Foster to the Scotch poet Robert Burns (4:236), by James Russell Lowell to the French politician and statesman Lamartine (7:113), and by Charles Dana to Memnon (2:159), the Egyptian god immortalized by Zeus. Foster's and Dana's lyrics appeared originally in *The Harbinger;* Lowell's was reprinted from his own journal, the *National Anti-Slavery Standard.*

Of the several lyrics expressive of moods, a surprising number—at least when one remembers the special nature of *The Harbinger*—were negative and even pessimistic in tone. These several poems lack the easy optimism and certainty that especially characterized the didactic verse. Much of this poetry concerned unrequited love, such as Mary Hewitt's "Love's Pleading" (4:259), in which the speaker pleads—seemingly to no avail—for love and praise from a loved one, and Anne C. Lynch's companion poems, "The Ideal" and "The Ideal Found" (3:28–29), in which the speaker states, in the first poem, that she did not believe her ideal in love existed in this world; and in the second, that though she had found her ideal, he rejected her. Thus, the speaker sadly concludes that the ideal remained a dream, as it had been before. Thomas Hood's "Ode to Melancholy" (2:236) only indirectly concerned unrequited love; the negativism of the poem derived from the poet's belief that "there's not a string attuned to Mirth / But has its chords of Melancholy." Hood's "To An Enthusiast" (2:346) is less negative than his "Ode," though it certainly was not cheerful. The poet says that he is not sure if he should admire or pity an enthusiastic person. He can only conclude that the enthusiastic person will experience the "ups and downs" of life more intensely than will other people.

Very few of the lyrics published in *The Harbinger* embodied what might be called the singing impulse, though the magazine did reprint two that were very patriotic: William Cullen Bryant's "Oh Mother of a Mighty Race" (4:69), and S. D. Robbins's "Our Country, Right or Wrong" (3:237). Bryant's poem chastised the cynical and those overly critical of America, while Robbins's poem adopted the attitude: "Our country shall be right, and right the wrong." Probably many of the poems discussed as didactic verse could be said to be expressive of the singing impulse if they had not been so obviously didactic in intent.

It would appear by now, perhaps, that the quality of the verse published in *The Harbinger* during the four years of the magazine's existence was not expecially noteworthy. Certainly it is true that in form and content, a good many of the poems may be characterized, generally, as being simplistic or provincial, not to mention heavy-handed. Often they are blaringly didactic; frequently they are overly sentimental. Given the ethos of the time, however, this is not so much a criticism as it is an observation—an important one, too, for it has more to do with early nineteenty-century American poetry than it does with *The Harbinger*. Indeed, one of the significant things to observe, by way of conclusion, about poetry in *The Harbinger* is that, while the magazine's ideological interests were chiefly social and economic in nature, the journal nevertheless became—unwittingly, to be sure—an extraordinary repository of American poems of the period. And while it is true that a majority of the poems were only reprints from a variety of sources, the really important point is that the poems themselves provide an interesting reflection of the age in which they were written (an age, we need not be reminded, that managed to produce poets such as Poe and Emerson and Whitman at the same time that it was embracing and applauding Longfellow, Bryant, Holmes, and Lowell), and so *The Harbinger* does, in fact, provide us today with the means for achieving a greater understanding of the state of American poetry—such as it was—in mid-nineteenth-century America.

6

Musical Criticism in *The Harbinger*

It is appropriate to conclude this discussion of *The Harbinger* by focusing on the one feature that continues to distinguish it ahead of any of the other periodicals associated with New England Transcendentalism,[1] a feature, in fact, that has resulted in the magazine's rightfully occupying a prominent place in any discussion today of the history of musical criticism in American journals and newspapers. That feature, of course, was its music criticism.

At a time when music criticism was anything but a popular or staple item in the fare offered by American journals and newspapers, *The Harbinger* regularly published a column of "Musical Reviews." Moreover, John S. Dwight, who was the principal author of the column, revealed in the numerous reviews that he wrote for the journal a breadth and depth of knowledge and appreciation in matters musical—both foreign and domestic—that was unusual to say the least, especially when one remembers that in America the seedbed for any serious study of music had been fallow indeed. As Dwight himself noted in his introductory column in the very first number of *The Harbinger,* there had been in this country "no composers; no great performances in our churches; no well-endowed and thorough academies to train the artist, or to educate the public taste by frequent hearings of the finest compositions, except in a very limited degree" (1:12).

Such a difficult situation did not prevent Dwight, however, from conducting a column that can only be described as extraordinary in many respects. In the nearly four years of the magazine's existence, he provided over one hundred (110, to be exact) essays, critiques, and reviews on subjects ranging from Beethoven to Leopold de Meyer, from the Boston Philharmonic Society to the New York Philharmonic Society, from the "traditional" school of music to the "new" virtuoso school, and from Italian opera to the Boston music teachers' conventions.

The music column was known in the first five volumes (from June 1845 to October 1847) as the "Musical Review," and it appeared approximately sixty-six times. During this period, when *The Harbinger* was still being published at Brook Farm, Dwight managed it almost singlehandedly. He did receive very occasional assistance from George W. Curtis, William W. Story, Christopher Pearse Cranch, and Albert Brisbane, Curtis contributing five items to the column, and Story, Cranch, and Brisbane providing just one apiece. Otherwise, Dwight supplied eighteen of the twenty items pertaining to music in the first volume, fifteen of twenty for volume 2, and seventeen of eighteen for the fifth volume. For the third and fourth volumes, he handled the column entirely by himself, providing along the way slightly more than a total of forty items.

In November 1847, it will be remembered, *The Harbinger* was transferred to New York City with the close of the fifth volume. There it immediately underwent a number of editorial changes designed to bolster dwindling subscription lists. One of those changes involved dropping the "Musical Review" in favor of an "Art Review," apparently because it was thought that the latter would be less specialized and would therefore have broader readership appeal. Whatever the actual reason, the "Art Review" column appeared right away in the first issue of the sixth volume in the number for 6 November 1847. It included articles by Charles Dana on painting, Elam Ives, Jr. on music in New York, and Parke Godwin on some of the New York theatres.[2] The "Art Review" column appeared seventeen times in the sixth volume, ten in volume 7, and only four in the incompleted eighth volume. Dwight, who did not move to New York with the transfer of *The Harbinger*, continued to report on musical affairs in Boston, and he eventually sent along more than twenty contributions before the magazine's demise in February 1849.

After *The Harbinger*'s collapse, Dwight, of course, went on to establish *Dwight's Journal of Music* (1852–81), a magazine that was very highly respected during the twenty-nine years of its existence, as well as one that continues to be cited today in works dealing with American music history. Somewhat surprisingly, such recognition has not been extended to *The Harbinger*, for it is almost never referred to in such works. Indeed, despite the fact that the Associationist journal contained, according to one critic, "the first noteworthy criticism of the ethereal art [of music] in the history of American journalism," and that it was, according to another critic, "one of the country's leading musical journals," it has been only infrequently acknowledged as such in the musical histories.[3] This omission has been compounded by the fact that, while there has always been nearly unanimous agreement that Dwight was the first important critic of music in America, such agreement seems for the most part to have been arrived at primarily on the basis of his later contributions, for the significant and formative part of his career during *The Harbinger* years has not been nearly so carefully examined as one might expect.[4] It is, then, one of the main intentions of this chapter to provide a few observations about the early John S. Dwight—his prejudices, for example, and his likes and dislikes—in order to contribute—however slightly—to a more informed and complete picture of the first noteworthy critic of music in America. Another intention, it goes without saying, is to illustrate the nature of the music criticism that was published in *The Harbinger*.

Before making any assessment of John Dwight the music critic, we should recall for a moment John Dwight the man. It is important to remember that Dwight was, after all, an individual committed to a specific social and economic program for the improvement of humanity, and that *The Harbinger* was being published during the frenetic 1840s when profound political and cultural changes were occurring in America. This is not to suggest that Dwight used the occasion of the "Musical Review" to proselytize the cause of Associationism and Fourierism, or to rant against institutions such as the American government. His reviews, as we shall see, were usually remarkably free from comments of a nonmusical nature. Rather, the point to be made is this: John Dwight may have been an idealist who lived for a considerable time in a utopian community (nearly four years, to be precise), but he was certainly never a man unable to hear the rhythm and beat of American society. His column, on occasion, subtly and importantly reflected this awareness, an awareness, surely, that must have had at least some influence on his musical tastes. We might therefore first characterize Dwight (as opposed to Dwight the music critic) by noting briefly his attitude toward industrialization and the war with Mexico, and toward the musical background of the American concertgoing public, three matters that were more than once referred to in his music column. Given the nature of the Associationist commitment—and specifically the Fourierist program for industrial reform—one would naturally expect Dwight. to have been sensitive to the increasing growth both at home and abroad of technology and industrialization. Indeed, Emerson himself had opened his important essay on *Nature* a decade before with a call for man to reestablish his original relationship to nature. Now, ten years later, Dwight thought that one effect of this "era of mechanical expansion" was, in the world of music specifically, the recent phenomenon of the virtuoso musician, who, in the case of the pianist, for example, was too often reducing the language of the composer to a "finger-drill." This was a subject about which Dwight would have a good deal to say (see below, pp. 130–36). For the immediate moment, however, the occasion was a review in the number for 8 August 1846 of three editions of musical works recently printed by the noted Boston publisher George P. Reed. The opportunity was as good as any for Dwight to complain generally that "the human race has turned its energies to making tools. . . . Instead of leading great lives, we are 'doing a great business;' instead of making characters and men, we are making machines, and even making machines of men" (3:140).

Dwight certainly did not have to look very far for examples of this tendency. Perhaps the most obvious one was the growing conflict with Mexico. We have already noted much earlier (see the chapter on "Social, Political, and Economic Matters in *The Harbinger*," pp. 56–58) that the editors of

The Harbinger took a vigorous and hard-line stand against the United States aggression in Mexican territory. What prompted Dwight's first reference to the Mexican War in the "Musical Review" was the occasion of his attendance at the first American concert in New York of Beethoven's Ninth Symphony (the "Choral Symphony"), on the way to which he had to pass a "dense, black sea of heads, a crowd of fifty thousand," who had gathered to support "the war summons of the President" (3:9). The crowd impressed Dwight as nothing more than a "gathering of fiends" anxious to unchain the fiercer, base passions that would "drown the voice of Love and Wisdom" that was only recently beginning to be heard in the world. He was therefore relieved to be able to leave the oppressive sounds of this gathering and enter into the "circle of light" where Beethoven and Mozart held forth, "*true* demagogues" themselves because they attuned mankind to harmony.

According to Dwight—and obviously most other Associationists as well—the problem with war—any war—was that it appealed only to man's base nature, to his most violent and brutal passions. War, Associationists thought, was nothing more than a way of nourishing these passions under the banner of an unprincipled patriotism. In the case of the present conflict, the eruption of these passions was not entirely surprising, however, for passions such as these were continually in strife in a competitive, commercial society. Truth be known, the current warfare—which the American government was trying to dignify by calling "*business*"—was nothing more than "war for the sake of war, for the sake of its mere animal excitment, for the sake of gratifying a base lust for power . . . and for the sake of no just cause, of no high sentiment or principle, of no real gain to anyone, of no good thing whatever!" (3:9).

Dwight himself was so sincere in these convictions that he even went so far on two later occasions to fire his own critical guns on the Boston Academy of Music and the American pianist Edward L. Walker for playing music that was too warlike. In an otherwise favorable and even enthusiastic review of "The Boston Academy of Music," which appeared in *The Harbinger* in the number for 21 November 1846, Dwight stated that, though he thought that the selection of music for the concert the week before "was certainly a rich one," there was "too much of the warlike for our taste" (3:381). The pieces in question were Peter Joseph Lindpaintner's *Overture Guerrière,* which contained a battle piece, and Italian composer Gaetano Donizetti's Overture to *La Fille du Régiment,* which was warlike and "full of the roll of drums." In times like these, Dwight said, "when a nation has gone mad with the old fever of conquest, . . . it certainly is desirable that music should not prostitute its divine faculties to the same base uses." He went on to point out that Beethoven's *Vittoria* Symphony, for example, was his only attempt to write martial music, and it was, the Bostonian quickly added, his only failure.

In his review of Edward L. Walker, which appeared a few months later in

the number for 27 February 1847, Dwight began by noting that the complimentary concert on 13 February 1847 at the Boston Melodeon was very
poorly attended, a fact that he said he wished he could attribute to the
presence in the program of a piece by Walker called the "Grand Triumphal
March of Monterey." This piece *The Harbinger* music critic roundly condemned because "it surely seemed a desecration of high art, to make it
minister to this poular madness, this fighting pseudo-patriotism, this great
shame of our nation" (4:187). Dwight added that he thought Walker had
acted thoughtlessly in accepting the first title suggested for the piece. Certainly a musician with so sacred a regard for art as Walker seemed to have
had should know that the Mexican War "never could inspire other music
than the grating sounds of hell."

Before concluding his review of Edward Walker, Dwight considerably
qualified his earlier observation that the concert had been given in the "chill
of an empty house" by stating that "as large an audience as is ever drawn out
in Boston by a piano forte Concert, were assembled." It would appear that
the number of people in attendance must have been small indeed, something
that Dwight might well have attributed to the failure of the American concertgoing public generally to appreciate serious music. He did not actually
make that point on this particular occasion, but he certainly did so on numerous others. In fact, he had even cautioned Walker himself several months
before in a review of the pianist's first Boston concert, which had been given
at the Melodeon on 15 April 1846. (It probably ought to be remarked at this
point, too, that we are obviously beginning now to move farther from the
consideration of John Dwight the man and closer to the more particular
consideration of John Dwight the music critic.)

To return, however, to Walker's concert, Dwight noted that much of the
excitment surrounding Walker's appearance in Boston had been caused by
"appeals to patriotic vanity on the score of the performer's being an American and 'self-taught,' as the phrase is" (2:315). Dwight then provided a
lengthy review of the event—and a positive one, it should be added—but not
before reminding both Walker and his readers that the "besetting sin of
Bostonians" was that they were "prone to go into rhapsodies about each
new-comer, and proclaim him the first genius in the world, until another
candidate arrives" (2:316).

Actually, Dwight had already criticized the Boston audience on similar
grounds almost a year earlier in only the third number of *The Harbinger*. At
that time, he attended a concert given by the popular Norwegian violinist
Ole Bull, held at the Melodeon on 21 June 1845. The audience, Dwight said,
"was only moderately large, justifying the remark that Bostonians are never
enthusiastic when an artist comes a second time; which proves that what
enthusiasm there is, is more for novelties, for signs and wonders, than for
Art" (1:44).

It was not only concerts given by individuals, however, which made clear the lack of sophistication of Boston audiences in musical affairs. At times, according to Dwight, Bostonians could be (and were) downright rude. Such was the case on the evening of 12 June 1847, when an Italian opera company was performing a series of operas in Boston. The announcement at the beginning of the program that the opera would be performed without the prima donna—Signorina Fortunata Tedesco—was greeted with much booing and hissing. The audience, Dwight reported, was eventually pacified, but only after everyone had been informed that they could receive a full refund if they chose not to remain for the performance. "This conduct," Dwight stated in his review, which appeared in the 19 June 1847 number of *The Harbinger,* "certainly reflects discredit upon our opera-going public; first for its want of generosity and of good manners; and secondly because it showed so little true appreciation of good music, as if they went to hear the prima donna, and recognized nothing worth their money or their time in the orchestra, chorusses and other singers, and especially in the composition of the opera itself" (5:26).

Dwight's annoyance with the Boston audience on these and other occasions extended, of course, to the American concertgoing public generally. Obviously, however, most concerts that he attended during *The Harbinger* years were in Boston, and he was therefore naturally more inclined to criticize audiences in that city. Nevertheless, there were a few opportunities to comment on "American audiences" as a whole, as Dwight did, for example, on 6 February 1847. In that number of *The Harbinger,* he informed his readers that his column that week included a translated article on Felix Mendelssohn that had been excerpted from a German journal. He prefaced the translation by stating that in order to realize "the idea of a true musical life" in this country, Americans needed to turn to Germany, for America was not yet able to provide "the highest conception of music realized." No doubt Dwight's readers were hardly surprised by that remark, for the Bostonian had been speaking of the Germans in reverential tones since the inception of the "Musical Review" column. In any event, Dwight then identified one of the reasons that he thought America had so far been unable to produce true musical artists, and that reason was the failure of the people to understand or support the real artist. How different was the case in Germany, where audiences sat silent and listened attentively and appreciatively to someone such as Felix Mendelssohn while he played his pieces. "How unlike," however, "the rude unmusical behavior of our audiences, who yawn and talk during the best passages, and spoil every delicate effect by the interruption of their gross and untimely applause!" (4:138).

Dwight thought that this kind of behavior was indicative of a lack of training and background in musical affairs, which, in turn, had a lot to do, he thought, with the increasing popularity here of the virtuoso musician and the "New School" of music. These are matters, of course, that bring us squarely to the consideration of John Dwight the music critic. We should state right away, then, what has perhaps already begun to be obvious: in matters musical, John Dwight was a purist who liked his classical "straight," so to speak. One does not have to read many of the "Musical Reviews" to recognize what Dwight made abundantly clear on numerous occasions: it was Beethoven and the German-related musicians that generally represented anything resembling an absolute standard of musical art. It may appear surprising that someone such as Dwight—who was obviously committed to a progressive and utopian scheme for the social and economic improvement of humanity— would have so immediately become such a confirmed spokesman for the classic "school" of music. The fact is, of course, that nothing could have been less surprising, if, at the same time, nevertheless ironic. As a thoroughgoing Associationist, Dwight had little choice but to be critical of an activity that valued the individual over the group. Indeed, it was this very issue of solitude versus society that had irreconcilably divided the ranks of the Transcendentalists in 1840 when Emerson felt required to refuse Ripley's request to join his then nascent Brook Farm community.

The best brief definition of what Dwight regularly referred to as the old and new schools in music appeared in *The Harbinger* in the number for 14 November 1846, though Dwight himself did not author this statment. Instead, he provided a translation of an article by a correspondent of the popular German periodical *Schnellpost,* which, the Bostonian said, "expresses just our view of modern music," and which he incorporated as part of his own review of "Henri Herz" (3 : 365).

Henri Herz (1803–88) was an Austrian composer and pianist who was generally regarded as the founder of the new, or modern, school of music. According to the *Schnellpost,* it was Herz who had paved the way for such other virtuosos as Sigismond Thalberg (1812–71), another Austrian pianist and composer, Franz Liszt (1811–86), the Hungarian child-prodigy composer and pianist, and Frederic Chopin (1810–49), the Polish composer and pianist. The old, or classic, school, on the other hand, dated back to the Germans Johann Sebastian Bach (1685–1750) and his son, Johann Christian Bach (1735–82), and it had become well established by such figures as the Austrian-born composer Franz Joseph Haydn (1732–1809), his fellow Austrian composer and violinist, Wolfgang Mozart (1756–91), and the noted German composer and pianist, Ludwig van Beethoven (1770–1827).

There was no doubt, the correspondent of the *Schnellpost* stated, that the modern musical masters were far more popular than the composers of the older school, for, among other things, the aim of the new school was "to secure the applause of the mass, to be the *lion* (hero) *of the day.*"And there was no denying, too, that in terms of "the mechanical use of tone-effects, in point of finger-facility and tasteful delivery," the moderns had wrought some rather dramatic effects using such instruments as the piano and violin. Their music, typically, was agreeable and even captivating, which largely explained why it was more sought after, Dwight himself stated, than the earnest, well-studied, and difficult music of the older school. Too many virtuosos, however, had fallen into the "province of the artificial" and had "sinned against aesthetic rules of taste" by striving so relentlessly to transform a single instrument so as to make it a "sort of compendium of all the others." Such a pursuit showed not only a failure of understanding, but it precluded, as well, any consideration of the very important musical matter of how best to unite and harmonize form with substance. It was this recognition which characterized the work of the classic composers, and which resulted in their work's being predominated by a "depth of thought" and a "power of pure harmony" that was rarely found in the work of the moderns.

The translation and inclusion in *The Harbinger* of this brief article from the *Schnellpost* certainly must have struck many of the regular readers of the "Musical Review" column as being unnecessary and even redundant, for Dwight had been routinely elaborating the same points himself right from the start of his column. In fact, he had already provided his own very extensive discussion of the new school of pianists and violinists a year before the article from the *Schnellpost* was translated and reprinted in *The Harbinger*. For the close of the first volume of the Associationist journal, Dwight wrote an article on "The Virtuoso Age in Music," which was so lengthy that it had to be printed in two installments in the consecutive numbers for 15 and 22 November 1845. It proved to be one of the longest pieces that Dwight would write for the "Musical Review," and it may be considered his definitive statement on the subject in *The Harbinger*.

What prompted the remarks on "The Virtuoso Age in Music" was, Dwight said, the arrival in Boston of the "*Trismegistus* among pianists," Leopold De Meyer, who was "heralded by his own biography in thick gilt-edged pamphlet, detailing his whole career of European triumphs, and making a book no wise inferior to the Arabian Nights for marvellous entertainment" (1:362). The fact was, Dwight said, that the musical heavens had been so dazzlingly illuminated recently by "a long meteoric shower of solo-players, 'virtuosos'" that the more "quiet orbs" to which he had been inclined to look up had been practically extinguished. It was therefore time to make a few remarks about this age of the "hundred-handed Briareuses of the piano."[5]

Dwight began his discussion by saying that he respected the new school, not only because some true geniuses were currently working in it, but because the mechanical finger-school had, at times, "produced soul-stirring fantasias and true pictures of marvellous ideal beauty" (1:363). He would therefore, try, he stated, to present both positive as well as negative points about the new school, though he would detail the latter first, he added, because essentially the origins of the new school were monstrous and illegitimate: *"It is music to satisfy the demands of extraordinary skill; and not skill to satisfy the demands of music."*

Specifically, there were five ways by which the modern school was degrading the art of music, and these were (1) by making it nothing more than

an exhibition of personal skill; (2) by making the music selected for performance subservient to the overriding end of exhibition; (3) by unnaturally
encouraging the musical performers to become too individualistic in a
medium the backbone of which was concerted, cooperative effort; (4) by
establishing a false musical standard for beginners; and (5) by reinforcing a
spirit of discontent that was already everywhere evident in contemporary
life (1:362–64; 378).

The way in which, first, the modern virtuoso compromised the true aim of
the art of music and made it, instead, merely an exhibition of his own skill
was obvious enough. One did not attend one of these performances to enjoy
the intrinsic value of the music itself—to be "transported into the ideal world
of harmony." One went to see the performer; he was all. The music was
nothing but the scenery and backdrop, and it was invariably selected and
arranged so as best to accent the virtuoso's abilities. In fact, everything that
he did was intended for effect. Dwight himself dramatized this point by
recreating for his readers what the rehearsed opening moments of such a
performance might have been like. (There's certainly no reason either not to
regard the portrait as an accurate one.) The passage here quoted is lengthy,
but it represents some of Dwight's most inspired critical writing:

> Do not be impatient for the entrance of the virtuoso. Precisely in the
> fullness of time, not a moment before or after the folding doors in the back
> of the stage fall open of their own accord, and forth advances, amid
> deafening applause, the tall dark form of the master, like a calm magician
> stepping forth upon the troubled sea, which he will soon tranquillize. He is
> dressed in elegant black, with the utmost precision. His air is that of the
> exquisite and the [Nicolò] Paganini combined; pale and rapt and all ab-
> stracted from this world, and yet so courtier-like in attitude and attire, that
> he seems waited upon in his sublime carelessness by invisible graces, who
> send him forth all curled and perfumed, like young Ascanius from the
> hands of Venus. With what complacency of sublime vanity he smiles
> down upon his audience, and distributes gracious little bows, accepting
> the applause as something his by right! And true enough; he need not
> concern himself; the victory is already won; he has spell-bound that many-
> headed monster, the public, by the very magnetism of his presence; and
> now perhaps he will condescend to amuse himself a little with his violin,
> and let the monster hear. He draws out fitful snatches of melody from the
> strings, just as his humor prompts him; and, by a sort of instinct, orchestra
> and all things chime in properly, for it is a magic influence; and now you
> shall go into ecstasies, you shall taste the very delirium of musical sensa-
> tion, to reward you for yielding yourselves in such implicit faith to him.
> [1:363]

Dwight was obviously warmed to his subject at this point, and he turned
his attention now to his second objection of the modern school: the subservi-
ence of music to exhibition. One striking fact about the virtuoso, Dwight
said, was that, while he claimed to be able to play anything, he never did

actually play anything of Beethoven, Bach, or Mozart! Invariably, the audience was required to listen to some fantasia, or more commonly, some piece of the virtuoso's own composition. Dwight added that he wanted it to be clear that he was not suggesting that the only true calling of the artist was to interpret the music of the older composers: "Certainly we will not object to the artist, if he will produce as good, or better music of his own" (1:364). It was not unreasonable to suppose, however, that if the modern virtuoso truly had the "soul of Art" in him, he would gladly postpone his own satisfaction for an hour or so in order to participate in some "genuine quickening converse" with the classical masters. Perhaps, though, the fault was really with the American public, for in musical matters it seemed always to prefer that which glittered to that which was genuine. Wherever the actual blame, it was clear that the modern virtuoso did not play for the glory of music, but only to glorify himself. In fact, the unwillingness of the contemporary artist to "lose himself in a joint effort with others to bring out some noble work" was, Dwight stated, yet a third serious weakness of the new school: "True Art can entertain no egotism." True art was characterized by a spirit of disinterestedness. In music, the ultimate object was to capture "the idea, the spirit, the conception of the beautiful whole" that was inherent in any good piece of music. The modern virtuoso, however, was preoccupied only with the estimation of the public; he was rarely if ever willing to become, for example, a part of a quartette or an orchestra, even though the music being performed might be Handel's *Messiah* or a symphony by Beethoven. Such preoccupation and unwillingness, Dwight concluded his third objection, could only prove fatal to the best interests of musical art.

Dwight's fourth objection to the new school was that it had already begun to establish something of a false standard of art, that standard being "that difficulty should be the chief desideratum in composition." Dwight said that he was especially concerned about the effect that such a false standard would have on young music students. At the very least, it would divert their attention from the true aim of music, which was to understand and express the sentiment that was in the music itself. Certainly the aim was not just to perform some difficult musical feat, though that was, in fact, precisely what many younger pianists were trying to do, equating as they were, difficulty with merit. These students should realize, however, that they could achieve a familiarity with the works of Beethoven or Mozart in half the time expended trying to conquer some brilliant musical set by Herz or Thalberg. Such an endeavor was surely the "purest and most refined and intellectual of all enjoyments."

Finally, though, Dwight indicated that, when all was said and done, he was really not all that surprised by the enormous popularity of the virtuoso musician, for it was, he claimed, indicative of an age of discontent, an age in which people, through a kind of general despair over the state of contemporary society, sought out those enjoyments which would temporarily alleviate

a "morbid restlessness, a *despairing* discontent!" This final criticism of the
new school was, of course, nothing more than a repetition of the more
generalized criticism of a capitalistic and increasingly more industrialized
American society that echoed through the pages of *The Harbinger* during the
four years of its existence. For the immediate moment, however, Dwight
characterized the "*despairing* discontent" of the age as a "convulsive activity, a straining after novelty, a craving for the wonderful and the intense in
literature, in art, in religion, in fortune-hunting, in every thing: Every thing is
for *effect*" (1:378). Dwight continued: "Hence the sweeping speculations in
trade, which turn men's heads; hence the highly-colored extravagance of
French novels; hence the amazing apparitions of the wizard Paganini, of the
hundred-handed Briareuses who smite the piano with fanatical fury, till it
resounds through all its length at once, with the fullness of an orchestra."

Thus Dwight concluded his remarks on the deficiencies of the new school
of music. He had obviously mounted what could only be called a vigorous
and penetrating critique of the phenomenon of the virtuoso age of musicians.
It will be remembered, however, that he had also promised his readers that
he would devote some time to a consideration of the positive contributions
of the new school, and so he now turned his attention to just that matter.

Certainly it seems unlikely that any of the regular readers of the "Musical
Review" column in *The Harbinger* would ever have expected Dwight willy-
nilly to condemn the new school, for among those contemporary artists
associated with it were Sigismond Thalberg, Franz Liszt, and Frederic Chopin. Dwight was simply too intelligent and perceptive a critic of music not to
recognize or appreciate the musical achievements of men such as these.
That Dwight did, in fact, is noteworthy, if only because his praise of Thalberg, Liszt, and Chopin indicates that the Bostonian was always ready to
praise genuine musical talent and ability, regardless of parochial considerations such as, for example, a musician's affiliation with a particular music
school.

Actually, Dwight had only the most enthusiastic things to say about Thalberg, Liszt, and Chopin. For example, Thalberg, *The Harbinger* music critic
thought, inspired in a person a grand sense of impressiveness. The sym-
metry and tone-architecture of his work reminded one of St. Peter's Cathedral or the cathedral of Milan, with their splendid halls and magnificent
domes that seemingly reached into the very heavens. Thalberg's music was
"a multiplying mirror, reflecting countless light. It is suggestive of all splen-
dor" (1:3799). More "soul-stirring," however, even than Thalberg was
Franz Liszt, that young musical Bacchus from Hungary who was "drunk
with the glories of his Art." Liszt was, Dwight said, the Paganini of the
piano: "His music is possessed; it laughs and raves and shudders with the
very frenzy of genius, and hurries all on with it in its uncontainable impulse." It was Chopin, though, who, of these three, was the most delicate,
spiritual, and sentimental. Because this was so, it was always refreshing to

return to him after the rush and glitter of Thalberg or Liszt. Chopin's music seemed compounded of spirit voices: "It is like the fragrance of flowers," Dwight said; "we seem to breath it . . . till we reel in a drowsy oriental languor."

There was yet a second important aspect of the modern school of music, Dwight acknowledged, and that was the extent to which virtuosos such as Liszt and Paganini had developed the very natures of their instruments. According to Dwight,

> each instrument has its peculiar genius, surely, corresponding to something in the soul of the Art. Art is developed not only by its own impulse from within, but also by hints and suggestions from without. Thus outward nature had as much to do with the invention of language as the mind itself had. So music originates in the soul and in the sounds of nature equally. He who wins a new order of tones from a string, a tube of wood or brass, at the same time quickens a new creative impulse in the mind, and adds to the composer's wealth. [1:379]

The virtuoso school of musicians had already considerably aided the development of modern music because anyone who discovered new tones or qualities in an instrument was helping musical art. As language had helped to quicken human thought, so did recent instrumental accomplishments help the development of musical art. In this regard, Dwight said, one might consider that the Italian composer and musician Nicolò Paganini (1782–1840) had been "*born* for the violin," that it was his destiny to unseal the secret musical springs of his instrument in order that the spiritual world hidden between the hollow pieces of wood be revealed. Certainly it could not be argued that the tones he elicited from the violin were pure. Indeed, Paganini was so accomplished that one never heard the strings or the scrape of the bow when he performed. There was nothing but tone, tone so pure and elevated that it was like a "disembodied spirit."

Dwight had certainly said a great deal about contemporary music in his lengthy two-installment essay on "The Virtuoso Age in Music," which helped to close out the first volume. He certainly had many other opportunities, of course, to add to his remarks, although he chose instead to devote most of his attention in subsequent volumes of The Harbinger to those musicians and musical affairs that mattered most to him, namely, the Germans—really, Ludwig van Beethoven—the Italians—especially Italian opera—and the Americans—specifically the increasing development of American interest in serious music. This is not to suggest that Dwight never again spoke of virtuosos such as Ole Bull or Paganini. His notices and reviews of new musical publications, for example, are sprinkled with remarks about men such as these, as well as about figures such as Chopin and Liszt, and he even devoted two or three individual reviews to Leopold de Meyer. Henri Herz also received this same individualized treatment.[6] It was the Germans, however, who most represented to *The Harbinger*'s music critic the fulfillment of musical accomplishment, and, to Dwight, the Germans meant first Ludwig van Beethoven.

It has already been noted earlier in this chapter that Dwight had only the highest regard for the German and Austrian composers. His admiration for them reverberated in the "Musical Review" as a popular refrain might linger in one's mind. Thus on one occasion we learn that Mozart is "tender, mystical, and sad," and on another that he "certainly is Love." Haydn is "sunny and genial," and he plays in the "sphere of calm, pure, domestic joy." Schubert has written symphonies that are for angelic ears. Handel's music, especially his *Messiah*—which, by the way, seems to have been Dwight's favorite piece of music—was filled with the "pure, unlimited, humanitary sentiment" that would someday lead to Univeral Friendship. Beethoven was strong, inspiring, and proud at the same time that he was tender. He was the aspiring Promethean spirit always longing for new triumphs.

It was especially this latter quality of Beethoven that the Associationist Dwight found very appealing. The spirit of yearning—of never-ceasing aspiration—that Dwight thought so characterized the German's music, impressed the Brook Farmer more than a little. In fact, it was precisely this striving for the infinite which enabled Dwight, early in the first volume, to proclaim: "Beethoven's is the music of this age" (1:154). Beethoven's music represented "the high hour of Human Brotherhood; the triumph of the grand unitary sentiment, into which all the passions and interests of all human hearts are destined finally to blend" (3:11). Once the present age began better to understand itself, it would appreciate Beethoven more fully because such appreciation would be nothing more than the realization that the German's music was prophetic of the worldwide social-reform movement that was then stirring at home and abroad. Thus an appreciation of Beethoven was something to be awaited with great anticipation, for it would signal an awareness of "the deeper soul of the age." Presently, the continued popularity of virtuosos like Leopold de Meyer indicated the "superficial outside character of the times."

For Dwight, then, Beethoven was nothing less than a "presentiment of coming social harmony." The Bostonian so referred to him in the number for 30 August 1845 in a review of "Music in Boston During the Last Winter. No. IV" (1:189). On this occasion the German was characterized as the seventh note in the musical scale, the note that "cries for the completion of the octave." It was this very note, Dwight then said in an elaboration of his metaphor that is a reminder again just how pervasive was the influence of the Swedish theologian and philosopher Emanuel Swedenborg,[7] whose

> correspondence is the passion of the soul for Order, the purified ambition, which no longer inverted and seeking only self-aggrandizement, contemplates a glorious hierarchy of all humanity, in which each, feeling his true place, and filling it, and felt in it, may in one act help to complete and

enjoy the universal accord, and thus, in the only conceivable manner, satisfy the craving of each single soul to embrace the Infinite at once.
[1:189]

This was obviously high praise indeed, and it should be noted that in every one of the numerous reviews that directly or indirectly had to do with Beethoven, Dwight was consistently enthusiastic in his praise of the German composer and musician.[8] This was certainly not the case, of course, with all the composers that Dwight treated in his column, as the reviews of the Italian musician Camillo Sivori illustrate very well.

Camillo Sivori (1815–94), who had been a student of the popular Italian virtuoso Nicolò Paganini, first performed in Boston in November 1846 after a series of successful concerts in different European capitals, as well as in New York City. Dwight attended all three of Sivori's Boston concerts, which prompted two consecutive reviews of the violinist, in the numbers for 14 and 21 November 1846. Dwight appended an apology to his first review for speaking "so tamely" of an artist "who has moved us as no other" (3:364). Apparently Dwight attended Sivori's second concert about the same time that his first article was going to press. The difference between the first and second reviews, however, was less one of enthusiasm than it was of qualification. Dwight was left after the first performance with a feeling of "unmingled satisfaction," for the Italian was clearly a skilled musician whose melodies were "graceful and full of sentiment," and whose tone was "of the utmost purity." One week later, Dwight would declare: "Sivori has clearly proved himself the greatest violinist who has visited this country" (3:380). Attending the second and third of Sivori's performances confirmed "beyond a doubt, that we were in the presence, not merely of a wonderful performer, but of a great Artist."

After these initial reviews, Dwight did not have the occasion to discuss Sivori again until almost a year later. At that time, the Italian was making an American tour with the so-called father of the modern virtuoso school of music, the Paris-trained Austrain pianist, Henri Herz. Dwight did a review for *The Harbinger* of their first two concerts together in Boston, which took place on 21 and 24 October 1847. The review appeared in the Associationist journal in the number for 30 October 1847. By this time, however, Dwight's enthusiasm for Camillo Sivori seems to have cooled somewhat, for beyond some obvious observations (the concerts were well attended, the audiences were spirited, the selections were engaging), he had very little to say about Sivori. The Bostonian noted once again that Paganini's pupil had played mostly works that had been originally composed by his master, and that they were, in fact, the same ones that Sivori had played the year before when he last performed in Boston. Nevertheless, Dwight was prepared to say— despite efforts by some New York critics to discredit the Italian's musical abilities (for unexplained reasons)—that Sivori "still commands all the admiration and sympathy which his masterly skill as a violinist, as well as his modest, musician-like deportment, excited on his former visit" (5:327).

Actually, these remarks on Camillo Sivori were to be John Dwight's last for the "Musical Review" column. With the close of the number for 30 October 1847, the fifth volume was completed, and *The Harbinger* was transferred to New York City. Dwight remained in Boston, where he continued to provide material for the Associationist journal until its demise in February 1849. In fact, his first contribution to the newly formed "Art Review" column was an article on "Herz, Sivori, and Knoop in Boston" (13 November 1847). The purpose of the review, however, was not to elaborate any remarks that the Bostonian had earlier made on Camillo Sivori. It was, instead, Dwight said, to record "our rare and heart-felt satisfaction at the return of [George] Knoop, the master violoncellist, perhaps the truest artist who has been among us."

Knoop had teamed up with Herz and Sivori in early November 1847, and the three musicians had begun performing a series of concerts in New York and Boston. Dwight did make a few brief remarks about Sivori in his review of 13 November 1847, but his original enthusiasm for the Italian had obviously waned considerably, so much so, in fact, that his relatively lengthy review of the second Boston concert of these three men—which took place on 10 November 1847, and which was reviewed in *The Harbinger* in the number for 27 November 1847—contained only a brief and superficial remark about the Italian musician.

Far more extensive than his handling of Camillo Sivori was Dwight's treatment of the Italian opera. These reviews, in fact, are among the most interesting that he wrote for the "Musical Review" column. For one thing, they contain some important critical assessments about such Italian composers as Gaetano Donizetti and Giuseppe Verdi. For another, they include valuable remarks about many of the leading operatic performers who were appearing at the time in Boston and New York. Finally, the reviews are punctuated with a very definite sense of excitement, for Dwight wrote most of them within a few days of having attended the performance under consideration. This excitement was probably due more, however, to the arrival in Boston of an Italian opera company, the first ever to visit that city. For all of its cultural advantages at the time, even Boston had not been able to boast of anything resembling a resident, professional Italian opera company. The arrival of one in April 1847 was therefore an important occasion. Dwight was understandably excited.

In the number for 17 April 1847, the Bostonian had written a piece for the "Musical Review" on "The Italian Opera in New York." In it, he noted that the troupe that had been performing in that city for the past several months had been organized in Italy by a Signor Sanquirico. He remarked that the company had, for the most part, "confined themselves within the monotonous range of the modern Italian opera" (4:294), concentrating, as they had, chiefly on the work of Donnizetti and Verdi. Dwight added that he had not yet himself had any opportunity to hear the music of Verdi, though he had recently heard in New York, he said, the very last part of *I Lombardi*. Based on such a fragmentary hearing of only one of his operas, Dwight stated that he was reluctant to express any of his impressions, since they had been so hastily formed. His most general impression, though, concerned Verdi's style, which was, he said in characteristically perceptive fashion, "altogether a new style for Italian music. . . . It is distinguished by full and bold harmony, by new and startling modulations, [and] by very elaborate orchestral accompaniments." Dwight said further that he thought that Verdi's attempt to infuse his music with strength and depth was commendable, given the weak and sentimental nature of so much of modern Italian opera. Still, he added, "We . . . cleave to [Giacchino Antonio] Rossini, so far as Italian opera goes; while we would not give one good German 'Don Juan,' or *'Der Freyschütz,'* or 'Fidelio,' for the whole of them" (4:295).[9] He then concluded his article by briefly praising the tenor of the opera, the soon-to-be-popular Signor Benedetti, and the prima donna, Signora Barili, and he said that he trusted that the modest success of this opera company would eventually lead to its being permanently established in New York, as well as in cities such as Boston.

Just two weeks after this column, Dwight excitedly announced in the "Musical Review" for 1 May 1847 that, while he and his fellow Bostonians had been vainly waiting to hear Signor Sanquirico's opera troupe, a second Italian opera company—this one originating in Havana, Cuba, and numbering seventy-three persons in all—had arrived in Boston, complete with their own orchestra, choruses, costumer, and scene painter. Dwight apologized for being able on the present occasion only to "notice" their opening performance—which took place at the Howard Athenaeum on 23 April 1847 before a full and enthusiastic house—though he nevertheless managed to provide an elaborate summary of Verdi's *Ernani,* a somewhat detailed critical analysis of the opera, and several remarks on the principal singers, among them, the prima donna, Signorina Fortunata Tedesco, and the tenor, Signor Natale Perilli. Dwight's "notice" ("The Italian Opera in Boston—Verdi's 'Ernani' ") actually ran to four and a half columns.

Thus began in May 1847 a series of reviews in *The Harbinger* on the Italian opera in Boston and New York that continued right up to the final numbers, for the opera quickly became an important part of the social and cultural life of those cities. That was due, in part, to the growth of new and successful opera companies, such as the Sequin Opera Company—which had been founded in 1838 by the English opera singers, Arthur and Ann Sequin—and Madame Bishop's Operatic Company—which had been established by the soprano, Anna Bishop (who had run away from her composer-conductor husband, Henry Rowley Bishop) and the celebrated harpist, Robert Nicolas Charles Bochsa.[10] No doubt, too, the development of new opera houses contributed significantly to the opera's growing popularity. Palmo's Opera House, for example, had been built in New York City in 1847, as had been the impressive Astor Place Opera House.

While these developments were occurring, Dwight was continuing to guide and direct the "Musical Review." His columns from May 1847 to November 1847 were filled with remarks about such matters as the Havana troupe and their performances of Verdi's *Ernani,* Pacini's *Saffo,* and Bellini's *Norma,* about musical affairs in New York, and about several of the leading singers in both of the major cities. For the number for 7 August 1847, Dwight turned his column over to George W. Curtis, who provided a piece on "The Italian Opera in New York," which was actually an essay on the relative strengths and weaknesses of the New York–based Palmo Company—as Signor Sanquirico's troupe was usually referred to since they performed in Palmo's Opera House—and the Havana company, which had, by the time of Curtis's article, become quite well established in Boston.

Dwight himself was in no real position to speak very authoritatively about the nature of the contribution of the Palmo troupe (though he did on several occasions attend the opera in New York), but he did not hesitate to praise what he took to be the very positive effect of the Havana company in his home city of Boston. For example, upon the completion of the first season, in June 1847, Dwight stated in the number for 19 June 1847 that the Hispano-Italian troupe "have taught Bostonians a new delight; they have given them a meaning to the familiar word opera; and they have been met with an enthusiasm which ensures another meeting, and to good opera evermore hereafter a true welcome and support" (5:27). Dwight added that he was especially impressed that his fellow Bostonians had showed such discriminating judgment by regularly appreciating Verdi and Pacini over the "weak sentimentality" of Donizetti and Bellini. The Havana troupe, Dwight would say a few months later, had taught a good many people in Boston that opera was "one of the indispensable good things of life" (5:267).

It was stated at the very beginning of this chapter that it seemed appropriate to conclude any extended discussion of *The Harbinger* by examining its musical criticism, for that was one of the journal's most distinguished features. It might likewise be said now that it is only appropriate to conclude any extended treatment of the musical criticism in *The Harbinger* by examining the handling of those musical matters that were natively American, for Associationists considered America to be the providential site for the comprehensive social-reform program that they advocated. Music, John Dwight had said in his introductory notice to the "Musical Review" that appeared in the very first number of *The Harbinger,* was "one of the outward accompaniments, expressions and instrumentalities of the greatest movement which ever yet engaged Humanity; of which this our America, the common gathering place of all nations, is destined to become the theatre" (1:13). The more that Americans learned to respect and appreciate music as an art form—the more that Americans learned themselves to create their own musical art—the sooner would the grand unitary movement of Associationism begin to be realized.

Thus Associationists were watching the development of musical affairs in America very closely. Dwight himself would complain in his introductory remarks that as yet in America there were no composers, no academies for musical training, and no great musical performances being given in our churches, but he would also state that he thought encouraging signs were everywhere to be found:

> Some excellent societies in our cities are learning the love of what is great and permanent, by their attempts to perform it; the number of appreciating listeners is sure to grow; singing-schools "for the million" are unlocking the outer musical sense for all, that, if they have a soul this channel to it need not be obstructed; the real virtuosos come from Europe to give us a touch of their quality, having in their turn discovered that Jonathan has learned-how to spend money for music; and finally, much excellent music is printed here, which our young ladies (and young men, too—they learn the piano), study in lieu of the "Battle of Prague," and other trash in which music masters dealt so long. [1:12]

Though Dwight did not specifically identify them here, the "excellent societies" to which he referred in this remark would undoubtedly have included the Handel and Haydn Society of Boston, the Harvard Musical Association, and the Boston Academy of Music, for in subsequent numbers of The Harbinger he would refer to them quite often.[11]

The Handel and Haydn Society, which was established in 1815, was certainly not the first choral or orchestral society to be founded in America, but it did have the distinction of being the oldest musical association in Boston.[12] More importantly, it had, John Dwight stated in the fourth volume of The Harbinger, "intrinsically the highest claims of any society in Boston to the public patronage" (4:252) because it dealt almost exclusively in the production of the great oratorios of such important composers as Handel and Haydn, as well as those of Felix Mendelssohn. This was an opinion that Dwight retained throughout The Harbinger years, for in one of the closing numbers of the Associationist journal he remarked that the society had "done more than anything else to introduce the knowledge of the great composers in New England" (8:30). Despite this obviously high regard for the Handel and Haydn Society, Dwight surprisingly never took the opportunity to devote a specific column to it. All of his remarks about the society were incorporated in his more general articles on "Music in Boston," a title that he used with some regularity whenever he wanted to discuss several musical matters.[13]

One probably would expect that the Harvard Musical Association would have received substantive treatment in the columns of one of its founders,

but Dwight provided extended remarks on the musical association that he
and several fellow Harvard graduates had established in 1837 only on four
occasions. Certainly the most noteworthy of these was an article titled "Mr.
Cranch's Address," which appeared in the second volume of *The Harbinger,*
in the number for 17 January 1846. This column actually was a reprinting
(though not entirely an accurate one) of Christopher Pearse Cranch's
"Address Delivered Before the Harvard Musical Association, August 28,
1845," which Dwight complained had been printed (at the request of the
association for its membership only) in too limited an edition, considering
that its "doctrines are so true, its spirit so exalted and so pure, its feeling of
music so profound and genuine" (2:88).

Cranch's *Address* is indeed an important document for what it reveals
about a Transcendental approach to an interpretation of the art of music,
but, for our present purposes, Dwight's own introductory remarks are even
more interesting. For one thing—for reasons that are not clear—he chose
not to identify himself as one of the founders of the Harvard Musical Association. It is possible, of course, that he simply did not consider the establishment of the association so very important, a possibility that would seem to
be supported by the casual manner in which he recollected the occasion:
"The Harvard Musical Association," he said, "was formed some five or six
years since, by those graduates of Harvard College who had musical remem-
brances of their *Alma Mater* and of one another."

On the other hand, all of Dwight's remarks about the association indicate
that he thought it was providing an invaluable opportunity for Bostonians to
hear the "choicest" quartettes of Beethoven, Mozart, and Haydn. In an
earlier review about the 1844–45 season, for example, he stated that the
series of eight chamber concerts that had been given by the association had
marked a "real progress in musical taste. For the first time in our city, a truly
musical and constant audience [which numbered, by the way, approximately
150 persons] assembled to enjoy music of that form which may be called the
quintessence of music" (1:123).

Dwight made virtually the same point in the third and fourth volumes of
The Harbinger in, respectively, "Chamber Concerts of the Harvard Musical
Association" (3:394–95) and "The Harvard Musical Association" (4:124),
just as he had done in the second volume in his remarks preceding the
reprinting of Cranch's *Address*. It was only in the Cranch column, however,
that Dwight took time to recall what he conceived to be the objects of the
Harvard Musical Association. There were three:

> Its objects were, first, to enjoy a musical reunion among the other
> festivities of the annual commencement; secondly, to accumulate a fund,
> to be applied some future day to a musical professorship in the college,
> and thereby procure an academic sanction to the indispensableness of this
> beautiful art as a branch of any liberal education; and thirdly, and gener-
> ally, to elevate the taste for music in our land, by making it an avowed and

corporate interest of men of intelligence and education, by attaching respectability to the musical profession, equal to that enjoyed by any literary profession, by collecting libraries, establishing schools, concerts,
critical reviews, &c. [2:88]

The nature of the musical experience provided by the orchestra of the
Boston Academy of Music was obviously dramatically different from that
afforded by the quartette of the Harvard Musical Association, but since, like
the association, the academy often featured the grand symphonies of such
masters as Beethoven and Haydn, the classically-minded John Dwight was
bound to be enthusiastic over those performances. At least he was enthusiastic about them during the 1844–45 season when the Boston Academy
of Music had performed several of Beethoven's symphonies, among them
the First, Second, Fifth (in C Minor), Seventh, and Eighth. He stated that
such a program represented a "bold undertaking" for a New England city in
the respect that most people would have presumed an American orchestra
incapable of successfully performing the music of a composer who was
"many years in advance of our [American] musical culture" (1:154). The
academy was to be applauded, Dwight said, for running such a risk of failure
and criticism, the positive results of which, however, had been several: the
Boston audience had been introduced to a true sense of the grandeur of
Beethoven; the public's taste and appreciation of good music had been
elevated; and a real enthusiasm for the most important of classical composers had been generated.

Dwight's treatment of the Boston Academy of Music, however, was not
always so encouraging. It would not be wrong to observe that his critical
assessments of the academy were sometimes shaped by the nature of the
particular program that was being produced, although, in most cases, it
would be more precise to say that Dwight usually just spoke forthrightly and
honestly. He thought, for example, that the academy's handling of the
Seventh Symphony during the 1846–47 season (on 6 February 1847, to be
exact) was "the best performance of a Beethoven Symphony to which we
have ever listened in Boston" (4:186). Just a month earlier, he had criticized
that same orchestra for its handling of selections from Gaetano Donizetti,
especially his *Zanetta:* "We think we never heard it played so badly; it was
one blur from the beginning to end" (4:76).

Interestingly enough, however, it was not to be Dwight but William W.
Story who supplied the "Musical Review" with the most specific criticism of
the Boston Academy.[14] As the 1845–46 season drew to a close, Story, in
March 1846, contributed a piece on the "Sixth Concert of the Boston
Academy," which began by charging the academy orchestra with performing
concerts that not only were tame, but that catered merely to fashionable
taste as well. He elaborated the charge in a passage that provides an interesting historical overview of the Boston Academy of Music:

The directors of the Academy began with the design of elevating the standard of musical taste, by the performance of classical pieces in a thorough manner, and although their concerts were but ill-attended at first, they soon got a hold upon the people, and nourished a better taste, and finally became fashionable. But no sooner were they fashionable, than they ducked to fashion; their popularity became their bane; their original object was lost sight of, and the whole view of directors seems to have been to make pleasing and popular concerts, which in their opinion could only be done by pandering to a medium and uneducated taste. From Mozart and Haydn and Spohr they fell down to Auber, and then slipped a stage lower in wearisome solos by second rate performers, dropping finally so low as school-boy and school-girl chorusses, which were roared as soft as if they were cooing dove-songs. Beethoven was always kept as the lion of the occasion, and was brought out in the second part as a sop to the appetites of those, who were bored to death by the first slap of the performance. [2:204]

Apparently, the directors of the Boston Academy were not impressed by Story's remarks, for Dwight himself had occasion to note—in "The Prospects for the Season," which appeared in the 17 October 1846 number of *The Harbinger*—that he had heard that Story's well-intentioned criticisms had been taken quite too seriously by the Academy. Dwight said that he included the criticisms in his column because "we thought true criticism, given in good faith, to be a work of real friendship," and he added that no antagonism had been intended for the Academy, "whose labors we have always recommended and encouraged, and whose downfall we should regard as a most irreparable loss to the musical treasures of Boston" (3:301).

The founder of the Boston Academy of Music had been none other than Lowell Mason (1792–1872), the unexcelled musical entrepreneur of the nineteenth century who was the first American to preach the doctrine of music for the masses. His influence continues to be felt today, of course, in those schools throughout the United States where students receive singing instruction at public expense. Indeed, such education was the *raison d'être* behind the founding of the Boston Academy of Music in 1832, the establishment of which, it would appear, could not have been more timely. In the very first year of operation, Mason enrolled approximately 1,500 students who, in return for free music lessons, promised to attend the music sessions that would be conducted by Mason and his assistants, George J. Webb and Samuel A. Eliot. Mason quickly realized, however, that in order to disseminate his ideas fully, he needed trained teachers who could carry his methods to classrooms and churches throughout New England. Thus in 1834, he conducted the first of what would become annual teachers' conventions for this purpose. These were so successful that by 1838, according to one musical historian, there were already 134 people (representing ten states) attending the several-day convention at the Boston Academy of Music, and by 1849 attendance had grown to 1,000 people.[15]

John Dwight estimated that there were between 300 and 400 teachers of singing, leaders of choirs, and choristers in attendance when he reviewed the Teachers' Convention for 1845 for the 20 September 1845 number of *The Harbinger,* his first notice of the popular movement started by Lowell Mason.[16] His last notice—"Boston Academy of Music. Teachers' Institute for 1848," which appeared in the seventh volume in the number for 26 August 1848—stated that no fewer than 700 persons participated in a concert that was the climax of the 1848 festival. In addition to these observations, Dwight also provided on these two occasions considerably more substantive remarks on Mason and the "singing schools for the million," though in neither instance did he summarize his critical assessments as well as he did in an article on "Teachers' Conventions in Boston" (5:203–5), which appeared in the 4 September 1847 number of *The Harbinger.*

In this review, the Bostonian stated that Mason and his annual teachers' convention already had produced three good effects. First was the "influence upon those engaged in it." Only good, Dwight said, could result from having persons—"of but ordinary culture and but little leisure"—engaged in singing the choruses of such composers as Handel and Mendelssohn. Acquainting Americans with the music of the great masters was nothing less than an introduction to the "most exalted, most refined productions of the most refining of all acts." A second important result was the "influence upon musical taste and practice throughout the country." Dwight said that it pleased him to know that at the end of every musical convention, hundreds of participants would "go back to give the same tone to their respective circles and communities. The [musical] standard is thus rising throughout all the land." Finally, the third good effect, Dwight stated, was "a tendency to some organic unity in the multifarious musical aspirations of this [the American] people." The conventions conducted by Lowell Mason at first attracted only teachers, but it did not take long before some of Boston's leading choirs began to attend as well. These, in turn, were followed by many talented musicians, including even several accomplished virtuosos. Such cooperative effort and universal harmony of musical interests could someday possibly produce a great musical festival in American such as those in London, Birmingham, and in parts of Germany. Whether it ever would or not, Dwight said, one thing was certain: "Not until the interests of musical people can be reconciled in one, shall we hear great music." Mason and his schools were a promising sign that such a reconciliation might, in fact, someday occur.

For Dwight, there would be many more opportunities in subsequent years to examine in the columns of *Dwight's Journal of Music* such promising signs as this. The Bostonian would be forced to write his last music review for *The Harbinger,* however, in the number for 3 February 1849, which was just one week before the journal's demise. It goes without saying, of course, that the years during which *The Harbinger* was published may not have been many, but they certanly were exciting and eventful ones. This was especially the case in the musical world. New York and Boston, as we have seen, each were discovering the nature of their developing musical identity. A brand-new school of musical virtuosos was sweeping through Europe and the United States, dazzling enthusiastic audiences with their musical abilities. Americans were being introduced for the first time to the enjoyment of opera by rival Italian opera companies that were attempting to establish themselves in cities such as New York and Boston. Americans generally not only were being introduced to the great oratorios and symphonies of the important European composers, but they were being taught these compositions—not to mention natively American ones—as well.

The point, of course—and it is an important one to make by way of conclusion—is that these and other musical matters did not go unnoticed by John Dwight and *The Harbinger*. On the contrary, it is fair to say that the "Musical Review" remains our most detailed record of musical affairs in America between mid-1845 and early 1848. And what an impressive record it is. John Dwight may have had his personal preferences (which is certainly very much in keeping with the so-called American critical tradition) but they rarely if ever prevented him from writing criticism that was judicious, discriminating, careful, and precise. It is not necessary to read many of Dwight's reviews to realize that the Bostonian obviously loved music, just as he obviously loved writing about it. The reviews are almost never labored or forced. Instead, they are lively throughout, and they are always informative.

This is all the more remarkable when one remembers that Dwight was writing musical criticism for *The Harbinger* in something of a critical vacuum. There was at the time, after all, no critical tradition for music in America. No doubt this was due, in part, to the fact that few Americans in the first half of the nineteenth century had the background or experience to write informed musical criticism. In any event, what needs to be said is that Dwight went a very long way in helping to establish sound critical standards for musical criticism, standards that are still to be admired because they were, above all, serious and high-minded.

Thus, when all is said and done, it is not enough merely to say how fortunate it is that we have *The Harbinger* and such a full and informative record of musical activities in America in the mid-1840s. That record is unquestionably important, and it will undoubtedly benefit cultural historians for many years to come. Behind the record, however, is the man, and in this case the man was someone who—by the breadth of his knowledge, by his penetrating criticism, and by his candor and honesty—represented a serious challenge to Americans: recognize music as a vital art form, or there will never be a true cultural life in America.

Conclusion

It is interesting to note that, in his study of *The Periodicals of American Transcendentalism,* Clarence Gohdes decided not to devote separate chapters to his treatment of *The Western Messenger* (1835–41) and the *Dial* (1840–44). Instead, both of these important Transcendental journals are handled together in the opening chapter because, the authors says, there is such a "marked likeness in the contents of *The Western Messenger* and *The Dial*" in terms of their "origin, purpose, and lists of contributors." In addition, *"The Dial,"* it is stated, "was founded in 1840 because of the intense passion for self-expression which moved a select group of New England individualists. *The Western Messenger* had been founded a few years earlier for a somewhat similar reason; and [subsequently] . . . had been conducted on the very same principles as *The Dial*."[1]

The Harbinger is also treated in *The Periodicals of American Transcendentalism,* but it is discussed by itself in the middle of the book. No mention whatever is made of it in the opening chapter, and Professor Gohdes is quite right, of course, not to discuss the Associationist journal along with *The Western Messenger* or the *Dial,* even though *The Harbinger* would appear, in many important respects, to be quite similar to them. For example, one of the points made about *The Western Messenger* and the *Dial* is that both magazines shared the talents of an extraordinary group of contributors. There were Emerson, Margaret Fuller, George Ripley, William Henry Channing, James Freeman Clarke, John S. Dwight, and Frederic Henry Hedge. Many of these names sound familiar, no doubt, because—with the exceptions of Emerson and Fuller—all of them wrote for *The Harbinger.* Indeed, eleven of *The Harbinger*'s contributors, it was noted much earlier in this study, had written for the *Dial.*

Another point of similarity between *The Western Messenger* and the *Dial* is what might be called the exceptional literary merit of the two journals. In addition to the original publication of many poems and sonnets by such figures as, for example, Emerson, Henry Thoreau, and Jones Very, both periodicals published penetrating literary reviews on important figures ranging from Wordsworth to Harriet Martineau. In short, Gohdes has observed, *The Western Messenger* and the *Dial* made important contributions in the world of literary affairs.

A similar point, however, could certainly be made about *The Harbinger*, and, in fact, it already has been. There is no question that original verse was hardly one of *The Harbinger*'s strong suits, so to speak, but there is equally no argument that its musical criticism is the most noteworthy of the time. And while it is true that the Associationist magazine did not—as did both *The Western Messenger* and the *Dial*—undertake the job of translating German literature in order to introduce it to the American public, it did not do so because it was introducing that audience to French writers such as George Sand and Eugène Sue. In short, in matters aesthetic, *The Harbinger* would have to get marks as high as, if not higher than, any of the periodicals associated with New England Transcendentalism.

It goes without saying that *The Harbinger* too was founded by a select group of New England individualists who, like their fellow Transcendentalists who had conducted *The Western Messenger* and the *Dial,* were driven by an "intense passion for self-expression." This fact is so self-evident by now that it certainly needs no further development here, other than to repeat the obvious point that it was, of course, the nature of the passion itself that accounted for *The Harbinger*'s acquiring a character that was—when all is said and done—fundamentally different from that of *The Western Messenger* or the *Dial*. It would be a mistake, however, to presume—as it would certainly seem Emerson did—that that character was one "desperately sectarian" in nature. Despite the magazine's obvious attachment to Associationist doctrines, the spirit with which it was conducted was clearly anything but sectarian. *The Harbinger* may have been the official organ of Associationism in America, but it was no less a magazine representative of the liberal, progressive, and nonpartisan spirit that has always been the basis of the democratic principle in the United States.

Ironically, it was *The Harbinger*'s so-called sectarianism that resulted in its having such catholicity of interests. Since Associationism claimed to embrace all reform movements of the time, very few matters failed to arouse the interest of *The Harbinger*. We need only recall the magazine's detailed and careful reviews of books and journals, and its vigorous and bold remarks on political, social, and economic matters for evidence of this fact. Certainly it was no mere sectarian magazine that devoted such considerable attention to abolitionism, feminism, and the Mexican War. The men who conducted *The Harbinger* may have been committed to a visionary and utopian scheme, but the men themselves were not simply visionary dreamers and utopian idlers. *The Harbinger*'s record is a reflection of this fact. The American Union of Associationists, an organization that gave definition and direction to thousands of people who were theretofore united only by common sympathies, would likely neither have been created nor have thrived were it not for *The Harbinger*'s proddings and its organizational efforts. Similarly, the establishment of the Woman's Associative Union was the direct result of a small but determined editorial campaign conducted by the magazine for the purpose of enlisting the aid of women in the Associationist cause. *The Harbinger,* of course, was one of the earliest and most outspoken advocates of women's rights, and the Woman's Associative Union may be regarded as one of the first steps in the long developing radicalization of American women. Finally, the founding in 1845 of the Workingmen's Protective Union, and particularly its growth and development in the three years that followed, was influenced in no small way by the magazine's frequent essays on the necessity of united action among the laboring classes.

In many respects, then, *The Harbinger* not only was but continues to be an extraordinary magazine. If for some reason today we do not appreciate the quality of its musical criticism, if we do not admire the magazine's courage in being the first in America to publish the English translations of the allegedly immoral George Sand, then at least we should be struck by the frightening prophetic quality of many of its statements (as when, for example, it remarked: "and if both [the United States and Russia] could have full sweep, each on its own side of the ocean, . . . the civilized world would present the spectacle of two great military despotisms, armed to the teeth, and frowning on each other over the Atlantic" [5:301]). More than anything else, however, *The Harbinger* elicits from this writer a sense of affirmation, for the magazine stands as a record of a people's faith and courage in a social experiment, one, obviously, which failed, but one which failed with a sense of dignity all the same because of the manner with which the journal was conducted. *The Harbinger* never lost faith that democracy in its truest form could one day be made reality. Despite ever-present financial difficulties, a disruptive transfer from its original place of publication, a change in editorial staff, and frequent attacks from usually uninformed and prejudicial detractors, the magazine never suffered a spirit of defeatism; it never lost faith in itself nor in its plan of Association as the key to a better world. At a time when America was a good seedbed for nay-saying, when Hawthorne was saying "No! in thunder" to the society around him and Melville was remarking that all men who said yes were liars,[2] *The Harbinger* emerges as one of the supreme statements in American history of the everlasting yes. For these reasons, then, the magazine has marked a niche for itself in the annals of the American people. But perhaps even more important is the fact that *The Harbinger* stands as a continuing reminder—and an especially timely one today—of the need to keep alive the spirit of liberalism that has always been such a vital part of the American democratic tradition.

Notes

Introduction

1. This point is dramatically illustrated in Joel Myerson, *Brook Farm: An Annotated Bibliography and Resources Guide* (New York: Garland Publishing, Inc. 1978). Myerson lists 343 items that have to do with the Brook Farm community, only eighteen of which, however, deal directly with *The Harbinger*.

2. To date, the most complete and authoritative treatment of the *Dial* is Joel Myerson, *The New England Transcendentalists and the Dial* (Rutherford, N.J.: Fairleigh Dickinson University Press, 1980).

3. Quoted by George Willis Cooke, *John Sullivan Dwight: Brook-Farmer, Editor, and Critic of Music* (Boston: Small, Maynard and Company, 1898), pp. 103–4.

Chapter 1

1. The point was rather dramatically made in the pages of *The Harbinger* in two editorials that appeared, respectively, in the numbers for 14 and 21 March 1846. In "Fire at Brook Farm," Ripley painfully announced the burning down on 3 March 1846 of the long-awaited Phalanstery, which had been under construction since the summer of 1844. Ripley acknowledged that the loss represented "a severe trial of our strength. We cannot now calculate its ultimate effect. It may prove more than we are able to bear." He quickly added, however, that "the destruction of our edifice makes no essential change in our pursuits" and that "whatever be our trials of an external character, we have every reason to rejoice in the internal condition of our Association."

The occasion of the second column was a letter from one of the many supporters of the Associationist cause who had learned of the loss of the Phalanstery. The letter was an appeal to all Associationists to support the Brook Farm community in its time of urgent need. The correspondent noted: "Upon the firm establishment of the Brook Farm Phalanx, depends in no small degree, the advance of our whole Cause." He went on to state: "As Associationists we have a common interest in your Phalanx; we look upon the experiment you are making not only as decisive of *your* ability to realize our doctrines, but as a test of their universal practicability:—you are laboring for *us* as well as for yourselves—for Humanity as well as for us, and we cannot be true to our principles, unless in this, the hour of need and of trial we are faithful to you."

Here, obviously, was a perfectly opportune moment for Ripley to assert Brook Farm's vital and essential role and importance in the American Associative movement, which would thereby have enabled him to appeal vigorously for funds to offset some of the $7,000 loss incurred by the fire. Instead of doing so, however, he prefaced the correspondent's conviction that "it is now time to make the appeal," by stating that he did not altogether agree with the writer "in the importance which he attaches to the special movement at Brook Farm. . . . We have never attempted any thing more than to prepare the way for Association, by demonstrating some of the leading ideas on which the theory is founded. . . ; we have always regarded ourselves only as the humble pioneers in a work, which would be carried on by others to its magnificient consummation."

2. Henry L. Golemba, *George Ripley* (Boston: Twayne, 1977), p. 94.

3. A Fourierist Phalanx was a utopian community based on the ideas of François Charles Marie Fourier (1772–1837), a French reformer, economist, and social scientist, who outlined his ideas in several works, of which *Le Nouveau Monde Industriel* (1829–30) contains the fullest exposition. Fourier envisioned a society in which individuals would conduct their economic activities in phalanxes, groups consisting of 1,600 persons living in common buildings called "phalansteries" and subdivided into series and groups that worked cooperatively under elective heads. Despite the socialistic nature of Fourier's ideas, he did not advocate the community of property or abolition of the family. Brook Farm had neither the funds nor an adequate number of people to carry out Fourier's ideas.

4. These are Fourier's terms. *The Harbinger,* in a lengthy article entitled "Objections to Association" (3:283–87), explained the difference between a Group and a Series. But Albert Brisbane, probably the first American to preach the gospel of Associationism and Fourierism, explained it more succinctly in *Concise Exposition of the Doctrine of Association* (New York: J. S. Redfield, 1844), p. 44.

> A Group is a body of persons united from a taste for any occupation, whether of Industry, Art or Science, and who combine for the purpose of prosecuting it. . . . A full Group should be composed of at least seven persons, and form three divisions or three sub-goups, the center one of which should be stronger than the two wings or extremes. . . .
> A Series is distributed in the same manner as a Group: the Series are composed of a number of Groups, as Groups are composed of individuals and operate upon Groups as Groups upon individuals. A series must contain at least three Groups—a center and two wings: twenty-four persons is the least number with which a Series can be formed. . . .
> Suppose in an Association three varieties of some species of a peach or pear are cultivated; a Group would be occupied with each variety, and the three Groups united would form a Series of Peach or Pear Growers.

5. *Constitution of the Brook Farm Phalanx, Adopted May 1, 1845* (Boston, 1845).

6. Amelia Russell, "Home Life of the Brook Farm Association," *Atlantic Monthly* 42 (October 1878): 458–66.

7. Charles Crowe, "Fourierism and the Founding of Brook Farm," *Boston Public Library Quarterly* 12 (April 1960): 84.

8. Arthur E. Bestor, "Brook Farm 1841–1847. An Exhibition to Commemorate the Centenary of Its Founding," mimeographed (New York: Columbia University Libraries, 1941).

9. Clarence Gohdes, "A Brook Farm Labor Record," *American Literature* 1 (November 1929): 297.

10. John Humphrey Noyes, *History of American Socialisms* (Philadelphia: Lippincott, 1870), pp. 15–18.

11. Charles Crowe, *George Ripley: Transcendentalist and Utopian Socialist* (Athens, Ga.: University of Georgia Press, 1967), p. 180.

12. Marianne Dwight, *Letters from Brook Farm 1844–47,* ed. Amy L. Reed (Poughkeepsie, N.Y.: Vassar College, 1928), p. 52.

13. Ripley expressed this belief in articles for the 21 and 28 March 1846 numbers of *The Harbinger.* It should be noted, however, that just one month later, in a letter dated 18 April 1846, Ripley wrote the following to James T. Fisher, the recording secretary for the American Union of Associationists: "I have never thought that we had here the materials to do anything like justice to the sublime Associative idea; and on that account have often regretted that we have been placed so prominently in the movement." Ripley may have been perfectly serious, but we should nevertheless remember that he made this remark just a few weeks after the nearly completed Phalanstery had burned down. Ripley's letter to Fisher is part of the James T. Fisher Papers of the Massachusetts Historical Society.

14. Parenthetical references throughout the book are to volume and page number of *The Harbinger*.

15. It would appear that Associationists were never completely successful ridding themselves of this charge, for one of the most elaborate debates ever conducted in the pages of *The Harbinger* concerned Fourier's ideas about sexual relations between men and women in the Phalanstery. It occurred in volume 8, the last volume of the journal. The "discussion" involved a Rev. Alfred E. Ford, a "New-Churchman," and Henry James, Sr., who represented the Associationists. See "Love in the Phalanstery," 8: 12, 36; "The Marriage Question," 8: 99, 109; and "Remarks," 8: 13, 36, 44, 53, 60, 68, 77, 107, and 116. The reader might also wish to consult Raymond Lee Muncy, *Sex and Marriage in Utopian Communities* (Bloomington, Ind.: Indiana University Press, 1973), pp. 64–78.

16. The term *passions* is one that had a special meaning in the Fourierist lexicon. According to Victor Considerant, the leader of the French Associative School (Ripley provided the translations for *The Harbinger*), by the word *passion* "Fourier understands exclusively *the constituent tendencies of Beings, or the springs of action inherent in* their very nature" (4: 351). (Italics are Considerant's or Ripley's.) Each individual has five sensitive passions, which have as their object "Elegance, Riches and Material Harmonies"; four affective passions—paternity, love, friendship, and ambition; and three "Distributive and Directing Passions," the "Emulative," "Alternating," and "Composite."

17. It is interesting to remember that Fourier and Greeley were also the objects of some caustic remarks by the frequently acidulous Edgar Poe. Poe had written in "Fifty Suggestions" (*Graham's Magazine,* 1845) that the "High Priest in the East" of a "new sect of philosophers is Charles Fourier—in the West, Horace Greeley," and that the "only common bond among them is Credulity:—let us call it Insanity at once, and be done with it."

18. The climax of this ideological controversy was a formal debate between Greeley and the New York *Courier and Enquirer*. The debate was conducted in the New York *Tribune* and the *Courier and Enquirer*, and it consisted of twelve articles on the subject of Associationism that were published in full in both papers. See 4: 14.

19. The complete "Constitution of the American Union of Associationists"—with resolutions—may be found in Appendix A.

20. See 5: 28, 43, 58, and 73.

21. See 6: 84; 8: 92.

22. See 1: 189; 2: 44; 3: 143; 4: 14; 5: 31, 161, and 287.

23. See 3: 155 and 221; 6: 124; 7: 196.

24. It should be noted that, despite *The Harbinger*'s ideological orientation, it was nevertheless highly regarded by many of its journalistic competitors. For example, *Hunt's Merchants' Magazine* (New York) thought that the paper was "one of the most ably conducted and most readable weekly journals that comes to our office." The Boston *Atlas* stated, that while it could not "sympathize with the tenets of its conductors," it could not "but admire the kind and catholic spirit of brotherly love with which this journal is, for the most part, conducted." The *National Era* (Washington, D.C.) observed that *The Harbinger* was "an able periodical, liberal in tone, courteous in the style of its discussions, and comprehensive in its views." *Nineteenth Century* magazine (Philadelphia) remarked that the paper was "distinguished by its critical character, its elevated and serious tone, and its deep faith in the future perfection of the race." The Chicago *Daily Tribune* said that it spoke with confidence when it stated that "there is not a single newspaper in the Union which maintains so high a standard of literary taste." And the Cincinnati *Herald* said that "there is no periodical which we read with more pleasure or profit, and none to which we recommend the subscription of our readers with more satisfaction than the Harbinger." For the complete remarks from these and other journals, see 6: 104.

25. A good example of this ambiguity and confusion is illustrated by the word *passion*, a word that did not mean the same thing in the language of the Associationist School as it did in the language of everyday speech. *The Harbinger* noted that *passion* was a confusing word, vague in meaning, whose definition depended on the context in which it was used. The word

often connoted violence, for example, but just as often it suggested such sentiments as hope, joy, sadness, and even love.

In the Fourieristic sense, however, passion caused an individual to direct all his activity toward the accomplishment of good. Passions were "the springs of action inherent in [man's] very nature, . . . the primitive and natural forces which [produced] the free and spontaneous activity of the Human Being" (4:351). See also n. 14 above.

26. *Studies in the American Renaissance 1977*, ed, Joel Myerson (Boston: Twayne Publishers, 1978), p. 1.

27. Clarence Gohdes, *"The Present," The Periodicals of American Transcendentalism* (Durham, N.C.: Duke University Press, 1931), pp. 83–101.

28. *The Present* 1 (September 1843): 1–2.

29. See *The Present* 1 : 19, 52, 65, 129, 317, and 361, for example.

30. Octavius Brooks Frothingham, *Memoir of William Henry Channing* (Boston: Houghton Mifflin Company, 1886), pp. 7, 94.

31. Channing's *Memoir of William Ellery Channing* was published in 1848.

32. Cited in Gohdes, *Periodicals*, p. 87.

33. Donald Drew Egbert and Stow Persons, eds., *Socialism and American Life*, 2 vols. (Princeton, N.J.: Princeton University Press, 1952), 2 : 134.

34. Ibid., 1 : 175.

35. Ibid.

36. *The Present* 1 (October 1843): 70.

37. *The Phalanx* 1 (28 May 1845): 354–55.

38. Marianne Dwight, *Letters*, pp. 136–37.

39. There are several letters in the Dwight Brook Farm Papers of the Boston Public Library that are relevant in this context, especially the following: letter from Georgianna Bruce to Dwight, dated 18 January 1846; letter from James Kay, Jr., dated 2 March 1846; letter from John Orvis, dated 9 December 1846. The letters by Kay and Orvis may be found in Zoltan Haraszti's *The Idyll of Brook Farm* (Boston: Trustees of the Public Library, 1937), pp. 37–38 and pp. 45–46 respectively.

40. Cited in John Thomas Codman, *Brook Farm: Historic and Personal Memoirs* (Boston: Arena, 1894), pp. 144–46.

41. George Willis Cooke, ed., *Early Letters of George Wm. Curtis to John S. Dwight* (New York: Harpers, 1898), p. 234. This letter was dated 22 December 1845.

42. Judging from the correspondence of Ripley and Dwight, there seems to have been no great love between these two and Godwin. For example, shortly after *The Harbinger*'s transfer to New York, Ripley complained to Dwight, in a letter dated 7 and 8 December 1847, about certain difficulties in that city: no material had been received from W. H. Channing; Dana felt confined by the secular department of the paper; and Ripley himself was bogged down with details. Godwin, Ripley said, was "fruitful, genial, and altogether in earnest, but is not altogether inexhaustible; and without a stronger infusion of the Boston element, we cannot do justice to our ideal." Seven months later, in a letter dated 14 July 1848, Ripley informed Dwight that Godwin had just had a son, who, Ripley remarked, "I hope will not turn out . . . like its father." On 18 October 1848, with *The Harbinger* on the verge of collapse, Ripley told Dwight that Godwin "has never shown any vital paramount interest in it [*The Harbinger*] and does not love it well enough to write for it without a consideration."

After the magazine's demise, the New York Associationists considered the possibility of publishing a new journal. Apparently they had asked Ripley for his support, for he informed Dwight on 26 March 1849 that he could not work on any publication with Godwin, a man who was "too much of a Caliban or Cannibal, to make cooperation with him pleasant. Indeed, I don't see . . . how anyone can work under him, or over him, or with him, without extreme annoyance; and for himself he decidedly prefers to write or fight (which with him is pretty much the same thing) on his own." These letters from Ripley to Dwight are in the George Ripley Collection of the Boston Public Library.

Dwight, too, seems to have had his troubles with Godwin. Just three months before *The Harbinger*'s demise, Godwin wrote to Dwight on 8 December 1848, complaining that the latter had neglected his responsibilities as Boston editor. Godwin criticized Dwight for not restricting himself to his particular journalistic assignments: "I do not like to spend several hours," Godwin said, "in thinking out and writing on a subject," only to find out the following day that it was done by someone else. Moreover, Godwin added, "this morning again we receive from you[Dwight] a batch of News, most of which was ready for the paper two days ago." This letter is in the Dwight Brook Farm Papers of the Boston Public Library.

43. Letter from Ripley to Dwight, dated 22 November 1847, in the Ripley Collection of the Boston Public Library.

44. Letter from Ripley to Dwight, dated 18 October 1848, in the Ripley Collection of the Boston Public Library.

45. Ibid.

46. This announcement, "To the Associationsts of the United States," may be found in the James T. Fisher Papers of the Massachusetts Historical Society.

47. The following is representative of the type of item found in this column: "Salting the Sea: Barque George Henry, of Boston, from St. Martins for New York, was recently overtaken by a hurricane and compelled to throw overboard 100 tons of salt in order to ride out the storm" (8:23).

48. Next to Fourier, no other individual had such a direct effect on the magazine's ideology. Whereas Fourier was regarded as the authority on all matters pertaining to the material world, Swedenborg was considered the best interpreter of the spiritual world. Undoubtedly *The Harbinger*'s interest in Swedenborg was reinforced more than a little by its association with Henry James, Sr., himself the most articulate American proponent of Swedenborgianism at this time. For more on Swedenborg, see the chapter on "Literary Criticism in *The Harbinger*," pp. 91–96.

49. Since *The Harbinger* collapsed before the completion of the eighth volume, it was never indexed. However, for a complete list of all titles and authors of material that appeared originally (i.e., was not reprinted) in volumes 1–7, see Appendix B, "Checklist of Original Contributions to *The Harbinger*."

50. Place of residence is not repeated unless there was a change of address.

51. A review of Calvert's poetry reveals that he often used the initials "E. Y. T." to sign his verse. See *The Harbinger* 5:25.

52. Gohdes, *Periodicals*, p. 111.

53. George Joyaux, "George Sand, Eugène Sue and *The Harbinger*," *The French Review* 27 (December, 1953): 124.

54. Zoltan Haraszti, *The Idyll of Brook Farm* (Boston, 1937), p. 30.

Chapter 2

1. Nicholas V. Risanovsky, *The Teaching of Charles Fourier* (Berkeley and Los Angeles: University of California Press, 1969), p. 32.

2. That *The Harbinger* did not chronicle events at its own place of origin, the Brook Farm Phalanx—which was unquestionably one of the most important experiments in Associationist living in America—has been considered by some to have been one of the more serious weaknesses of the magazine. See, for example, John Thomas Codman, *Brook Farm; Historic and Personal Memoirs* (Boston, 1894), p. 264, and *The Harbinger* 1:192. In addition to several brief references to Brook Farm (1:47, 176, and 192; 2:94 and 174; 5:317), the magazine published only four articles that included substantial remarks about the West Roxbury, Massachusetts, community: "Fire at Brook Farm" (2:220); "To Our Friends" (2:237); "Correspondence" (2:299); and "How Stands the Cause?" (3:348). The reason for this may be explained simply by

the fact that the editors of the magazine considered the paper the organ of Associationists throughout the United States rather than the mouthpiece of Brook Farm (1:47). The editors took the stand that Brook Farm was a center of influence in the Associationist movement, but that it was not *the* center of that movement: "We have never attempted any thing more than to prepare the way for Association . . . [and] we have always regarded ourselves [at Brook Farm] only as the humble pioneers in a work, which would be carried on by others to its magnificent consumation" (2:237).

3. The two principal groups of socialists vying for power in the French Revolution of 1848 were the Fourierists (i.e., Associationists) and the communists. Though the ideological base of these two groups was similar—each accepted the principle of mutual cooperation for the interest of all—their objects and methods were considerably different. Specifically, the communists advocated the establishment of a society in which the profits resulting from an individual's labor would be turned over to the state. The state, then, would distribute those profits as it saw fit, without any special regard for the individual who helped secure them. According to *The Harbinger,* the communist system failed to recognize individual abilities, it reduced ambition to indifference, and it discouraged talent. Thus the magazine minded being tarred with communism, however indirectly, because its very *raison d'être,* and indeed that of Associationism, was based on the belief that the rewards of an individual's labor were directly proportionate to the amount of capital, skill, or labor an individual had invested in securing those rewards. See 5:93; and 7:12, 13, and 26.

Chapter 3

1. For a discussion of these various movements, see Alice Felt Tyler, *Freedom's Ferment: Phases of American Social History to 1860* (Minneapolis, Minn.: University of Minnesota, 1944), parts 2 and 3. This chapter deals directly only with those matters which were of major importance to *The Harbinger,* as determined by the attention they received in the pages of the magazine. Those matters not discussed in this chapter, but which received at least some attention in *The Harbinger,* are the following: the anti-rent movement ("Young America—Anti-Rentism," 1:174; untitled remarks, 1:352; "The Anti-Rent Question," 5:105; and Charles Dana's remarks in review of James Fenimore Cooper's *Satanstoe,* 1:122, *The Chainbearer,* 1:411–12, and *The Redskins,* 3:123, a trilogy concerned with the anti-rent wars in New York in the 1840s); rehabilitation of convicted criminals ("Reform of Criminals," 1:60); educational reform ("Education," 2:62; 3:110); the free-soil movement ("Reform Movements Originating Among the Producing Classes," 2:110; "Homestead Exemptions," 5:55; "Homestead," 5:107; "National Reform," 5:274); the California Gold Rush ("The Golden Age," 8:52); housing reform ("The Tenant's League," 6:148; "The Tenant Movement," 6:156); the Irish famine ("The Famine in Ireland," 4:301; "The Irish Trouble," 7:124; "Potatoes from Ireland," 8:36); moral reform ("Moral Reform," 1:124 and 141); temperance ("Temperance Reform," 1:91). See also "Union of All Reformers, For One Great Reform," No. 1 and No. 2, 1:134 and 1:245 respectively.

2. Joint-stock proprietorship was a financial arrangement not unlike that which exists between stockholders and corporations today. Prospective members of communities such as Brook Farm and Hopedale (Milford, Massachusetts) purchased negotiable shares of stock in the enterprise. (The original shares of stock at Brook Farm were sold for $500.00 apiece. The earliest "Articles of Association" [1841] at the West Roxbury community indicate that, among others, George Ripley committed himself to purchasing three shares, and Nathaniel Hawthorne pledged to buy two.) Whenever a stockholder wished to convert his stock it was offered to other stockholders. If the community prospered, dividends were paid to stockholders.

3. For a more detailed discussion of this kind of verse, see the chapter on "Poetry in *The Harbinger,*" pp. 115–17.

4. For a complete slate of the original officers of the American Union of Associationists, see Appendix A.

5. See, for example, "Cassius M. Clay's Appeal" (1:317); "Cassius M. Clay, His Notions of Association" (1:415); "Cassius M. Clay and *The Harbinger*" (2:95); "Weekly Gossip" (7:86); and a review of *The Writings of Cassius Marcellus Clay* (7:127).

6. No new party was ever formed along the exact lines proposed by the Liberty League, but it should be noted that the Liberty League did merge in 1848 with the Free-Soil party, a political organization that originated in opposition to the extension of slavery in the territories acquired by the Mexican War. See p. 60.

7. In an essay entitled "Waste, Waste, Waste!," which appeared on 31 July 1847, *The Harbinger* estimated that the United States was spending $1,000,000 a week to support the war effort. Whether or not this figure was an exaggeration, the magazine complained on this occasion because so much money was being spent to support the war, but Associationists could not raise the $500,000 which would enable them to build an experimental model Phalanx that would establish a social order wherein there would be no war, oppression, or slavery.

8. Tyler, *Freedom's Ferment*, p. 544.

9. *The Harbinger* also published a lengthy editorial essay that compared Henry Clay (1777–1852), the Virginia-born statesman, with John Q. Adams (1767–1848), the sixth President of the United States. The occasion of the "Reception of Henry Clay—Obsequies of John Q. Adams," which appeared in the number for 18 March 1848, was Clay's arrival in New York City just a few days before the funeral tribute in that same city to Adams. *The Harbinger* used this occasion to draw one of the more insightful parallels ever made on these two great political figures, one from the South, the other from the North, whose political careers were continually in apposition throughout the first half of the nineteenth century. See 6:156.

Chapter 4

1. For a discussion of *The Harbinger*, Charles Fourier, and Associationism, see chapter 1, pp. 16–24, and chapter 2.

2. Unless otherwise noted, dates of publication of works by American and European authors refer to the American edition.

3. Despite the generally egalitarian attitude of Associationists, all literary reviews in *The Harbinger* were written by men.

4. Brisbane's *The Phalanx* and Channing's *The Present* were the immediate predecessors of *The Harbinger*. See chapter 2, pp. 000–00.

5. In addition to these men, the following individuals reviewed books for *The Harbinger*: S. P. Andrews, Walter Channing, James Freeman Clarke, George Foster, E. P. Grant, Everett Ives, Henry James, Sr., Osborne Macdaniel, and John Orvis.

6. No American dramatists were treated in the literary-reviews column. The reader may wish to examine, however, the "Art Review" column in volumes 6–8, which included several items on the New York theaters.

7. Perry Miller, ed., *The American Transcendentalists: Their Prose and Poetry* (Garden City, N.Y.: Doubleday & Co., 1957), p. 101.

8. Ibid., p. 148.

9. Dwight, as well as his associates on *The Harbinger*, never showed the slightest appreciation of Poe's labors in this area.

10. Miller, *The American Transcendentalists*, p. 188.

11. Charles Crowe, *George Ripley: Transcendentalist and Utopian Socialist* (Athens, Ga.: University of Georgia Press, 1967), p. 158.

12. Perry Miller, *The Transcendentalists: An Anthology* (Cambridge, Mass.: Harvard University Press, 1950), p. 450.

13. Perhaps it should be remembered here that John Dwight tried to enlist Emerson's aid when *The Harbinger* was just getting underway, but he refused Dwight's request for a contribution or two on the grounds that he could not aid a journal that had chosen a "patron." He also told Dwight that he was saddened by the fact that the "scholars and philosophers" had no "literary organ or voice" that was not "desperately sectarian," and he concluded by telling him that so long as *The Harbinger* was sectarian, he would "respect it at a distance. If it should become catholic, I shall be found suing for a place in it." See George Willis Cooke, *John Sullivan Dwight: Brook-Farmer, Editor, and Critic of Music* (Boston: Small, Maynard & Co., 1898), pp. 103–5. For a somewhat more detailed account of Emerson's refusal to be involved in his friend Ripley's Brook Farm community, see Gay Wilson Allen, *Waldo Emerson: A Biography* (New York: The Viking Press, 1981), pp. 363–65.

14. *Journals of Ralph Waldo Emerson*, ed. E. W. Emerson and W. E. Forbes (Boston: Houghton Mifflin Company, 1911), 5:473–74.

15. This is not the first time that Dana had occasion to comment on the "school" of "transcendental philosophy." In a review in the number for 15 November 1845 of *Studies in Religion* (1845)—a work that was an "offshoot" of "that remarkable intellectual and moral phenomenon, New England Transcendentalism," by an author whose name was not cited—Dana condemned Transcendentalism as a philosophy, and he denounced its proponents as well. Regarding the philosophy, "Its doctrine and tendency," Dana said, "are extreme individualism. It sunders the man from his fellows, and even doubts whether it is necessary that he should have any fellows at all. In a word, it teaches a perfect *spiritual* selfishness" (1:362). Of the school's leader Waldo Emerson, Dana admitted that, though his ideas often were lofty and his paradoxes brilliant, he was nevertheless "eminently a one-sided and unbalanced man vainly endeavoring after equilibrium," which is interesting criticism indeed, coming, as it did, from a man representing a group that had essentially the same charge leveled at them on numerous occasions. In any event, Dana was pleased to observe that young people associated with the "new school" were "generally short lived and that their number is not at present increasing."

16. Robert Spiller, *The Cycle of American Literature* (New York: Macmillan Company, 1955), p. 34.

17. It should be noted that Godwin probably would not have included William Cullen Bryant, friend of Halleck and contemporary of the Knickerbocker group, among those American writers who had been "greatly over-rated." Although *The Harbinger* never formally reviewed Bryant, Godwin used the present occasion to cite him as an example of the kind of poet Halleck could have become had he ever developed the poetic abilities earlier evidenced in his "Burns" and "Marco Bozzaris." Godwin thought Halleck to be a direct contrast to Bryant, insofar as poetic ability was concerned. He felt that to the extent that Halleck, over the years, had carelessly and even wantonly misused his talent, Bryant had nourished and developed his.

18. Sidney P. Moss, *Poe's Literary Battles* (Durham, N.C.: Duke University Press, 1963), p. 190. For a detailed discussion of the events that, according to Moss, lead to Poe's downfall as a critic, see pp. 190–248 of this work.

19. In his reply to Dwight's review, Poe referred to Brook Farm as "Snook Farm," and he said that *The Harbinger* was the "most reputable organ of the Crazyites." This remark Poe intended as a compliment. See the *Broadway Journal* 2 (13 December 1845): 357–59.

20. *The Works of Orestes A. Brownson*, comp. Henry R. Brownson. (Detroit, Mich.: Thorndike Nourse, 1884), 9:551.

21. The reviewers of *A Fable for Critics* and *The Biglow Papers* are not identified because the reviews appeared in the incompleted and thus unindexed eighth volume, yet it seems certain that both reviews were written by the same individual. For one thing, at the end of the review on *The Fable*, the reviewer stated that he had intended to notice *The Biglow Papers* on the present occasion, but limitations of space prevented him from doing so. For another thing, the style of both reviews is quite similar.

22. It does seem odd, however, that *The Harbinger* failed to review Cooper's *The Crater* (1847), a utopian novel that dealt with Fourier's ideas.

23. Immediately after Dana published the first of his three reviews on Cooper's trilogy (on *Satanstoe*), he was charged with "taking equivocal ground" on the issue of inherited property by *Young America*, an organ, according to Dana, of the "National Reformers." The charge provided Dana an occasion to elaborate his earlier remarks, which he gladly did in *The Harbinger*, in the number for 23 August 1845 in an essay titled "Young America—Anti-Rentism" (1:174).

24. Quoted by James D. Hart, *Oxford Companion to American Literature* (New York: Oxford University Press, 1956), p. 466.

25. Frank Luther Mott, *A History of American Magazines, 1741–1850* (Cambridge, Mass.: Harvard University Press, 1957), 1:368.

26. Ibid., p. 777.

27. See pp. 71–72.

28. *The Harbinger* also published an excerpt from a highly complimentary review about Hunt and his magazine, which was written by N. P. Willis for the *Broadway Journal*. See *The Harbinger*, 2:80.

29. Mott, *American Magazines*, 1:751.

30. See 5:28–30; 43–46; 58–60; 73–76.

31. Miller, *The Transcendentalists: An Anthology*, p. 49. It should be remembered, too, that American interest in Swedenberg dated back to the late eighteenth century. At that time, James Glen and Francis Bailey—two of the earliest and most vigorous proslytizers in this country of Swedenborgian doctrines—lectured, conducted reading circles, and printed various tracts and pamphlets on Swedenborg. By 1840, there were already several thousand Swedenborgians living in the United States, and they could be found in every state in the Union. For a comprehensive discussion of Swedenborg and his followers in America, see Marguerite Beck Block, *The New Church in the New World* (1932; reprint, New York: Octagon Books, 1968).

32. See, respectively, Alexander Kern, "The Rise of Transcendentalism" in *Transitions in American Literary History*, ed. Harry Hayden Clark (Durham, N.C.: Duke University Press, 1953), p. 272, and Miller, *The Transcendentalists: An Anthology*, p. 53.

33. Quoted in Ralph L. Rusk, *The Life of Ralph Waldo Emerson* (New York: Columbia University Press, 1949), p. 118. See also Clarence Paul Hotson, "Sampson Reed, A Teacher of Emerson," *New England Quarterly* 2 (April 1929): 249–77.

34. *The Correspondence of Emerson and Carlyle*, ed. Joseph Slater (New York: Columbia University Press, 1964), p. 109.

35. Block, *The New Church*, p. 145.

36. Ibid.

37. "Historic Notes of Life and Letters in New England," in *The Complete Works of Ralph Waldo Emerson*, ed. Edward Waldo Emerson, 12 vols. (Boston: Houghton, Mifflin, 1904), 10:330.

38. Amelia Russell, *Home Life of the Brook Farm Association* (Boston, Mass., 1900), p. 93.

39. Marianne Dwight, *Letters from Brook Farm: 1844–1847*, ed. Amy L. Reed (Poughkeepsie, N.Y.: Vassar College, 1928), p. 123.

40. *"Omnia hodie stant provisa, et parata, et expectant diem"* (prologue to *Regnum Animale*, 1744, sec. 23). Cited in Clarence L. F. Gohdes, *The Periodicals of American Transcendentalism* (Durham, N.C.: Duke University Press, 1931), p. 128.

41. Ripley's remark is especially interesting when remembered in the larger context of his earlier role in the so-called Transcendental movement. German writers generally had had, of course, a powerful influence on Harvard Divinity School students such as Ripley in the 1830s. As early as January 1832, for example, Ripley himself had written a review for *The Christian Examiner* (11:373–80) of Charles Follen's "Inaugural Discourse." (Follen had been appointed to the Harvard faculty in 1831 to teach German. In 1835, his appointment was not renewed.) Ripley had also written a two-part essay on Johann Gottfried von Herder, which appeared in *The Christian Examiner* in the numbers for May 1835 and November 1835. A few months

later—March 1836—he published in *The Christian Examiner* again an important essay on Friedrich Schleiermacher.

42. Cited in Crowe, *George Ripley*, p. 233.

43. Foster's assertion, as well as Dana's reaction, are perhaps more interesting when one remembers that the two men were associates in producing the first two volumes of *The Harbinger*.

44. Crowe, *George Ripley*, p. 68.

45. Cited by Joseph Slater, "George Ripley and Thomas Carlyle," *PMLA* 48 (June 1952): 342.

46. For a more detailed discussion of the Ripley-Carlyle correspondence and relationship, see Slater's article cited above.

47. Letter from Ripley to Carlyle, dated 29 December 1836. Cited in Slater, "George Ripley and Thomas Carlyle," p. 344.

48. Thomas Carlyle, *Past and Present* (Boston: Charles C. Little & James Brown, 1843), p. 294.

49. In addition to the three reviews and the Carlyle letter reprinted from the *Tribune*, Ripley briefly cited Carlyle on three other occasions in *The Harbinger*. In an 1845 editorial, for example, Ripley quoted Carlyle on England's indifference to the fact that, while her warehouses were full of shirts, the backs of English workers were bare. Ripley added: "The thing is, to bring the shirts and the backs together" (1:34). In 1846, Ripley again quoted Carlyle on the evils of a laissez-faire economy (3:167), and in 1848, he printed an extract of a letter from Thomas Cooper in which the Chartist poet told of an evening at Carlyle's when the company had been "up to the ears in Fourierism, Communism, . . . etc. . . . Carlyle came out nobly, and backed me up like a man" (7:21).

50. See *The Harbinger* 2:139 and 234; 3:27 and 379; and 4:11.

51. George Joyaux, *The French Review* 27 (December 1953): 124.

52. See, for example, *The Christian Examiner* 42 (March, 1847): 209; and the *Literary World* 1 (February 6, 1847): 8.

53. Howard Mumford Jones, "American Comment on George Sand, 1837–48," *American Literature* 3 (January 1932): 390.

54. George Joyaux," George Sand, Eugene Sue and *The Harbinger*," *The French Review* 27 (December 1953): 131.

Chapter 5

1. Gohdes, *Periodicals*, p. 131.

2. *Whittier Correspondence*, ed. John Albree (Salem, Mass.: Essex Book and Print Club, 1911), p. 94. The "piece" Dana alluded to was "The Moral Warfare," which was, by the way, printed correctly.

3. Emerson's importance in the development of American poetry has only recently begun to be recognized and appreciated. Among the worthwhile treatments of Emerson the poet in the larger context of the development of American poetry are Roy Harvey Pearce, *The Continuity of American Poetry* (Princeton, N.J.: Princeton University Press, 1961), pp. 153–64, and Donald Barlow Stauffer, *A Short History of American Poetry* (New York: E. P. Dutton & Co., 1974), pp. 93–102. Especially valuable is Hyatt H. Waggoner, *American Poets from the Puritans to the Present* (Boston: Houghton Mifflin Company, 1968), pp. 90–114.

4. If the categories seem especially broad, it is because they are necessarily so. If *The Harbinger* had published only a very few poems—as its immediate predecessor *The Present* did—there would be little difficulty discussing them. Because, however, the magazine printed so much verse—considerably more, in fact, than any of the other Transcendental journals, such as *The Western Messenger* or the *Dial*—it would be quite difficult to discuss the poetry in any organized way without elastic categories such as the ones used in this chapter.

5. Though the index to volume 1 cites Dana's poem as appearing originally in *The Harbinger*, it actually made its first appearance in *The Present*, in the number for 15 November 1843.

6. Sterling F. Delano, "A Rediscovered Transcendental Poem by Frederic Hedge," *American Transcendental Quarterly* 29 (Winter 1976): 35–36.

7. Pearce, *American Poetry*, pp. 24–42. It is interesting to remember, too, that Henry Thoreau's first verse submission to the *Dial* was titled "Elegy." See Joel Myerson, *The New England Transcendentalists and the "Dial"* (Rutherford, N.J.: Fairleigh Dickinson University Press, 1980), p. 39.

8. Lewis G. Sterner, *The Sonnet in American Literature* (Philadelphia: University of Pennsylvania Press, 1930), p. xii.

Chapter 6

1. In his study of *Music and Musicians in Early America* (New York: W. W. Norton, 1964), Irving Lowens has stated that *"The Harbinger* was far and away the most important medium through which Transcendental-colored ideas about music were disseminated" (p. 253). Lowens goes on to note that all but twenty-six of the 183 items dealing with music that appeared in the journals associated with New England Transcendentalism were published in *The Harbinger*. See his "A Check-List of Writings about Music in the Periodicals of American Transcendentalism (1835–50)," Appendix C, pp. 311–21.

2. Dana, it should be noted, would later contribute seven articles for the "Art Review" column on the 1847–48 Italian opera season in New York. Ives, who provided four reviews for the new column (all for volume 6), was the only professional musician to write music criticism for *The Harbinger*. His own work had been favorably reviewed by John Dwight on three separate occasions. (See 2:43–44; 2:317–18; and 4:124–25.) Godwin, however, managed only one article on music—"The Philharmonic Concert"—which was published in the number for 11 March 1848.

3. The remarks are those, respectively, by Clarence Gohdes, *The Periodicals of American Transcendentalism* (Durham, N.C.: Duke University Press, 1931), p. 113, and Lowens, *Music and Musicians in Early America*, p. 253.

4. Regarding Dwight's importance as a critic of music, he has been described, for example, as the "foe of humbug, of charlatanism, and though he made some grave errors, he generally knew what he was talking about" (John Tasker Howard, *Our American Music* [New York: Thomas Y. Crowell, 1954], p. 218); and he has been referred to as the "pioneer of musical criticism in America" (Henry Charles Lahee, *Annals of Music in America* [1922; reprint, Freeport, New York: Books for Free Libraries Press, 1970], p. 37); as "America's first real music critic" (Irving Sablosky, *American Music* [Chicago and London: University of Chicago Press, 1969], p. 74); as "the first really significant and influential American music critic and arbiter of taste" (H. Wiley Hitchcock, *Music in the United States: A Historical Introduction* [Englewood Cliffs, N.J.: Prentice-Hall, 1969], p. 129); and as the "keenest critical intelligence [in the 1840s] on the entire American scene" (Lowens, *Music and Musicians in America*, p. 252). With the exception of Lowens—who provides some insightful and substantive remarks on Dwight's music theory in the context of New England Transcendentalism—none of these works offers more than the brief observations alluded to above.

5. Dwight's allusion is to Greek mythology, and it was aptly chosen. Briareus, who appears in book 1 of Homer's *Iliad,* was "the creature of the hundred hands" who helped Thetis unbind Zeus after he had been subdued by the other Olympians. See the translation by Richmond Lattimore, *The Iliad of Homer* (Chicago and London: University of Chicago Press, 1951), p. 69, 400–406.

6. For Dwight's reviews of Leopold de Meyer, see "Leopold de Meyer," 1:396–97; "Review," 2:11–12; and "De Meyer Again in Boston," 3:317–18. For the reviews of Henri Herz,

see "Henri Herz," 3:364; "Henri Herz in Boston," 4:42–43; and "Herz, Sivori, and Knoop in Boston," 6:11.

7. Dwight did not speak so figuratively when, in his introductory remarks in the very first number of *The Harbinger,* he said: "The scale of musical tones is only the scale of the human Paissons, or motive springs of action, as that scale is repeated in the sphere of sound and of the ear" (1:13). For a fuller account of Emanuel Swedenborg, see the chapter on "Literary Criticism in *The Harbinger,*" pp. 91–96.

8. See, for example, 1:329–32; 2:3; 2:361–63; and 3:9–11.

9. Given Dwight's great love for German music, it was inevitable that he would compare—although usually not directly—Italian and German opera. Not only did he do so here, he did so on other occasions as well. In an article on "The Opera in Boston" (5 June 1847), for example, Dwight praised Giuseppe Verdi because his "music always makes us stronger." Then he complained that, while "we yield to no one in the extent of our preference of the great German music (and especially the most German of all, Beethoven and Schubert) to all other; . . . we think some of our friends are even blinded by a good prejudice when they condemn 'the Verdi trash' as a weak dilution of Donizetti. Whatever may be his faults, whatever he may lack, he certainly has nothing in common with Donizetti, Mercadanti or Bellini" (4:409).

10. Madam Bishop and Robert Bochsa first seem to have performed in Boston on 9 September 1847, when they gave a concert at the Tremont Temple. Dwight's review of the performance, "Madam Bishop and Bochsa," appeared in *The Harbinger* in the number for 11 September 1847. (See 5:235–36.) He had much earlier reviewed the Sequins in the number for 8 November 1845. (See 1:348–49.)

11. The reader may also be interested in Dwight's remarks on the Boston Philharmonic Society (1843–63). His most substantive comments may be found in two columns, both of which were published in the fourth volume: see the "Boston Philharmonic Society," 4:77, and 185–86.

12. Lahee, in *Annals of Music,* p. 295, identifies twenty-one choral or orchestral associations that were established before the Boston Handel and Haydn Society.

13. See, for example, 1:329; 2:76; 4:251. See also 8:30. It might be noted here, too, that in addition to the "Music in Boston" feature, the "Musical Review" occasionally included a "Music in New York" column as well. Christopher Pearse Cranch acted as the correspondent for one such article (1:59–60); and William W. Story sent along three (1:412–13; 2:139–40; and 2:235–36). The subjects of these pieces covered the musical spectrum, ranging, as they did, from the New York Philharmonic Society concerts, to Ole Bull, to Mozart, to Signor Sanquirico's New York–based Italian opera company.

14. Story's review, which appeared in two consecutive installments in the numbers for 7 and 14 March 1846, is also interesting for its elaboration of what might be called a Transcendental theory of music. See especially the number for 14 March 1846, 2:218–20.

15. Howard, *Our American Music,* pp. 136–41. Dwight himself cited the figure of twelve for Mason's first class in 1834. See 5:203.

16. It seems appropriate here to note that Dwight also wrote a review on Lowell Mason's son, William, for the 18 April 1846 number of *The Harbinger* (2:298–99). In addition to Lowell and William Mason, Dwight discussed only two other American musicians: the American pianist Edward L. Walker was reviewed twice (2:315–17; 4:187), and Elam Ives, Jr., who was mentioned earlier in this chapter (see n. 3 above), was reviewed three times.

Conclusion

1. Clarence L. F. Gohdes, *The Periodicals of American Transcendentalism* (Durham, N.C.: Duke University Press, 1931), pp. 17–37.

2. *The Letters of Herman Melville,* ed. Merrell R. Davis and William H. Gilman (New Haven, Conn.: Yale University Press, 1960), p. 125.

Appendix A

Constitution
of the
American Union of Associationists

[Adopted May 1846]

Constitution

I. The Name of this Society shall be the AMERICAN UNION OF ASSOCIA-TIONISTS.

II. Its purpose shall be the establishment of an order of Society based on a system of

Joint-Stock Property;
Cooperative Labor;
Association of Families;
Equitable Distribution of Profits;
Mutual Guarantees;
Honors according to Usefulness;
Integral Education;
Unity of Interests;

which system we believe to be in accordance with the Laws of Divine Providence, and the Destiny of Man.

III. Its Method of operation shall be the appointment of agents, the sending out of lecturers, the issuing of publications, and the formation of a series of affiliated societies, which shall be auxiliary to the parent Society, in holding meetings, collecting funds, and in every way diffusing the Principles of Association, and preparing for their practical application.

IV. Any person may become a member of this society by signing its Constitution, or that of any affiliated society.

V. An Anniversary meeting of this Society shall be held at times and places duly appointed, when officers shall be chosen for the ensuing year.

VI. The Officers shall be a President, five or more Vice Presidents, two Corresponding Secretaries, one Domestic and one Foreign,—a Recording

163

Secretary, a Treasurer and seven Directors, who shall constitute the Executive Committee of the Society, and shall be responsible for its general management; it shall also be their duty to fill all occasional vacancies in the offices of the Society.

VII. This Constitution can be amended at any anniversary meeting, by a vote of two thirds of the members present.

On motion, Messrs. OLIVER JOHNSON, CHANNING, BRISBANE, JAQUES, and DANA, were appointed a Committee to nominate officers for the Society whose Constitution had just been adopted.

The Committee nominated the following persons as Officers of the Society, who were unanimously elected.

PRESIDENT.

HORACE GREELEY, New York.

VICE PRESIDENTS.

PELEG CLARKE, Coventry, R.I.

FREDERIC GRAIN, New York.

E. P. GRANT, Canton, O.

JAMES KAY, JR., Philadelphia.

CHARLES SEARS, N.Am. Phalanx.

BENJAMIN URNER, Cincinnati.

H. H. VAN AMRINGE, Pittsburg, Pa.

DOMESTIC CORRESPONDING SECRETARY.

WILLIAM H. CHANNING, Brook Farm.

FOREIGN CORRESPONDING SECRETARY.

PARKE GODWIN, New York.

RECORDING SECRETARY.

JAMES FISHER, Boston.

TREASURER.

FRANCIS GEO. SHAW, West Roxbury.

DIRECTORS.

GEORGE RIPLEY, Brook Farm.

CHARLES A. DANA, Brook Farm.

ALBERT BRISBANE, New York.

OSBORNE MACDANIEL, New York.

EDMUND TWEEDY, New York.

JOHN ALLEN, Brook Farm.

JOHN S. DWIGHT, Brook Farm.

The same committee in compliance with the directions of the Convention, also reported the following Resolutions, which were discussed and adopted.

I. *Resolved,* That we—the Associationists of the United States of America—desiring the sympathy and aid of the wise and good of all denominations and parties in teaching and applying the sublime doctrine of UNIVERSAL UNITY; and fearing that calumnies, systematically circulated in regard to Association, have prejudiced many well meaning persons against this, as we believe, Providential movement; do now, once again, announce our distinctive purpose and policy to be, the establishment of an order of society based upon a system of Joint-stock Property,—Co-operative Labor,—Association of Families,—Equitable Distribution of Profits,—Mutual Guarantes,—Honors according to Usefulness,—Integral Education,—UNITY OF INTERESTS,—which system we are confident is in accordance with the Laws of Divine Justice and the Destiny of Man.

II. *Resolved,* That it is our hope and trust, as it is our prayer, that the Kingdom of God will come, and His will be done on earth as it is in heaven; that it is our wish and aim to cherish in the hearts and embody in the acts of communities and individuals, the Spirit of Christ, which is LOVE; that we seek the formation of human societies wherein the New Commandment may be perfectly obeyed, and all disciples be members one of another in truth and in deed; that we call upon Christians of all sects, to unite in the holy and humane effort of establishing Universal Brotherhood, of putting away forever from Christendom and the world the forms of inhumanity which now disgrace earth, degrade man and outrage Heaven, such as Slavery,—War,—Legalized Murder,—Poverty,—Licentiousness,—Intemperance,—Commercial Fraud,—Industrial Anarchy,—Ignorance,—Duplicity, private and public,—dishonesty of all kinds, individual and national, and of substituting in their place Mutual Kindness the earth over; and finally, that we look with joyful confidence to a time, near at hand, when the Doers of the Will of God shall be made at-one with their Heavenly Father and with their brethren, in a Holy, True, Loving, Universal Church.

III. *Resolved,* That the Constitutions and Laws of this Nation and of its several States, assert principles of liberty and equality, which would secure the rights of every man, woman, and child to life, liberty, and the pursuit of happiness, if they were practically embodied in actual life; but that they are not thus embodied any where, because the fundamental rights to labor and to property have not been acknowledged and respected; that the result is, political feuds growing ever fiercer, wasting the energies and resources, the time, the talents, the character and principle of citizens, and arraying them more and more into two great parties of Capital and Labor, Money and Men; that it is a mockery for a Republic not to seek what its name implies—the Common Wealth; that this Nation is nevertheless manifestly designed to be a Nation of United Freemen, where the remnants of Barbarism, Slavery, Serfdom, Caste, will be utterly banished; where Woman will possess, as she surely ought, like privileges with Man; where Industry will be raised to its just dignity, and usefulness will alone be honored; and that in its system of confederated Townships, Counties, States, this people has been wonderfully and providentially prepared for that very Union of Freemen, which Association proposes as its Ideal of True Government.

IV. *Resolved,* That in the mighty Reforms which are every where agitating Society, and moving men on all sides to protest against the continuance of transmitted social wrongs, and to assert the claims of every human being to brotherly kindness, we hail the sign of an inspiration of Heavenly Love; that we rejoice to see the growing union among these various movements of Humanity, and gladly pledge our earnest co-operation in fulfilling their designs; but that we earnestly warn our fellow philanthropists that the disgraceful degradations of Man which every where prevail, can be remedied only by cutting down and tearing up by the roots the temptations and difficulties, the collisions and hostilities which our present system of Isolated Life inevitably engenders; and that we summon them to unite with us in laying as the very corner-stone of the Temple of Society, Perfect Justice and Universal Love.

V. *Resolved,* That in this hour of national disgrace, when this so-called free and Christian Republic is seeking by force of arms to rob a sister republic of province after province that she may extend over it to the Pacific and the Isthmus of Panama slave institutions and slave labor,—we do solemnly utter our horror and detestation of ALL War, and especially of such an iniquitous war as the present; that in this war, as in all others, we see an evidence that only a radical substitution of Co-operation for Conflict in all relations of Social Life, can do away with this most impious and unnatural custom of human butchery and wholesale destruction of all earth's blessings; that we hereby pledge ourselves, in no way to aid the Government of these United States, or of the several States, in carrying on war against Mexico; and that we will raise the White Flag above the National Flag, in sign that we are only and always Peace-Keepers and Peace Makers.

VI. *Resolved,* That the attempts at practical Association, which have been commenced in various parts of the United States, having in most cases been undertaken with insufficient resources to insure complete success, and on too limited a scale to illustrate fully the divine principles of Associative Unity,—ought not by any want of success with which they may have been attended, to discourage the hopes of the advocates of our holy cause; but on the contrary, the social results already obtained, should inspire them with a warmer faith in the truth and value of their principles, impel them to a more determined energy for their promulgation, and lead them to new efforts for their realization, with materials adapted to insure their certain and speedy triumph.

VII. *Resolved,* That we hold it our duty, as seekers of the practical unity of the race, to accept every light afforded by the providential men whom God has raised up, without committing ourselves blindly to the guidance of any one, or speaking and acting in the name of any man;—that we recognize the invaluable worth of the discoveries of Charles Fourier in the Science of Society, the harmony of that Science with all the vital truths of Christianity, and the promise it holds out of a material condition of life wherein alone the spirit of Christ can dwell in all its fulness;—but "Fourierists" we are not, and cannot consent to be called, because Fourier is only one among the great teachers of mankind; because many of his assertions are concerning spheres of thought which exceed our present ability to test, and of which it would be presumption for us to affirm with confidence; and because we regard this as a holy and providential movement, independent of every merely *individual* influence or guidance, the sure and gradual evolving of Man's great unitary destiny in the Ages.

VIII. *Resolved,* That the time has arrived for an earnest, vigorous, and persistent effort for the propagation of our principles; that our present duty as Associationists is, with zeal and patience to disseminate the truths relating to the Combined Order of Society and the Social Destiny of Man, which have been implanted in our souls; waiting with confident faith in Providence for the time of their realization, whensoever that time may arrive; and that we hail with hope, as we commence with resolute determination and deep trust in God and the truth, the organization which we have this day formed; and we do solemnly call upon all friends of Humanity to second and forward its operations.

Appendix B

Checklist of Original Contributions to *The Harbinger*

This appendix is a checklist of original contributions to *The Harbinger*. It is arranged alphabetically by author, and chronologically by volume, number, and page(s). Its purpose is to enable the reader to understand more clearly the exact nature and extent of a specific individual's contribution to *The Harbinger*, something that is presently quite difficult to do because, among other things, the indexes to volumes 1–7 are arranged only by title; they include reprinted as well as original items; they rely on abbreviated and often misleading rather than exact titles; they do not always cite every item that actually appeared in a particular volume; and they often are inaccurate in the matter of page locations.

The Harbinger collapsed, of course, before the completion of the eighth volume, which is why the editors never compiled an index for volume 8. The reader might want to see, however, Sterling F. Delano and Rita Colanzi, "An Index to Volume VIII of *The Harbinger*," in *Resources for American Literary Study* 10 (Autumn 1980): 173–86.

It should be noted that translations of foreign writings (mostly of French prose and German verse) are not included in the checklist because they did not seem properly to fit the category "original contributions." *The Harbinger*'s correspondence (of which there was a considerable amount, especially in the last three volumes), seemed not to fit that category either, so neither is it included, except, that is, when such correspondence obviously served as a regular feature of the Associationist journal, as it certainly did, for example, in the case of George G. Foster's "Letter From Broadway," or James John Garth Wilkinson's "Letter From London."

Finally, titles throughout are cited exactly as they originally appeared, although I have routinely regularized the punctuation for purposes of clarity and consistency.

168

Anonymous

1.1.7	Lewis, *Plato Against The Atheists* [review]
1.2.25.	[trans. Calvert], *Correspondence Between Schiller and Goethe* [review]
1.10.160	Progress At The West
1.11.171.	Richter, *Flower, Fruit, and Thorn Pieces* [review]
1.14.221.	Hazard, *Essay on the Philosophical Character of Channing* [noticed]
1.15.235.	[not given], *The Hermit of Warkworth;* Foque, *The Two Captains* [noticed]
1.18.284.	[not given], *Adventures of Captain Simon Suggs* [noticed]
1.22.348–49.	*Norma* in Boston
1.25.395.	Thierry, *The Historical Essays* [review]
2.8.125.	A Demand [poem—signed "Portia"]
2.15.233.	Hunt, *Stories From The Italian Poets* [review]
2.17.270–71.	The Integral Phalanx
2.17.271.	New Orleans
2.18.283.	To _____ [poem]
2.19.298.	[not given], *The Common School Drawing Master* [Part I—review]
3.1.12.	The Unknown Friend [poem]
3.6.85.	Reflections on Boston Common [Eliza A. Starr?]
3.7.102.	The Catholics and Associationists
3.7.108.	Peace on Earth [poem—signed "S.J."]
3.21.334.	Prospects of *The Harbinger*
3.21.336.	Workingmen's Protective Union
3.25.395.	The Fall of the Leaf [poem—signed "X."]
3.25.396.	The Morning Mist [poem—signed "X."]
4.9.138–40.	Music in Germany [musical review]
4.13.204–05.	The Fate of Women! [poem—signed "X."]
4.13.205.	The Frozen Cascade [poem—signed "X."]
4.17.272.	Model Phalanx
4.20.314.	The Village Girl [poem—signed "*"]
4.21.325.	Signs of the Times [on poets in Cuba]
4.21.333.	Convention in New York
4.22.347.	Love Unfulfilled [poem—signed "***"]
4.22.347.	Wright, *The Past: An Air With Variations* [musical review]
4.22.351.	A Woman's Call to Women
4.24.383–84.	Promising Signs
4.25.395–96.	To Elizabeth Barrett [poem—signed "***"]
5.2.27.	The Spring-time of the World [poem—signed "R.H.B."]
5.4.63.	Communist Movement
5.14.218.	Thalberg, *Viola* [musical review]

5.15.235.	Madam Bishop and Bochsa [musical review]
6.17.130.	Nichol's Principle of Assurance
6.20.153.	Political Affairs
6.21.167.	*North British Review* [review]
6.22.175.	*The Pictorial History of England*[review]
7.1.1.	A Song of Faith [poem—signed "E.B.B."]
7.2.12.	"Fourier an Infidel" [writer identified only as "Fox"]
7.6.45.	The New Era of Industry
7.7.53.	Comfort
7.8.62.	The Greek Slave [musical review—signed "W.H.F."]
7.11.81.	Progress; June; A Song [poems]
7.12.89.	A Communion Hymn [poem—signed "*₊*"]
7.22.173.	Protective Union Convention
7.26.204.	Germania Musical Association [musical review]

John Allen

5.8.123–24.	Capital, Its Rights
5.20.317–18.	Prospects in Western New York

S. P. Andrews

3.2.24–27.	Kraitsir, *Significance of the Alphabet* [review]

Albert Brisbane

1.2.20–21.	Movement in Favor of a Social Reformation
1.2.29–31.	The Question of Slavery
1.4.61–63.	What Do The Workingmen Want?
1.5.75–77.	The Collective Unity
1.10.157–59.	The Collective Unity, No. II.
1.13.203.	Smith, *Lectures on Clairmativeness* [review]
1.18.284–86.	The Universality of Providence
1.24.375.	Fourier's Writings
1.25.398–400.	Theory of the Human Passions
2.5.78–79.	Association, What Is It?
2.7.97–98.	Theory of Human Passions. No. II
2.7.110–12.	Reform Movements Originating
2.10.159–60.	Theory of the Human Passions. No. III
2.11.163.,65.	Theory of the Human Passions. No. IV
2.11.174–175.	Progress in France

2.12.190–91. Religious Movement in Germany
2.13.193–95. Theory of the Human Passions. No. V
2.13.200–203. The American Associationists
2.14.222–24. Religious and Social Movements
2.15.238–39. Spread of Our Principles in France
3.3.44–46. The Organization of Labor No. I
3.4.59–62. The Organization of Labor No. II
3.6.92–95. Interest on Capital
3.7.108–10. The Organization of Labor No. III
3.10.157–60. The Organization of Labor No. IV
3.11.172–74. The Organization of Labor No. IV continued
3.16.253–56. Government—The Church—Marriage
3.18.287–88. Industrial Reform
3.23.365–68. False Association Contrasted With True Association
3.25.396–99. The Conservative Principles of Order in Society
4.9.133. Appalling Distress
4.12.188–90. National Era—Christ and Association—Destiny of Man
4.12.191–92. Error Corrected
4.13.206–7. The Viennese Children
4.15.235–36. The Sufferings and Wrongs of Ireland
4.18.284–87. The Different Modes of Acting on Society, and the Classes
that Represent Those Modes
4.19.299–301. The Liberator
4.19.301–2. The Famine in Ireland

George H. Calvert ["E.Y.T."]

4.3.43. Dream No More [poem]
4.9.141. Aspiration [poem]
4.9.141. The Lost, Found [poem]
4.12.188. The Loved Departed [poem]
4.13.205. Why Are Poets Sad? [poem]
4.15.236. Burns [poem]
6.24.184. The God and the Bayedere [poem]

William Ellery Channing

3.8.123. The Ice Ravine [poem]

Walter Channing

2.23.357–58. Sargent, *An Address on Pauperism* [review]

William F. Channing

2.11.165–66.   The Progress of Science

William Henry Channing

1.2.24–25.	The Fountain in the Palace: A Story Told to Brook Farm Children
1.2.28–29	Anniversary Week
1.4.60–61	Reform of Criminals
1.6.81.	The Ins and Outs, A Dialogue
1.6.91–93.	The Temperence Reform
1.7.111.	Many United in One
1.8.124–26.	Moral Reform
1.9.141–42.	Moral Reform [continued]
1.15.237–39.	Association in the U.S.A. No. I
1.18.301–3.	Association in the U.S.A. No. II
1.20.317–19.	Cassius M. Clay's Appeal
1.24.376.	Whewell, *The Elements of Morality* [review]
2.15.231–33.	Taylor's Address at Miami University [review]
2.23.365–67.	Unity in Catholicity in the Church
2.25.393–95.	Peace the Principle and Policy of Associationists
2.25.395–97.	Labor for Wages
3.1.14–16.	To the Associationists of the United States
3.3.43–44.	Hawthorne, *Mosses From An Old Manse* [review]
3.4.64.	Affiliated Societies
3.5.77–80.	Objections to Association—No. I
3.6.89–92.	Objections to Association—No. II
3.6.95.	Woman's Function in the Associative Movement
3.8.124–26.	Objections to Association—No. III
3.17.269–71.	To "The American Union of Associationists"
4.4.59–60.	Gloria in Excelsis
[4. 15. 240.	See note at end of Appendix]
5.3.33–38.	The Optimist—The Cynic—The Seer
5.16.253–54.	Othello—Jealousy
6.1.6.	How the World Lives
7.26.202.	Fourier and His School [coauthored with Parke Goodwin and John S. Dwight]

Otis Clapp

1.5.70–72.   The Family Sphere

James Freeman Clarke

2.15.234.   *Keats' Poetical Works* [review]

Joseph J. Cooke

5.5.65–67.   A Personal Experience
6.3.17.   Sayings and Doings in Providence [Rhode Island]
6.4.26.   Sayings and Doings in Providence
6.6.41.   Sayings and Doings in Providence
6.8.57.   Voice of the Press
6.8.59.   Sayings and Doings in Providence
6.9.65.   Sayings and Doings in Providence
6.11.85.   Sayings and Doings in Providence
6.16.125.   Letter from Providence
6.21.166.   Letter from Providence

Christopher Pearse Cranch

1.4.59–60.   Music in New York
1.7.108.   A Glimpse of Light [poem]
1.10.170.   On the Ideal in Art
1.11.172.   The Minstrel's Curse [poem]
1.15.233–34.   Natural Curiosity: "The Voice of Thy Brothers' Blood Crieth
               From the Earth"
1.22.347.   Autumn [poem]
2.2.29.   Athanasia [poem]
3.6.89.   The Music World [poem]
3.6.89.   Sonnet on the Mexican War [poem]

George W. Curtis

1.17.263.   Autumn Song [poem]
1.24.381.   To _____. [poem]
1.26.412–13.   Music in New York
2.4.59–60.   Dirge [poem]
2.9.139–40.   Music in New York
2.11.173–74.   DeMeyer in New York
2.15.235–36.   Music in New York
2.20.318.   The Railroad [poem]
3.3.44.   Destiny [poem]

4.10.142.	Letter From Rome
5.4.49–50.	Letter From Italy
5.9.136–39.	The Italian Opera in New York

Charles A. Dana

1.1.7–8.	Vestiges of the Natural History of Creation
1.1.8.	Auf Wiedersehn [poem]
1.2.25–26.	[not given], *The Philosophy of Evil* [review]
1.2.27.	Ad Arma [poem—see n. 5, p. 161]
1.2.31–32.	Commerce
1.3.43.	*La Phalange* [review]
1.3.48.	Irish Repeal
1.3.48.	Abandonment of Children in Boston
1.4.58.	Hawthorne, *Journal of An African Cruiser* [review]
1.4.64.	Amusing Remarks of *Albany Citizen* on Association
1.4.64.	Universality of Humbug
1.5.73–74.	Poe, *Tales* [review]
1.5.74–75.	Odd Fellowship
1.6.90.	Downing, *The Fruits and Fruit Trees of America* [review]
1.6.90.	Whittier, *The Stranger in Lowell* [review]
1.6.93–95.	Social Movement in Germany
1.7.107.	[not given], *The Bustle* [notice]
1.7.107.	Mowatt, *Evelyn* [review]
1.7.108.	Jerrold, *Time Works Wonders* [review]
1.7.109.	Social and Political Science
1.8.122.	[not given], *Natalia and Other Tales* [notice]
1.8.122.	Cooper, *Satanstoe* [review]
1.8.123.	Les Attractions Sont Proportionelles Aun Destines [poem]
1.9.138.	Godwin, *Tales from the German of Heinrick Zschokke* [review]
1.9.138.	Hood, *Prose and Verse* [review]
1.9.139.	Bremer, *The Parsonage of Mora* [review]
1.9.139.	[not given], *Pen and Ink Sketches* [notice]
1.10.151–53.	Anthon, *A System of Latin Versification* [review]
1.11.172	Tupper, *The Crock of Gold: A Rural Novel* [review]
1.11.174–76.	Young America—Anti-Rentism
1.12.185–86.	Scoresby, *American Factories and Their Female Operatives* [review]
1.12.186–88.	Miles, *Lowell As It Was, and As It Is* [review]
1.13.203.	[not given], *Margaret* [review]
1.13.204–7.	Cassius M. Clay—Slavery
1.14.221.	Hood, *Prose and Verse* [notice]

1.14.221.	Bush, *The Soul* [review]
1.14.223–24.	Doherty, *The Religious Question* [review]
1.16.251–53.	Civilization: The Isolated Family
1.17.262–63.	*The National Magazine, and Industrial Record* [review]
1.17.263.	Von Humboldt, *Cosmos* [review]
1.17.263.	Howitt, *The Improvisatore* [review]
1.17.267.	Labor in Lowell
1.18.283–84.	Mathews, *Big Abel and the Little Manhattan* [review]
1.19.304.	To Christians
1.20.316.	Simms, *The Wigwam and the Cabin* [review]
.335–36.	The World's Convention—The Industrial Congress
1.22.347.	Worcester, *A Letter to the Receivers of the Heavenly Doctrines of the New Jerusalem* [review]
1.22.349–51.	The Translator of the Wandering Jew
1.22.352.	The Philadelphia Ledger
1.23.362.	[not given], *Studies in Religion* [review]
1.24.377–78.	Bush, *The Swedenborg Library,* Part I [review]
1.24.384.	The Ivory Christ
1.25.393–94.	Andrews and Boyle, *The Complete Phonographic Class Book* [review]
1.25.400.	Godwin, *The Teachers of the Nineteenth Century* [announcement]
1.26.411–12.	Cooper, *The Chainbearer* [review]
1.26.412.	Forester, *Trippings in Author-Land* [review]
2.2.27–28.	*The American Review* [review]
2.2.28–29.	Lester, *The Jesuits* and *The Roman Church and Modern Society* [review]
2.2.29.	Hunt, *The Foster Brother* [notice]
2.3.39–42.	Sumner, *The True Grandeur of Nations* [review]
2.4.59.	Maturin, *Montezuma, The Last of the Aztecs* [review]
2.4.59.	Norman, *Rambles by Land and Water* [review]
2.4.59.	Wilkinson, *The Grouping of Animals* [review]
2.4.60.	The Bankrupt [poem]
2.5.74–75.	Foster, *The Poetical Works of Percy Bysshe Shelley* [review]
2.9.137–38.	Perdicaris, *The Greece of the Greeks* [review]
2.9.139.	*The Quarterly Journal and Review* [review]
2.9.139.	Dickens, *The Cricket on the Hearth* [review]
2.9.139.	Erotis [poem]
2.10.157.	[not given], *Over the Ocean* [review]
2.10.157–58.	Parker, *The Idea of a Christian Church* [review]
2.10.158–59.	Clapp, *The Pioneer* [review]
2.10.159.	Memnon [poem]
2.11.172–73.	Cheever, *The Defence of Capital Punishment* [review]
2.11.173.	Longfellow, *The Belfry of Bruges and Other Poems* [review]

2.11.176.	The Alphadelphia Tocsin on Fourier's Cosmogony
2.13.203–4.	Lester, *The Artists of America* [review]
2.14.217.	Godwin, *Tales from the German of Heinrich Zschokke* [review]
2.14.217–18.	Arnold, *The Modern Eleusinia* [review]
2.14.218.	Simms, *The Wigwam and the Cabin* [review]
2.14.218.	Lowell, *Poetry for Home and School* [notice]
2.14.222.	The New York Express on Labor
2.15.233–34.	Titmarsh, *Notes of a Journey from Cornhill to Grand Cairo* [review]
2.15.234.	Dickens, *Travelling Letters* [review]
2.16.249.	Hazlitt, *Table Talk* [review]
2.16.249–50.	*The Democratic Review* [review]
2.17.263–66.	Melville, *Typee* [review]
2.17.268.	Bush, *Professor Bush's Reply to R. W. Emerson* [review]
2.17.268–69.	*First Book of Andrews' and Boyle's Series of Phonotypic Readers* [review—see above]
2.17.269.	*The New Church Advocate and Examiner* [review]
2.17.270.	How Does God Take Care Of The Poor?
2.18.282.	[not given], *Thiodolf, The Icelander* [review]
2.18.282.	Burritt, *Sparks From the Anvil* [review]
2.18.282–83.	Jesse, *Memoirs of the Pretenders and Their Adherents* [review]
2.18.283.	List, *Outlines of Astronomy* [review]
2.19.298.	[not given], *The Retrospect and Other Poems* [review]
2.20.312–14.	James, *What Constitutes the State?* [review]
2.20.314.–15.	Swedenborg, *The Apocalypse Explained* [notice]
2.20.315.	Hall, *The Wilderness and the War-Path* [review]
2.20.318–19.	Labor For Wages
2.20.319–20.	New Politics
2.20.320.	Modern Philosophy
2.22.344–45.	[Not given], *Self-Formation* [review]
2.22.345–46.	Mountford, *Martyria* [review]
2.22.346.	*The Bankers' Weekly Circular and Statistical Record* [review]
2.22.349–50.	New Social System
2.22.350–51.	The Swedenborgian Association
2.22.352.	Mortality of English Laborers
2.22.361.	Mitchell, *A System of Classical and Sacred Geography* [review]
2.23.364–65.	Progress of Society
2.24.378–81.	The Social and Religious Movements
2.24.383.	Interest on Capital

2.25.391–92.   Fremont, *Narrative of the Exploring Expedition to the Rocky Mountains* [review]

2.25.400.   *The Practical Christian* [notice]

2.26.408–9.   *The Quarterly Journal and Review* [review]

2.26.412.   *The Spiritual Magazine* [notice]

3.1.8–9.   Graham, *Henry Russell* [review]

3.1.9.   Orme, *Uncle John* [review]

3.2.29–30.   Letter From A Factory Laborer

3.2.31–32.   Signs of Progress

3.3.44.   Requier, *The Old Sanctuary* [review]

3.4.63.   The Swedenborg Association

3.5.71–75.   Swedenborg, *The Animal Kingdom, The Principia, The Economy of the Animal Kingdom;* Wilkinson, *Remarks on Swedenborg's Economy of the Animal Kingdom* [review]

3.5.75–76.   Parker, *A Sermon of War* [review]
          3.5.80.

3.5.80.   Lectures in Lowell and Worcester

3.7.104–7.   Corselius, *Hints Towards the Development of a Unitary Service* [review]

3.7.107.   Ballou, *Christian Non-Resistance* [review]

3.7.107–8.   *The American Review* [review]

3.7.110–11.   Education

3.7.112.   Industrial Feudalism

3.8.120.   Arnold, *A First Latin Book* [review]

3.8.123.   Cooper, *The Redskins* [review]

3.8.127.   Civilization Encourages the Fine Arts

3.9.138–39.   *Columbian Lady's and Gentleman's Magazine* [review]

3.9.139.   Barrow, *Voyages of Discovery and Research Within the Artic Regions* [review]

3.9.139–40.   Webster, *An Oration Delivered Before the Authorities of the City of Boston . . . July 4, 1846* [review]

3.9.140.   *The Swedenborg Library,* Nos. 23 & 24 [review]

3.9.140.   Thompson, *Recollections of Mexico* [review]

3.9.140.   [not given], *Philosophical Theories and Philosophical Experience* [review]

3.9.142–43.   The Other Side of the Picture

3.9.143.   Attacks on the Doctrine Association

3.11.168–69.   Keppel, *the Expedition to Borneo of H.M.S. Dido for the Suppression of Piracy* [review]

3.11.169.   Maxwell, *Captain O'Sullivan* [review]

3.12.185–88.   Michelet, *The People* [review]

3.12.188.   Sue, *Martin the Foundling* [review]

3.12.188.   Hazen, *The Grammatic Reader* [review]

3.12.191.	The Lowell Union of Associationists
3.12.191–92.	Poverty and Its Lesson
3.13.203–4.	Beecher, *The Evils Suffered by American Women and American Children* [review]
3.13.204–5.	Warburton, *Hochelaga, or England in the New World* [review]
3.13.205.	Bush, *Statement of Reasons for Embracing the Doctrines and Disclosures of Emanuel Swedenborg* [review]
3.13.205.	Plumber, *Lyrica Sacra* [review]
3.14.218.	[not given], *Father Darcy* [review]
3.14.220–21.	Daniel Webster on Labor
3.15.232–35.	Kraitsir, *First Book of English for Children* [review]
3.15.235.	Coggins, *The Chaplet* [review]
3.15.237.	[not given], *Laveton Parsonage: A Tale* [review]
3.15.237–39.	Has It Come To This?
3.15.239.	The Largest Liberty
3.16.252.	[not given], *The Wreck of the Glide* [review]
3.17.267.	Joyslin, *Clement of Rome* [review]
3.17.267.	*Comstock's Phonetic Magazine* [review]
3.18.281–83.	Sumner, *The Scholar, The Artist, The Jurist, The Philanthropist* [review]
3.18.288.	Freedom and Its Friends
3.24.383–84.	Swedenborg Association
4.13.203–4.	*The Literary World* [review]
4.13.204.	Bailey, *American Progress* [review]
4.16.25.	Wilkinson, *Posthumous Tracts of Swedenborg* [review]
4.20.314–18.	Celebration of Fourier's Birthday in New York
6.1.2.	European Affairs
6.1.3.	Illustration of Civilization
6.1.5.	Page's Pictue of Ruth
6.2.9.	European Affairs
6.2.11.	Foreign Art Intelligence
6.3.17.	Affairs in Mexico
6.4.25.	European Affairs
6.4.30.	The Opera at Astor Place
6.4.30–31.	Foreign Art Intelligence
6.6.45.	The Position of Mexico
6.7.53–54.	The American Art-Union
6.8.57.	Affairs in Mexico
6.9.65.	European Affairs
6.9.70.	The Italian Opera in New York
6.10.73.	[Affairs in Mexico]
6.10.78.	The Italian Opera
6.11.81.	[Affairs in Mexico]

6.12.89.	European Affairs
6.12.89–90.	[Affairs in Mexico]
6.12.94.	The Opera at Astor Place
6.12.94–95.	Foreign Art Intelligence
6.12.95.	Bronte, *Jane Eyre* [review—see also 6.24.189]
6.13.97.	The Mexican Question
6.13.101.	The Opera at Astor Place
6.13.103.	*Illustrirter Kalendar für 1848* [review]
6.14.105.	European Affairs
6.14.105.	Shall We Have Peace?
6.16.121.	Review of the Week.
6.16.126.	The Opera at Astor Place
6.17.129.	Review of the Week
6.17.134–35.	Von Humboldt, *Kosmos* [review]
6.18.137.	Review of the Week
6.18.143.	The Italian Opera
6.18.143.	A Fine Collection of Paintings
6.19.145.	European Affairs
6.20.159.	[not given], *The Bachelor of the Albany* [review]
6.21.161–62.	European Affairs
6.21.167.	Foreign Art Intelligence
6.24.184–86.	European Affairs
6.25.198.	Webber, *Old Hicks the Guide* [review]
6.26.200.	European Affairs
7.1.1.	European Affairs
7.3.17.	European Affairs
7.4.25.	European Affairs
7.5.33.	European Affairs
7.6.41–42.	European Affairs
7.7.49.	European Affairs
7.9.65.	European Affairs
7.10.73	European Affairs
7.11.81–82.	European Affairs
7.11.84–85.	Editorial Correspondence
7.13.97.	European Affairs
7.13.101–2.	Editorial Correspondence
7.18.137.	European Affairs
7.21.161.	European Affairs
7.23.180.	European Affairs

Augustine J. H. Duganne

1.16.251.	Labor! [poem]
1.20.313.	The Mechanic [poem]

1.22.348.	"Vorwarts, Bruder! Vorwarts!" [poem]
6.5.33.	Unhappy Marriages
6.13.98.	Who Owneth America's Soil [poem]
6.26.200.	The New World for Columbus [poem]
7.11.91.	The World's Lie [poem]

John S. Dwight

1.1.8.	Goethe, *Essays on Art* [review]
1.1.11.	*Consuelo*. By George Sand
1.1.12.	Musical Review [Introductory]
1.2.26–27.	Gems of German Song
1.3.41–43.	Child, *Letters From New York* [review]
1.3.44.	Work, While It Is Day [poem]
1.3.44–45.	Ole Bull's Concert
1.5.77–78.	The Floral Procession in Boston
1.7.105–7.	Cranch, *Poems* [review]
1.8.123–24.	Music in Boston During the Last Winter
1.8.126–28.	New Symptoms in Fashionable Literature
1.9.139–41.	Concerts of the Boston Academy
1.9.141.	Reed's Publications
1.10.154–57.	Boston Academy—Beethoven's Symphonies
1.12.188–89.	Boston Academy—Beethoven's Symphonies
1.15.235.	Wilson, *The Genius and Character of Burns* [review]
1.15.236.	The Four Streams From The Fountain [poem]
1.15.236–37.	Teachers' Convention for 1845
1.16.248–51.	Goethe, Essays on Art [review]
1.17.264.	Johnson's Musical Class Book
1.17.264.	Bertini's XXV Etudes
1.17.264.	Six Songs by Telfourd
1.17.264–66.	Individuality in Association
1.18.284.	Day and Night [poem]
1.21.329–32.	Music in Boston
1.21.333–35.	Fourier's Writings
1.22.348.	Recent Musical Publications
1.23.362–64.	The Virtuoso Age in Music
1.23.364–66.	Eugene Sue
1.24.376–77.	Lester, *The Artist, The Merchant, and The Statesman* [review]
1.24.378–81.	The Virtuoso Age in Music [continued]
1.24.381–83.	Eugene Sue, No. II
1.25.396–97.	Leopold De Meyer
1.26.410–11.	Poe, *The Raven and Other Poems* [review]

2.1.11–12.   The Biography of Leopold De Meyer
2.1.12–13.   Reed's Publications
2.1.13–14.   Fourier's Cosmogony
2.2.25–27.   Bailey, *Festus* [review]
2.3.43–43.   Farquhar, *Geraldine* [review]
2.3.43–44.   Ives, *et. al., The Beethoven Collection of Sacred Music* [review]
2.4.56–57.   Carlyle, *Oliver Cromwell's Letters and Speeches* [review]
2.4.62–64.   Education
2.5.75–76.   Gilfillan, *Sketches of Modern Literature* [review]
2.5.76.   Lester, *The Artist, The Merchant, and The Statesman* [review]
2.5.76–77.   Music in Boston
2.5.77.   Reed's Publications
2.6.88–90.   Mr. Cranch's Address
2.6.91.   Ditson's Publications
2.6.92–94.   The Perfectionist
2.7.109.   New Edition of Handel's "Messiah"
2.8.122–23.   Holmes Life of Mozart
2.8.124–25.   Emblem [poem]
2.8.127.   Goethe's Autobiography
2.11.175–76. Association the Body of Christianity
2.9.298–99.   Mason, *Deux Romances Sans Paroles* [review]
2.20.315–17. Mr. Edward L. Walker
2.20.317–18. Ives's Publications
2.21.333–34. Reed's Publications
2.22.347–49. The Inauguration of President Everett
2.23.360–61. Hood, *Poems* [review]
2.23.361–63. Great Concert in New York
2.23.363.   Beethoven's "Adelaide"
3.1.9–11.   The Festival Concert in New York
3.1.12–13.   Celebration of Fourier's Birthday in Paris
3.2.27–28.   Dickens, *Pictures From Italy* [review]
3.3.46–48.   Meeting of The "American Union of Associationists" in Boston
3.4.58–59.   "Father Heinrich" in Boston
3.5.76–77.   New Publications of Oliver Ditson
3.8.121–23.   Jameson, *Memoirs and Essays Illustrative of Art, Literature, and Social Morals* [review]
3.9.140–41.   New Publications of George P. Reed
3.10.152–53. Darley and Standbridge, *Cantus Ecclesiae* [review]
3.12.188–91. Objections to Association—No. V.
3.13.205–8.   Objections to Association—No. VI.
3.14.215–16. Motherwell, *Minstrelsy, Ancient and Modern* [review]

4.3.42–43.   Henri Herz in Boston
4.3.43–44.   Convention of Associationists in Christmas Week
4.4.57–58.   Child, *Fact and Fiction* [review]
4.4.58.   Walton, *Lives* . . . [review]
4.4.61–62.   The Juvenile Choirs of Harmony
4.5.76.   Boston Academy of Music
4.5.77.   Boston Philharmonic Society
4.5.78–79.   The Convention in Boston
4.6.91–94.   Emerson, *Poems;* Channing, *Poems;* Story, *Poems* [review]
4.7.106–9.   [Emerson, Channing, and Story review continued]
4.8.121–22.   Sand, *Jacques* [review]
4.8.123–24.   Boston Academy of Music
4.8.124.   Harvard Musical Association
4.8.124–25.   Zingarelli, *The Mozart Collection of Sacred Music* [review]
4.8.125–27.   Fourier's "Three Distributives"
4.9.138.   List, *Outlines of Botany* [review]
4.12.185–86.   Boston Philharmonic Society
4.12.186–87.   Boston Academy of Music
4.12.187–88.   Mr. Edward L. Walker
4.13.202–3.   Weiss, *Unity and Peace* [review]
4.13.204.   Whittier, *The Supernaturalism of New England* [review]
4.14.219–20.   Andrews and Boyle, *The Primary Phonotypic Reader* [review]
4.14.220–21.   Howitt, *Ballads and Other Poems* [review]
4.15.236–39.   The Seven Scourges
[4.15.240.   See note at end of Appendix]
4.15.239–40.   Cookery
4.16.251–52.   Music in Boston
4.16.252–54.   Social Science
4.16.254–55.   Suggestions to Affiliated Societies
4.17.269–70.   Fourier Among the Cardinals
4.19.294–95.   The Italian Opera in New York
4.19.295–96.   More Chamber Concerts in Boston
4.19.296.   Maretzek, *Le Pas des Fleurs, Le Pas des Moissonneurs, Les Petits Danseuses Quadrilles;* Adam, *Le Pas Hungrois de Drapeaux* [review]
4.19.296.   Willis, *New Set of Glenmary Waltzes* [review]
4.19.297–98.   Celebration of Fourier's Birthday in Boston
4.21.327–29.   Swedenborg, *Outlines of a Philosophical Argument on the Infinite and the Final Cause of Creation* [review]
4.21.329–31.   *Tracts for the Times.* No. I [review]
4.21.331.   The Italian Opera in Boston—Verdi's "Ermani"
4.22.346.   The Italian Opera in Boston—First Week
4.22.346.   Mason, *La Capricieuse* [review]

4.22.348–51.   The Grounds of Association in the Nature of Man
4.23.361–63.   Second Week of the Opera in Boston—Pacini's "Saffo"
4.24.379–81.   The Grounds of Association in the Nature of Man—No. II
4.25.394–95.   Concerts of the Italian Troupe in Boston
4.25.395.   Italian Opera in New York
4.25.397–400.   The Grounds of Association in the Nature of Man—No. III
4.26.408–9.   The Opera in Boston
4.26.409–10.   Convention of Associationists in Boston
5.1.6–10.   *Tracts for the New Times*. No. II [review]
5..2.25.   Calvert, *Poems* [review]
5.2.25–27.   Italian Opera in Boston
5.2.27.   [review of Handel's "The Messiah" and Haydn's "The Crea-
     tion," arranged by Vincent Novello]
5.2.28–30.   The American Review's Account of the Religious Union of
     Associationists
5.3.43–46.   [The American Review's Account . . . No. II]
5.4.58–60.   [The American Review's Account . . . No. III]
5.5.69–71.   Channing, *Conversations in Rome* [review]
5.5.71–72.   [ed. Godwin], *The Auto-Biography of Goethe* [review]
5.5.72.   Songs from "Sappho"
5.5.72–73.   From a Young Composer
5.5.73–76.   The American Review's Account of the Religious Union of
     Associationists—No. IV
5.5.79.   Lectures in Albany
5.6.88.   [trans. Ford], *Guardian Spirits* [review]
5.6.89–92.   Integral Education. No. I
5.7.108–10.   Integral Education. No. II
5.9.140–44.   Integral Education. No. III
5.9.144.   Circulate the Tract!
5.10.151.   High Life in England
5.10.153–56.   The Good Time Coming
5.10.156–58.   The Shakers at New Lebanon
5.10.158–59.   Fourierism in an Old Book
5.11.171–73.   Briancourt, *The Organization of Labor and Association*
     [review]
5.11.174–76.   The Shakers at New Lebanon [continued]
5.12.184–85.   Mendelssohn's Songs Without Words
5.12.185.   The Publications of G. P. Reed
5.13.203–5.   Teachers' Conventions in Boston
5.13.207–8.   Does Passional Attraction Exclude Conscience
5.14.217–18.   Madam Anna Bishop
5.14.218.   Signora Biscaccianti
5.14.218.   Great Festival
5.14.219–20.   Tide Marks

E. J. Eames

George G. Foster

1.9.134.	Letter From Broadway—No. III
1.9.137–38.	Dr. Buchanan the Neurologist
2.5.73.	Letter From Broadway—No. V
2.6.92.	To _____ [poem]
2.7.99.	The Baby's Epitaph [poem]
2.21.327–28.	Letter From Broadway—No. VII

Edward Giles

7.19.146.	Labor and Evil

Parke Godwin

1.1.10–11.	The Oregon Question
2.9.138–39.	Everett, *Critical and Miscellaneous Essays* [review]
2.15.231.	Letter From Broadway—No. VI
2.16.248–49.	Van Amringe, *Association and Christianity* [review]
4.23.363.	A Letter to Joseph Mazzini on the Doctrines of Fourier
6.1.5.	The Theatres
5.1.5.	Introductory
6.1.6.	The New York Election
6.2.11.	Theatres
6.2.12.	Free Trade, Free Soil, Free Labor, and Free Speech
6.2.12.	The Conditions of England
6.2.15.	James, *Life of Henry the Fourth* [review]
6.3.20.	Pope Pio Nono
6.3.20.	The Morals of New York
6.3.21.	Epigram [poem—to P. B.]
6.3.22.	Theatres
6.4.28.	A Thanksgiving Article
6.4.28–29.	The National Reformers
6.4.29.	A Good Move
6.5.36.	Pauperism
6.5.36.	More Fourierism. The State of Ireland.
6.5.38–39.	The Theatres
6.5.39.	Halleck, *The Poems of Fitz Greene Halleck* [review]
6.6.44.	Good Words from and for the Pulpit
6.6.44.	[Association:] Is It Needed?
6.6.47.	Theatres
6.6.47.	Schlegel, *The Philosophy of Life, and the Philosophy of Language* [review]
6.7.52.	Christian Union

6.7.54.	Thompson, *Theatrical Amusements;* Sawyer, *A Plea for Amusements* [review]
6.8.60.	Christmas
6.8.63.	*The Poems of Nathaniel Parker Willis* [review]
6.8.63.	Nicholson, *The Stranger's Welcome to Ireland* [review]
6.9.68.	Sound Doctrines in a High Place
6.9.68–69.	Pictures of Civilization
6.10.76.	What Associationists Propose
6.10.76.	Symptoms of Progress
6.10.78.	The Theatres
6.10.78.	Beecher, *A Discourse on Thanksgiving Day* [review]
6.10.79.	[not given], *The Pictorial History of England* [review]
6.10.79.	[not given], *Republication of the Foreign Reviews* [review]
6.10.79.	*Chapman's American Drawing Book* [review]
6.11.84.	Mr. [Orestes] Brownson on Association
6.11.84.	A Small Blast—from Tayler Lewis [see also 6.14.108 below]
6.11.86.	Carey, *The Past, the Present and the Future* [review]
6.12.92.	What Associationists Propose
6.12.92.	Mr. King's Lectures
6.12.95.	[not given], *Scenes and Characters from the Comedy of Life* [review]
6.13.100.	The Power of Concentration
6.13.100.	Taking the Alarm
6.14.108.	An Objection Answered
6.14.108.	[A reply to] Professor [Tayler] Lewis
6.14.108.	Honora Shepherd
6.15.116.	Social Health
6.15.116–17.	The Virtue of a Warm Blanket
6.15.119.	Lamartine, *History of the Girondists* [review]
6.16.124.	*The Observer* Again
6.16.124–25.	Death of Mr. [Thomas] Cole
6.17.132–33.	Mutual Assurance
6.17.133.	The Univercoelum
6.18.140.	Lodging Houses
6.19.148.	The Tenants' League
6.19.150.	The Philharmonic Concert
6.19.151.	Ruxton, *Adventures in Mexico* [review]
6.20.154–55.	The Influence of Evil
6.20.156.	The Tenant Movement
6.20.156.	The Land Question in the New York Legislature
6.21.164.	Wages Slavery
6.21.164–65.	Another Good Movement
6.22.172.	The Great Event
6.22.172–73.	Political Economy
6.23.179.	American Sympathy with France

6.24.187.	It Goes On
6.24.187.	The Fourierism of the French Revolution
6.25.195.	Let Not Your Hearts Be Troubled
6.26.203.	Interdering with Trade
6.26.203.	Politics and Socialism
6.26.206.	Bronte, *Wuthering Heights* [review]
7.1.4.	Woman's Rights
7.2.12.	The State of France
7.3.20.	The Newspapers and the French Revolution
7.3.20.	Better Views
7.3.20–21.	A Civilized Example
7.3.21.	French Affairs
7.3.23.	Channing, *Memoirs of William Ellery Channing*[review]
7.4.28.	The French Elections
7.4.29.	Getting Up in the World
7.4.31.	Von Talvj, *Geschicte der Colonization von New England* [review]
7.4.31.	Lamartine, *History of the Girondists* [review]
7.5.36.	The Prospect in France
7.5.36–37.	Political Economy
7.6.44.	The Progress of Principles
7.6.44.	Parties in France
7.7.52.	Our Politics
7.7.52.	Edinburgh Review
7.7.52.	The American Review
7.8.60.	The Problem of the Age
7.9.68.	A Few Facts
7.9.70.	Roelker, *The Constitutions of France* [review]
7.10.76.	Lamartine and Ledre Rollin
7.11.84.	The French Revolution As We View It
7.12.92.	The French Outbreak
7.13.100.	Mad Dogs! Look Out!
7.13.103.	Lytton, *Harold, the Last of the Saxon Kings* [review]
7.13.103.	Bremer, *Brothers and Sisters* [review]
7.13.103.	Stewart, *Treatise on the Lungs* [review]
7.14.108.	The Great Political Question
7.15.116.	Industrial Armies
7.15.116.	Mr. Mann's Speech
7.16.124.	The Irish Trouble
7.16.124.	So Say We
7.19.148.	Revolutions in Europe
7.19.148–49.	The Hunger Academy
7.19.149.	Truth in High Places
7.20.156.	Objections to Association
7.21.164.	National Workshops

7.22.172.   Social Changes
7.22.173.   A New Picture
7.23.181.   The Right to Labor
7.24.188.   The Organization of Labor
7.25.196.   The Observer Once More
7.25.198.   De La Roche's Napoleon
7.26.202.   Fourier and His School [coauthored with John S. Dwight and
                William H. Channing]

E. P. Grant

1.14.220.   Spooner, *The Unconstitutionality of Slavery* [review]
1.18.283.   Hurlbut, *Essays on Human Rights and Their Political Guar-
                anters* [review]
2.15.239.   Albert Gallatin on Labor
3.8.118–20.   Spooner, *Poverty: Its Illegal Causes and Legal Cure* [review]

Horace Greeley

1.20.315–16.   Duty of Associationists to the Cause

Frederic Henry Hedge

3.14.219.   The Hanging Moss [poem]

Thomas Wentworth Higginson

1.21.332.   Tyrtaeus [poem]
2.17.269–70.   The Railroad [poem]
3.2.28.   Holiness Unto The Lord [poem]
3.3.44.   Hymn of Humanity [poem]
3.4.59.   Hebe [poem]
4.6.94.   Dawn and Day [poem]
4.8.125.   De Profundis Clamavi [poem]
4.8.125.   Sonnet [poem]
5.4.58.   Earth Waits For Her Queen [poem]

Elam Ives

6.1.5.   Music in New York

6.2.15.	*American Musical Times* [review]
6.3.22.	Mr. Burke's Concert
6.3.23.	[ed. Kingsley], *The Harp of David* [review]

Henry James, Sr.

6.1.4.	Bushnell, *Views of Christian Nurture* [review]
6.2.15.	Bush and Barrett, *Davis's Revelations Revealed* [review]
6.4.28.	Observations on *The Observer*
6.5.39.	James, *The Convict* [review]
6.7.54.	*The New Jerusalem Magazine* [review]
6.8.61.	The New Jerusalem Magazine
6.14.111.	Warren, *Now and Then* [review]
6.14.111.	James, *The Last of the Fairies* [review]
6.16.126.	*The New Church Repository and Monthly Review* [review]
6.17.132.	Fourier and Swedenborg
6.18.140.	Swedenborg and Fourier
6.26.203.	Theological Differences in Association
6.26.205.	*New Church Repository* [review]
7.3.22.	Morell, *On the Philosophical Tendencies of the Age* [review]
7.4.29.	Dr. Channing and the Moral Life
7.9.69.	The Divine Life in Man
7.10.78.	*Swedenborg's Posthumous Philosophical Tracts*—No. 1; J. E. Le Boys Des Guays, *Letters to a Man of the World; New Jerusalem Magazine* [June 1848]; *New Church Repository* [July 1848] [review]
7.11.86.	Benevolence Not the Divine Life in Man
7.13.100.	Practical Morality and Association
7.13.102.	*The Harbinger* and the (Self-Styled) New Church
7.15.116–17.	*The Harbinger* and Sectarianism
7.16.125.	Human Freedom
7.17.133–34.	Human Freedom—No. II
7.18.140.	*The Harbinger* and "B.F.B."
7.19.150–51.	James, *Gowrie* [review]
7.20.156.	The New York *Evangelist*
7.22.172–73.	Is Human Nature Positively Evil?
7.24.189.	The Origin of Nature, or Creation not Arbitrary
7.25.197.	*The Observer* and Hannequin
7.26.202–3.	Love and Marriage

William H. Kimball

6.26.200.	"It is too Late" [poem]

Marx Edgeworth Lazarus

3.20.305–8.   Society—An Aspiration—Or the Actual and the Possible
3.21.325–30.   Society—An Aspiration [continued]
3.22.344–48.   Society—An Aspiration [continued]
3.22.355.   The Drama—Mrs. Mowatt
3.23.358–61.   Society—An Aspiration [continued]
3.24.369–71.   Society—An Aspiration [continued]
3.24.381–82.   Union of Associationists in the Church of Humanity
3.26.401–4.   Society—An Aspiration [continued]
4.1.7–9.   Society—An Aspiration [continued]
4.2.17–19.   Society—An Aspiration [continued]
4.3.38.   Society—An Aspiration [continued]
4.5.66–69.   Society—An Aspiration [continued]
4.6.87–89.   Society—An Aspiration [continued]
4.7.97–101.   Society—An Aspiration [continued]
4.7.109–11.   Statement of Principles
4.10.154–56.   Sketches of a Day in the Serial Order
4.11.161–65.   Sketches of a Day in the Serial Order [continued]
4.13.199–200. Cannibalism
4.14.216–19.   Cannibalism [continued]
4.16.249–50.   Cannibalism [continued]
4.17.259–63.   Cannibalism [continued]
4.18.276–78.   Cannibalism [continued]
4.18.279–82.   Results of Civilization
4.19.289–91.   Cannibalism [continued]
4.20.310.13.   Cannibalism [continued]
4.22.339–41.   Cannibalism [continued]
4.23.358–60.   Cannibalism [continued]
5.6.84–87.   Cannibalism [continued]
5.7.99–104.   Cannibalism [continued]
5.9.131–33.   Cannibalism [continued]
5.9.134–36.   Desperadoes of the Southwest
5.16.247–50.   Letter on Natural Classification
6.14.106.   Physiognomy—The Science of Incarnation
6.15.113.   Physiognomy—The Science of Incarnation [continued]
6.17.130.   Scriptural Analogies
6.19.146.   Scriptural Analogies—No. II
6.20.153.   Scriptural Analogies—No. III

James Russell Lowell

1.8.122.   To a Pine Tree [poem]
4.6.94.   *Si Descendero In Infernum Ades* [poem]

Osborne Macdaniel

1.1.15.	First Annual Meeting of the N.E. [New England] Working Men's Association
1.4.63.	Phonography
1.5.80.	The Fourth of July
1.6.95.	Anastatic Printing
1.19.293–95.	Artesian Wells
1.19.303.	Profligacy in Politics
1.24.380–84.	Etzler's Machinery
1.25.394.	Vail, *The American Electro Magnetic Telegraph* [review]
1.26.415–16.	Cassius Clay, His Notions of Association
2.1.14–15.	The President's Message
2.1.15.	The Workingmen's Protective Union
2.4.58–59.	[not given], *The History of Silk* [review]
2.6.95.	Cassius M. Clay and *The Harbinger*
2.14.216.	Bronson, *Elocution* [review]
2.18.281–82.	Brown, *An Appeal From the Old Theory of Grammar* [review]
2.19.298.	Smith, *A New Guide for Travelling Through the U.S.A.* [review]
2.19.302–3.	Celebration of Fourier's Birthday in New York
2.22.345.	Oram, *First Lessons in English Grammar and Composition* [review]
2.23.358–60.	Comstock, *A Treatise on Phonology* [review]
4.1.10.	Mandeville, *A Course of Reading for Common Schools* [review]
4.1.11.	Wright, *Primary Lessons* [review]
5.16.256.	The Smithsonian Bequest
5.17.270.	Another Convert
5.18.287–88.	The New York *Tribune*
6.13.102.	Williams, *The Middle Kingdom* [review]

William H. Muller

7.2.9.	A Word to the Church in Behalf of Social Reorganization
7.3.17.	A Word to the Church in Behalf of Social Reorganization [continued]

C. Neidhardt

5.12.190–91.	A Fourth of July Visit to the North American Phalanx

John Orvis

2.13.205.	Letter From Vermont
2.23.361.	Guenon, *A Treatise on Milch Cows* [review]
4.4.60–61.	Social Re-organization—No. I
4.6.95–96.	Social Re-organization—No. II
4.8.127.	Social Re-organization—No. III
4.8.127–28.	Lectures in Newburyport
4.9.142–43.	Social Re-organization—No. IV
4.11.174–75.	Social Re-organization—No. V
4.12.190–91.	Social Re-organization—No. VI.
4.16.255–56.	Social Re-organization—No. VI [continued]
4.17.270–72.	Social Re-organization—No. VII
4.19.302–3.	Our Lecturers
4.21.333–35.	Social Re-organization—No. VIII
4.21.335–36.	Lectures in Providence
4.24.381–83.	Social Re-organization—No. IX
5.4.50–52.	Trip To Vermont
5.5.68–69.	Trip to Vermont—No. II
5.6.95–96.	Social Re-organization—No. X
5.7.111–12.	Associative Lectures in Amesbury, Mass.
5.9.144.	The Committee of Thirteen
5.16.255–56.	Letter From New York State
5.17.285–87.	Our Prospects in New York
5.20.319–20.	The Liberty League
5.21.330–32.	The Liberty League [continued]

Frances S. Osgood

6.25.194.	Stanzas for Music [poem]

Jean M. Palisse

5.20.305–6.	Ballard Vale

E. W. Parkman

5.17.266.	Preliminary Movements

Mary Spencer Pease

6.11.82.	A New Year's Rhapsody

6.12.93.	Letter From Philadelphia
6.14.109.	Letter From Philadelphia
6.16.125	Letter From Philadelphia

J. H. Pulte

3.4.51–54.	The Political State of the World
3.5.68–71.	The Political State of the World [concluded]

George Ripley

1.1.8.	The Introductory Notice of *The Harbinger*
1.1.13–14	The Infidelity of Modern Society
1.1.14	Influence of Machinery
1.1.14.	*The Practical Christian*
1.1.15.	Build Up and Not Destroy
1.1.16.	The Prospectus of *The Harbinger*
1.2.32.	The Fourth of July
1.3.33–35.	Tendencies of Modern Civilization
1.3.45–47.	Andrew Jackson
1.3.47.	To Our Friends in Association
1.3.47.	Cassius M. Clay and William C. Bell
1.3.47–48.	Signs of Progress
1.3.48.	What Do You Propose?
1.5.79.	The *Voice of Industry* [notice]
1.7.107.	*The Farmer's Library and Monthly Journal of Agriculture* [review]
1.7.108–9.	Association in the West—The Integral Phalanx
1.7.110.	Progress of the Cause
1.7.110.	The True American
1.7.111.	*The Montreal Pilot* [notice]
1.9.142–43.	Trading and Farming
1.10.153.	Lyell, *Travels in North America* [review]
1.10.153–54.	*Hunt's Merchants' Magazine and Commercial Review* [review]
1.10.159–60.	The Commencement of Association
1.12.189–91.	The Assaults of the *New York Express*
1.12.191–92.	What Shall I Do For The Cause?
1.14.221–23.	Association: Will It Succeed?
1.16.253–54.	The Skaneatales Community
1.17.262.	Burdett, *Wrongs of American Women* [review]
1.17.262.	Morrell, *The American Shepherd* [review]
1.17.266–67.	Ornamental Farming

3.2.30–31. The Working Men's Movement
3.2.31–32. *Consuelo*
3.8.127. Association Meeting at Hingham, Mass [achusetts]
3.9.140. Forster. *The Statesmen of the Commonwealth of England* [review]
3.10.155–57. The *New York Observer* on Association
3.10.160. *Hunt's Merchants' Magazine*
3.11.167–68. Headley, *Napolean and His Marshals* [review]
3.2.170–72. The *New York Observer* on Association
3.11.175. Mrs. Powers and C. Edwards Lester
3.13.202–3. *The People's Journal* [review]
3.13.208. John A. Collins
3.14.217–18. Pond, *Swedenborgianism Reviewed;* Wood, *Lectures on Swedenborgianism* [review]
3.14.221–22. "War To The Knife"
3.14.222. How It Strikes A Stranger
3.14.222–23. Where Are We?
3.14.223. American Labor
3.15.236. *The Christian Examiner and Religious Miscellany* [review]
3.15.239–40. What We Wish
3.16.252–53. Influence of Association on Woman
3.17.267. Carlyle, *On Heroes, Hero Worship, and The Heroic in History* [review]
3.17.271. Movement in Wheeling, Va
3.17.271–72. Association in Lowell, Mass [achusetts]
3.17.272. To The Friends of *The Harbinger*
3.19.300. *The Whig Almanac and United States Register for 1847* [review]
3.20.316. Kipp, *The Early Jesuit Missions, in North America* [review]
3.20.319–20. Guarantyism
3.21.334–35. Association in Boston
3.21.335–36. Forms of Guarantyism
3.21.336. Well Done Wisconsin!
3.21.336. Onward Germany
3.22.352. We Cannot Breathe This Atmosphere!
3.23.361. Parker, *A Sermon of the Perishing Classes in Boston* [review]
3.23.268. What Is To Be Done?
3.24.377–78. Sampson, *Rationale of Crime* [review]
3.24.383. Signs of the Times
3.26.409–10. What Shall We Do?
4.1.13–14. Lectures on Association in Vermont
4.1.14–15. New York Controversy on Association
4.1.15. Aid From the West
4.1.16. Anti-Slavery at Washington

5.12.192.　　　[Notice on *The Chronotype*]

5.13.200–203.　Morrell, *An Historical and Critical View of the Speculative Philosophy of Europe of the Nineteenth Century* [review]

5.13.205–7.　　The French Associative Movement

5.14.222–24.　　Professor Bush and Davis the Clairvoyant

5.15.237–38.　　Opinions of the Foreign Press

5.16.254–55.　　Victor Hannequin's Lectures

5.16.256.　　　Movement in Cincinnati

5.17.265–66.　　The Paris Murder

5.17.269–70.　　Signs of the Times

5.17.271.　　　Unitarianism and Association

5.18.282–83.　　Obscurity of Associative Science

5.18.283–85.　　Crude Notions of Association

5.18.285.　　　Spirit of Trade

5.19.298–99.　　Sand, *The Journeyman Joiner* [review]

5.19.302–3.　　Morality of the Praslin Affair

5.19.304.　　　Protective Unions

5.21.328–29.　　Notice to Subscribers

6.1.4.　　　　*A Collection from the Newspaper Writings of Nathaniel Peabody Rogers* [review]

6.1.7.　　　　To the Affiliated Unions

6.2.12–13.　　New Movements

6.2.15.　　　Henry, *Campaign Sketches of the War With Mexico* [review]

6.2.15.　　　[ed. Follen], *The Child's Friend* [review]

6.3.17.　　　Presbyterianism

6.3.20.　　　Policy of Associationists

6.3.20.　　　Orson Murray and the Courts

6.3.21.　　　Victor Considerant

6.3.21.　　　New Work on Association by Hannequin

6.3.22–23.　　*Life of Jeremy Belknap* [review]

6.4.25.　　　A Friendly Hint

6.4.31.　　　Smith, *Narrative of an Exploratory Visit to . . . China* [review]

6.5.36–37.　　Relation of Associationists to Civilization

6.7.52.　　　Association and Science

6.7.52.　　　The Morals of Commerce

6.8.60.　　　The Late Chancellor Kent

6.9.69.　　　Christmas in Philadelphia [by Ripley?]

6.10.79.　　　[not given], *Water Cure in America* [review]

6.14.108–9.　　Victor Hennequin at Brussels

6.14.110–11.　Stallo, *General Principles of the Philosophy of Nature* [review]

6.14.111.　　　*The Nineteenth Century. A Quarterly Miscellany* [review]

6.15.116.　　　Is Association Impracticable?

6.15.116.   A Question Answered
6.15.119.   Cantagrel, *The Children at the Phalanstery* [review]
6.18.143.   Abbot, *A Summer in Scotland* [review]
6.19.150–51. Hedge, *Prose Writers of Germany* [review]
6.19.152.   *The Massachusetts Quarterly Review* [review]
6.19.152.   *Hunt's Merchants' Magazine* [review]
6.20.156.   Reception of Henry Clay—Obsequies of John Q. Adams
6.21.164.   The *Express* on Labor
6.21.165.   Revolution—Fourierism
6.22.172.   The Birth Day of Fourier
6.22.173.   Movements in Cincinnati
6.24.187.   *The Harbinger*
6.24.189.   Fourier's Birth Day in New York
6.25.195   Associative Bearings of the Revolution
6.25.196.   The Voice of Industry
7.1.6–7.   Hopedale Community
7.1.7.   *London Morning Chronicle* and Association
7.1.7.   Fourierism and Swedenborg Compared
7.4.29.   Taking It Cool
7.4.31.   The Artist Darley
7.5.36.   Victor Considerant and Louis Blanc
7.8.60.   The Movement in this Country
7.8.60–61.   An Inquiry
7.10.76.   Wisconsin Phalanx
7.11.85.   Retaliatory Postage
7.12.92.   Social Evils and their Remedy
7.12.93.   Falsehood in High Places
7.12.93.   A Rare Chance
7.13.101.   Sound Views of the Revolt in Paris
7.16.125.   Progress at the West
7.16.125.   *The Spiritual Magazine*
7.16.126.   DeVericour, *Modern French Literature* [review]
7.16.127.   [ed. Greeley], *Speeches and Addresses* [review]
7.16.127.   Carleton, *The Battle of Buena Vista* [review]
7.16.127.   Ranlett, *The Architect* [review]
7.16.127.   Chivers, *Search After Truth* [review]
7.17.132.   Proudhon's Financial Sketches
7.17.132.   Misrepresentations of Association
7.19.148.   Christianity and Socialism
7.19.150.   *The Massachusetts Quarterly Review* [review]
7.20.156.   Association and Infidelity
7.20.156.   Our Contemporaries
7.20.159.   Pellarin, *The Life of Charles Fourier* [review]
7.21.164.   Progress of Associative Principles

Samuel D. Robbins

Lewis W. Ryckman

J. A. Saxton

James Sellers, Jr.

Francis George Shaw

1.5.79.	Teaching Not Education
1.2.163.	Essays, By T. Parsons
1.11.172.	*The Medici Series of Italian Prose*—Vol. 1 [review]
1.14.220.	[not given], *Gertrude: A Tale* [review]
1.14.220–21.	Etzler, *Two Visions of J. A. Etzler* [review]
1.17.268–70.	The Women of the Boston Anti-Slavery Fair
1.20.316.	Cheever, *Wanderings of A Pilgrim Under the Shadow of Mount Blanc* [review]
1.22.345–46.	*The Medici Series of Italian Prose*—Vol. 2 [review]
1.22.346–47.	Dix, *Remarks on Prisons and Prison Discipline in the United States* [review]
1.22.347.	Manzoni, *I Promessi Sposi* [review]
1.22.351–52.	Children in Workshops Near Paris
1.25.394–95.	Kirkland, *Western Clearings* [review]
1.25.395–96.	[not given], *Prairiedom, Rambles and Scrambles in Texas* [review]
1.25.396.	Lover, *The O'Donoghue* [review]
2.18.284–86.	Political Economy: British Free Trade
2.18.286.	The French in Algiers
4.14.223–24.	The Writings of George Sand
6.8.63.	[ed. Child], *Rainbows for Children* [review]
6.8.63.	Miller, *The Boy's Winter Book* [notice]

Eliza A. Starr

5.17.266–67.	Angelina [poem]
7.2.9.	May Buds [poem]
7.7.49.	Napolean and His Infant Son [poem]
7.13.97.	Sonnet [poem]
7.18.142.	Practical Association

William W. Story

1.3.44.	The Future [poem]
1.4.55–58.	Athenaeum Gallery—Allston's Belshazzar
1.10.154.	To the Moon [poem]
2.1.13.	The Mountain Stream [poem]
2.2.30–31.	The Ivory Christ
2.9.142–44.	Mr. Emerson's Lectures in Boston
2.13.204–5.	Sixth Concert of the Boston Academy
2.14.218–20.	Sixth Concert of the Boston Academy
3.9.141–42.	Midnight [poem]

3.17.257–60.	A Letter From The Sea Shore
4.1.13.	Pledge [poem]
4.2.25.	The Ideal [poem]
4.2.25.	Longings [poem]
4.4.58.	*Stille Liebe* [poem]

H. H. Van Amringe

| 7.11.85. | Wisconsin and Wisconsin Phalanx |
| 7.12.93. | Wisconsin and Wisconsin Phalanx—No. II |

Owen G. Warren

| 6.20.155. | Hope On [poem] |
| 6.26.202. | Labor [poem] |

John Greenleaf Whittier

| 1.7.108. | To My Friend On the Death Of His Sister [poem] |

James John Garth Wilkinson

7.1.6.	Letter from London
7.2.14.	Letter from London
7.3.21.	Letter from London
7.5.37.	Letter from London
7.6.45.	Letter from London
7.8.61–62.	Letter from London
7.10.77.	Letter from London
7.23.180–81.	Progress

NOTE: The index to volume 4 lists William Henry Channing, George Ripley, and John S. Dwight as coauthors of these five items:

4.15.240.	[Anniversary Meeting of the American Union of Associationists]
4.18.287–88.	Societies
4.20.318–20.	Another Word to Our Friends
4.24.384.	The Convention in New York
4.25.385–92.	Annual Meeting of the American Union of Associationists

Bibliography

Allen, Gay Wilson. *Waldo Emerson: A Biography*. New York: The Viking Press, 1981.

Baer, Helene G. *The Heart Is Like Heaven: The Life of Lydia Maria Child*. Philadelphia: University of Pennsylvania Press, 1964.

Bestor, Arthur E., Jr. "American Phalanxes: Fourierist Socialism in the United States." Ph.D. dissertation, Yale University, 1938.

―――. "Brook Farm 1841–1847. An Exhibition to Commemorate the Centenary of Its Founding." Mimeographed. New York: Columbia University Libraries, 1941.

Blanck, Jacob. *Bibliography of American Literature*. 6 vols. to date. New Haven, Conn.: Yale University Press, 1955―.

Block, Marguerite Beck. *The New Church in the New World*. 2d ed., 1932. Reprint. New York: Octagon Books, 1968.

Boston. Boston Public Library. George Ripley papers.

Boston. Boston Public Library. John Dwight Brook Farm papers.

Boston. Massachusetts Historical Society. Brook Farm records.

Boston. Massachusetts Historical Society. James T. Fisher papers.

Brisbane, Albert. *Concise Exposition of the Doctrine of Association*. 8th ed. New York: J. S. Redfield, 1844.

―――. *Social Destiny of Man*. 2d ed., 1840. Reprint. New York: Augustus M. Kelley, 1969.

Brisbane, Redelia. *Albert Brisbane: A Mental Biography*. Boston: Arena, 1893.

Brownson, Orestes A. *The Works of Orestes A. Brownson*. 20 vols. Compiled by Henry F. Brownson. Detroit: Thorndike Nourse, 1884.

Cabot, J. Elliot. *A Memoir of Ralph Waldo Emerson*. Vol. 2. 2nd ed., 1887. Reprint. New York: AMS Press, 1969.

Carlyle, Thomas. *Past and Present*. Boston: Charles C. Little and James Brown, 1843.

Cary, Edward. *George William Curtis*. Boston: Houghton, Mifflin, 1894.

Codman, John Thomas. *Brook Farm; Historic and Personal Memoirs*. Boston: Arena, 1894.

Commager, Henry Steele. *Theodore Parker*. Boston: Little, Brown, 1936.

"Constitution of the American Union of Associationists, Adopted May 1846." *The Harbinger* 2 (6 June 1846): 410–11.

Constitution of the Brook Farm Phalanx, Adopted May 1, 1845. Boston, 1845.

Cooke, George Willis. *John Sullivan Dwight: Brook-Farmer, Editor, and Critic of Music*. Boston: Small, Maynard, 1898.

————, ed. *The Poets of Transcendentalism*. Boston: Houghton, Mifflin, 1903.

Cranch, Christopher Pearse. *Address Delivered Before the Harvard Musical Association, August 28, 1845*. Boston, 1845.

Crowe, Charles. "Fourierism and the Founding of Brook Farm." *Boston Public Library Quarterly* 12 (April 1960): 79–88.

————. *George Ripley: Transcendentalist and Utopian Socialist*. Athens, Ga.: University of Georgia Press, 1967.

Curtis, Edith Roelker. *A Season in Utopia; The Story of Brook Farm*. New York: Nelson, 1961.

Curtis, George William. *Early Letters of George William Curtis to John S. Dwight*. Edited by George Willis Cooke. New York: Harper and Brothers, 1898.

Dana, Charles A. *A Lecture on Association, in Its Connection with Religion*. Boston: Benjamin H. Greene, 1844.

Delano, Sterling F. "*The Harbinger* Reviews Its Transcendental 'Friends': Margaret Fuller, Theodore Parker, and Ralph Waldo Emerson." *Colby Library Quarterly* 17 (June 1981): 74–84.

Delano, Sterling F. "A Rediscovered Transcendental Poem by Frederic Hedge." *American Transcendental Quarterly* 29 (Winter 1976): 35–36.

Delano, Sterling F., and Colanzi, Rita. "An Index to Volume VIII of *The Harbinger*." *Resources for American Literary Study* 10 (Autumn 1980): 173–86.

Dwight, John S. *A Lecture on Association, in Its Connection with Education and Religion*. Boston: Benjamin H. Greene, 1844.

————. See also Boston. Boston Public Library.

Dwight, Marianne. *Letters from Brook Farm: 1844–47*. Edited by Amy L. Reed. Poughkeepsie, N.Y.: Vassar College, 1928.

Einstein, Alfred. *Music in the Romantic Era*. New York: W. W. Norton, 1947.

Emerson, Ralph Waldo. *The Complete Works of Ralph Waldo Emerson*. Edited by Edward Waldo Emerson. The Centenary Edition. 12 vols. Boston: Houghton, Mifflin, 1903–4.

————. *The Correspondence of Emerson and Carlyle*. Edited by Joseph Slater. New York: Columbia University Press, 1964.

————. *Journals of Ralph Waldo Emerson*. Edited by Edward Waldo Emerson and Waldo Emerson Forbes. 10 vols. Boston: Houghton Mifflin, 1909–14.

————. *The Letters of Ralph Waldo Emerson*. Edited by Ralph L.Rusk. 6 vols. New York: Columbia University Press, 1939.

Fertig, Walter L. "John Sullivan Dwight: Transcendentalist and Literary Amateur of Music." Ph.D. dissertation, University of Maryland, 1952.

Fisher, James T. See Boston. Massachusetts Historical Society.

Francis, Richard. "The Ideology of Brook Farm." *Studies in the American Renaissance 1977*. Edited by Joel Myerson. Boston: Twayne Publishers, 1978.

Frothingham, Octavius B. *George Ripley*. 2d ed., 1882. Reprint. New York: AMS Press, 1970.

————. *Memoir of William Henry Channing*. Boston: Houghton Mifflin Company, 1886.

————. *Transcendentalism in New England*. New York: Putnams, 1876.

"George Ripley and the Brook Farm Association." *Littel's Living Age* 12 (October 1860): 571–73.

Gohdes, Clarence L. F. "A Book Farm Labor Record." *American Literature* 1 (November 1929): 297–303.

————. *The Periodicals of American Transcendentalism*. Durham, N.C.: Duke University Press, 1931.

Golemba, Henry L. *George Ripley*. Boston: Twayne Publishers, 1977.

Haraszti, Zoltan. *The Idyll of Brook Farm: As Revealed by Unpublished Letters in the Boston Public Library*. Boston: Trustees of the Public Library, 1937.

The Harbinger. 8 vols. Vols. 1–4: West Roxbury, Mass.: Brook Farm Phalanx. Vol. 5: West Roxbury: American Union of Associationists. Vols. 6–8: New York: American Union of Associationists.

Hart, James D. *The Oxford Companion to American Literature*. 3d ed. New York: Oxford University Press, 1956.

Higginson, T[homas] W[entworth]. *Margaret Fuller Ossoli*. Boston: Hougton Mifflin Company, 1882.

Hillquit, Morris. *History of Socialism in the United States*. New York: Russell and Russell, 1965.

Hotson, Clarence Paul. "Sampson Reed, A Teacher of Emerson." *New England Quarterly* 2 (April 1929): 249–77.

Howard, John Tasker. *Our American Music*. New York: Thomas Y. Crowell, 1954.

"*Jacques,* by George Sand." *Literary World* 1 (6 February 1847): 8–9.

Jones, Howard Mumford. "American Comment on George Sand, 1837–48." *American Literature* 3 (January 1932): 389–407.

Joyaux, George. "George Sand, Eugene Sue and *The Harbinger*." *The French Review* 27 (December 1953): 122–31.

Kern, Alexander. "The Rise of Transcendentalism, 1815–1860." *Transistions in American Literary History*. Edited by Harry Hayden Clark. Durham, N.C.: Duke University Press, 1953.

[Kirby, Georgiana Bruce]. "Reminiscences of Brook Farm." *Old and New* 3 (April 1871): 425–38.

Lahee, Henry Charles. *Annals of Music in America*. 1922. Reprint. Freeport, N.Y.: Books for Free Libraries Press, 1970.

Lane, Charles. "Brook Farm." *Dial* 4 (January 1844): 351–57.

Lattimore, Richmond. *The Iliad of Homer*. Chicago: University of Chicago Press, 1951.

Lowens, Irving. *Music and Musicians in Early America*. New York: W. W. Norton, 1964.

Melville, Herman. *The Letters of Herman Melville*. Edited by Merrell R. Davis and William H. Gilman. New Haven, Conn.: Yale University Press, 1960.

Miller, Perry. *The Transcendentalists: An Anthology*. Cambridge, Mass.: Harvard University Press, 1950.

————, ed. *The American Transcendentalists: Their Prose and Poetry*. Garden City, N.Y.: Doubleday Anchor Books, 1957.

Moss, Sidney P. *Poe's Literary Battles*. Durham, N.C.: Duke University Press, 1963.

Mott, Frank Luther. *A History of American Magazines 1741–1850*. Cambridge, Mass.: Harvard University Press, 1957 [1939].

Muncy, Raymond Lee. *Sex and Marriage in Utopian Communities*. Bloomington, Ind.: Indiana University Press, 1973.

Myerson, Joel. *Brook Farm: An Annotated Bibliography and Resources Guide*. New York: Garland Publishing, 1978.

———. *The New England Transcendentalists and the DIAL*. Rutherford, N.J.: Fairleigh Dickinson University Press, 1980.

Noyes, John Humphrey. *History of American Socialisms*. Philadelphia: Lippincott, 1870.

Peabody, Elizabeth P. "Plan of the West Roxbury Community." *Dial* 2 (January 1842): 361–72.

Pearce, Roy Harvey. *The Continuity of American Poetry*. Princeton, N.J.: Princeton University Press, 1961.

Phalanx or Journal of Social Science, Devoted to the Cause of Association and Social Reform. 1 vol. New York: J. Winchester, 5 October 1843–28 May 1845.

Pochmann, Henry A. *German Culture in America: Philosophical and Literary Influences 1600–1900*. Madison, Wisc.: University of Wisconsin Press, 1957.

Poe, Edgar Allan. "The Harbinger." *Broadway Journal* 2 (13 December 1845): 357–59.

Pratt, Waldo Selden. *The History of Music: A Handbook and Guide for Students*. New York: G. Schirmer, 1907.

The Present. 1 vol. New York: September 1843–April 1844.

Riasanovsky, Nicholas V. *The Teaching of Charles Fourier*. Berkeley and Los Angeles: University of California Press, 1969.

Riggs, Lisette. "George and Sophia Ripley." Ph.D. dissertation, University of Maryland, 1942.

Ripley, George. See Boston. Boston Public Library.

Rusk, Ralph L. *The Life of Ralph Waldo Emerson*. New York: Scribners, 1949.

Russell, Amelia. "Home Life of the Brook Farm Association." *Atlantic Monthly* 42 (October 1878): 458–66.

———. *Home Life of the Brook Farm Association*. Boston: Little, Brown, 1900.

Sablosky, Irving. *American Music*. Chicago: University of Chicago Press, 1969.

Salisbury, Annie M. *Brook Farm*. Marlborough, Mass.: W. B. Smith, 1898.

Sams, Henry W., ed. *Autobiography of Brook Farm*. Englewood Cliffs, N.J.: Prentice-Hall, 1958.

Shepard, Odell. *Pedlar's Progress: The Life of Bronson Alcott*. Boston: Little, Brown and Company, 1937.

"Signs of the Times." *The Present* 1 (October 1843): 70.

Slater, Joseph. "George Ripley and Thomas Carlyle." *PMLA* 68 (June 1952): 341–49.

Socialism and American Life. 2 vols. Edited by Donald Drew Egbert and Stow Persons. Princeton, N.J.: Princeton University Press, 1952.

Spiller, Robert E. *The Cycle of Amerian Literature*. New York: Macmillan Company, 1955.

Stauffer, Donald Barlow. *A Short History of American Poetry*. New York: E. P. Dutton, 1974.

Sterner, Lewis G. *The Sonnet in American Literature*. Philadelphia: University of Pennsylvania Press, 1930.

Swift, Lindsay. *Brook Farm, Its Members, Scholars, and Visitors*. New York: Macmillan Company, 1900.

Tyler, Alice Felt. *Freedom's Ferment: Phases of American Social History to 1860*. Parts Two and Three. Minneapolis, Minn.: University of Minnesota, 1944.

Waggoner, Hyatt H. *American Poets from the Puritans to the Present*. Boston: Houghton Mifflin Company, 1968.

Wilson, James Harrison. *The Life of Charles A. Dana*. New York: Harper and Brothers, 1907.

"Writings of George Sand." *Christian Examiner* 42 (March 1847): 201–27.

Vogel, Stanley M. *German Literary Influences on the American Transcendentalists*. New Haven, Conn.: Yale University Press, 1955.

Index